THE NEW HORROR HANDBOOK

A.S. BERMAN

With love to Richard + Judy Berman, who brought forth the horror that is Your's Truly.

This book is dedicated to Pamela Norman, without whose love + support this book would not have been possible.

COVER + INTERIOR DESIGN
Pamela Norman
pnormandesigns@me.com

TEXT ©2009
A.S. Berman

PHOTOGRAPHY
[see page 228 for photo credits]

All rights reserved.

Published by:

bearmanormedia.com

Printed by:

lightningsource.com

The New Horror Handbook

A.S. Berman, author.

p.cm.

Includes bibliographical references + index.

ISBN 1-59393-144-1

1. Horror + popular culture, 1994-2008.
   2. Biography. 3. Horror + popular culture-History. I. Title.

10 9 8 7 6 5 4 3 2 1

CONTENTS

INTRODUCTION	04
PART ONE: GOT GUTS?	**08**
ELI ROTH [Cabin Fever, Hostel, Hostel Part II]	10
GREG MCLEAN [Wolf Creek, Rogue]	44
STEVE NILES [30 Days of Night, writer]	64
PART TWO: GOT SOMETHING YOU WANNA SAY?	**76**
VINCENZO NATALI [Cube, Splice]	78
GINGER SNAPS [Case Study]	96
JULIEN MAURY + ALEXANDRE BUSTILLO [Inside]	128
DARREN LYNN BOUSMAN [Saw II–IV, Repo! The Genetic Opera]	142
RUE MORGUE MAGAZINE	164
PART THREE: TOMORROW'S TERRORS	**188**
EMILY HAGINS [Pathogen, The Retelling]	190
SEAN CLARK [Horror's Hallowed Grounds, creator]	212
JOE MONKS [The Bunker]	220
ACKNOWLEDGEMENTS	229
INDEX	230

INTRODUCTION
BROKEN, BLOODIED + DESPERATE...

...a young woman drags herself along a sizzling blacktop beneath a wide blue sky. She only has minutes to live. She knows it, we know it, and we all know how it will end—we've seen it a thousand times before. But in this moment before a bullet puts paid to the struggles that have brought her to this place, she is beautiful.

The scene that graces the cover of this book may be one of the most intense ever screened in English-language cinema. It comes from Australian director Greg McLean's 2005 masterpiece *Wolf Creek*. Like all of the films discussed in this volume, it managed to bring a new quality to a type of film that had long since fallen into mind-numbing routine. It is a sterling example of the "New Horror."

While the genre is still no closer to being regarded as anything more than the suspense film's scumbag brother by the mainstream, it has nevertheless undergone a radical transformation over the last 15 years. Like most of us, the genre had to hit rock bottom—think recent PG-13 offerings at your local multiplex—before it came back swinging.

What, then, is the New Horror? Though disturbed minds can disagree, for the purposes of this book the New Horror is a film released in the last several years that delivers one or more of the following:

1 AESTHETIC APPEAL No matter how vicious the on-screen carnage, even its most disturbing scenes are rendered in a stunning, and unexpectedly appealing, way.

2. AN UNDERLYING MESSAGE And no, "stay the hell out of the woods" does *not* count. Rather, the movie uses an extreme style or story to underscore issues that affect a great many of us today.

3. HIDDEN DEPTHS The film's multilayered approach to its story and/or execution rewards repeat viewings with a greater understanding of the tale and its message.

WHAT AWAITS YOU WITHIN THESE PAGES

Certainly an exhaustive examination of horror cinema of the last 15 years would take up a good four volumes of this size at least. Instead, *The New Horror Handbook* seeks to explore the evolution of 21st century fright cinema by offering an in-depth look at several landmark filmmakers, allowing them to speak directly to their audiences as they reveal what went on behind the scenes of their greatest works. Though many of them are no strangers to the horror press, the level of detail you will find herein is unprecedented for the writers and directors in question. Some are controversial, others little known beyond their most famous works. Yet I believe that all are worth understanding by anyone who appreciates a good cinematic scare. And for those of you who are in the process of converting friends or family to the genre, you just might pick up an argument or two to help you along in that thankless task.

Finally, the last part of this book, Tomorrow's Terrors, takes a look at how the genre has inspired others to bring their nightmares to the screen, regardless of their backgrounds or the obstacles that stood in their way.

REVIEWS
Within each chapter, you will find movie reviews labeled
POSTMORTEM

SPOILERS

As most horror flicks succeed or fail on the strength of their endings, it serves little purpose to avoid discussing them here, much less discussing them with their creators. The reader is advised to see any film discussed in this book prior to reading its corresponding chapter. Go on...Netflix it.

HORROR: THE STORY SO FAR

The New Horror Handbook prides itself on being one of the first books of its kind to begin its chronicles not with Thomas Edison's *Frankenstein* silent, the Universal monster greats, nor even George Romero's *Living Dead* series. That's because the New Horror has very little to do with these classics.

While Frankenstein, Dracula and his pals remain nostalgic favorites for many, and the offal-chomping splendor of Romero's *Living Dead* pushed the envelope further still, they are all works very much of their days.

Since the mid- to late 1990s, horror cinema has matured beyond the simple splatter that characterized so many flicks of the '70s and '80s. There's no shortage of blood in modern offerings, but it's been leavened with themes that address modern concerns with such forces as globalization, tensions between haves and have-nots, and the alienating influences of technology.

While the works of Romero and John Carpenter in particular are often singled out as artistic responses to the carnage of the Vietnam conflict that dominated their formative years, today's directors have found greater demons to grapple with, many of them much closer to home.

The events of Sept. 11, 2001 were the warning bell that the gloves were off when it came to world violence and its impact on the First World. Operations in Vietnam were hell for anyone unlucky enough to be drafted. Yet, if a draftee's love of life and limb was strong enough, he kissed his mother, packed a bag and got the hell out of Dodge. Where do you go when planes are hitting New York skyscrapers and trains are blowing up in London? When street cleaners are bagging limbs and viscera in the capitals of the free world, Michael Myers is a cartoon and the living dead are quaint boogeymen for a quieter time.

I was working at *USA Today* on 9/11, in a Washington-area building that gave us a front-row seat to the plane that crashed into the Pentagon. That evening, National Guard troops patrolled the streets as we struggled to update the newspaper's Web site and soberly debated whether anyone would ever pay to see a dark or explosion-riddled film again.

Since then, mainstream horror films have, if anything, grown darker. They've turned their gaze from motiveless slashers to mediations on the hatred of white, privileged young people by "others"—be they Third World ghouls or First World pariahs. Frequently these murderous creatures are themselves victims, whether it's *Saw*'s cancer-ridden Jigsaw or the deadly intruder in the French phenomenon *Inside*. Sometimes, these films seem to say, we reap what we sow.

The manner of dispatch, too, has grown more extreme, giving rise to a subgenre that was quickly dubbed "torture porn" or "gorno." *(See p. 34 for a brief look at this trend.)* The former term originally referred to films that gradually build up an almost sexual tension that only reaches climax with the evisceration of victims on-screen—an idea similar to that behind the snuff films of myth, really. However, torture porn soon became a pejorative catch-all applied to any film that featured protracted, on-camera brutality.

But it wasn't all splintered limbs and agonized screams. After hitting the big time with his *30 Days of Night* comic series, for example, writer Steve Niles finally saw his masterwork hit the big screen in 2007. With director David Slade behind the camera, *30 Days* single-handedly gave the world one of its first truly terrifying vampire films.

In fact by May 2009, just as this book is going to press, horror cinema appears on the verge of another renaissance if this year's releases are anything to go by.

But that's a story for another time, and perhaps another volume of *The New Horror Handbook*. For now, it's time to go back to the beginning of the New Horror, starting with a name that's cursed as often as it's praised. Then again, if you're truly a bringer of nightmares to the big screen, how could it ever be otherwise? [NHH]

FUTURE TENSE
Just a few months before the text for this book was finalized, I caught a screening of the Swedish phenomenon *Let the Right One In*. Not only is it one of the best supernatural tales I've ever seen, it stands as one of the best examples I've come across of what the New Horror is all about—a work that uses elements of the horrific to highlight what it is to be human.

PART ONE

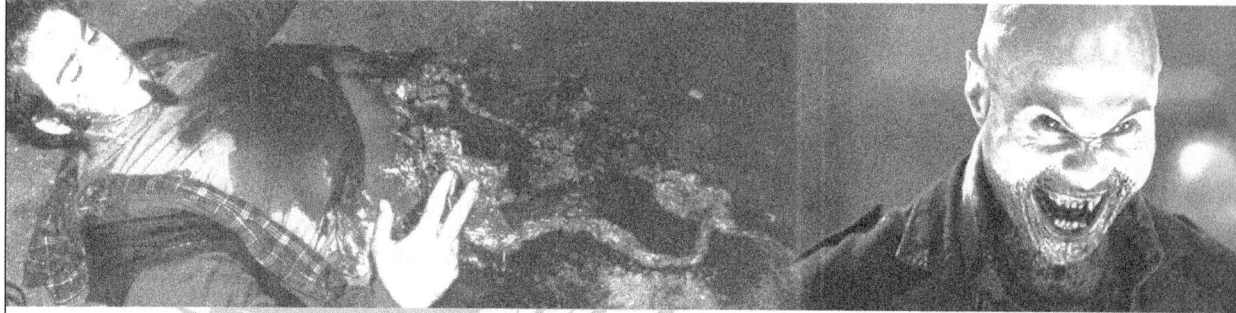

GOT GUTS?

During the first decade of the 21st century, the New Horror embraced the on-screen depiction of over-the-top suffering, an aesthetic quickly dubbed "torture porn" by the mainstream. While a great catch-all phrase for any film depicting ultrarealistic agony, it glosses over a fundamental change cinema has recently undergone.

The horror genre is forever engaged in a game of one-upmanship of the extreme, not only with the last fright flick, but also with the horrors that grace the nightly news. After the events of Sept. 11, 2001 and the world atrocities that followed, that became infinitely more difficult, and directors responded in kind.

The talents in this section each have brought an unprecedented edge and realism to horror, emphasizing the visceral price to be paid when opposing cultures collide. Though **Eli Roth** (p. 10) is often pilloried for his ultra-violent *Hostel* series, his films illustrated the dark ramifications of America's empire building years before the nation grew weary of the Iraq war.

Director **Greg McLean's** (p. 44) *Wolf Creek* and *Rogue* followed in a similar vein, revealing the inevitable chaos that comes when people fail to summon the proper humility when traipsing through lands not their own.

Lastly, comic book writer **Steve Niles** (p. 64), together with illustrator Ben Templesmith, gave vampires back their bite with the 2002 comic series *30 Days of Night,* basis for the 2007 film of the same name.

THE LENNY BRUCE OF BLOODSHED

ELI ROTH

THERE'S SOMETHING NOT QUITE RIGHT ABOUT ELI ROTH. AT LEAST NOT IF YOU BELIEVE HIS CRITICS. WHEN HE HIT THE TORONTO FILM FESTIVAL IN 2002 WITH *CABIN FEVER*, HIS FIRST FEATURE, HE WAS EMBRACED BY HORROR AND MAINSTREAM JOURNALISTS ALIKE AS THE PLUCKY HORROR FAN WHO HAD MADE A SLIGHTLY FREAKY, BUT GENUINELY EFFECTIVE, FLICK....

His infectious enthusiasm for classic grindhouse films and the whole moviemaking process, combined with *Cabin Fever's* against-the-odds success story, lent him instant street cred with horror buffs and starry-eyed entrepreneurs.

Still, critics being the wary beasts that they are, withheld judgment, waiting for Roth's next effort lest *Cabin Fever* prove to be a fluke. When *Hostel* finally emerged in 2005, things got a lot clearer.

It was, after all, a garish movie about obnoxious frat-boy types on a perpetual booty call, which gloried in the juxtaposition of torture and sex. "Torture porn" quickly entered the vernacular.

As for Roth himself, his enthusiasm in interviews and his apparent glee in describing his messy *mise-en-scene* coalesced into a single obvious conclusion: Roth himself was an obnoxious frat boy. Whatever artistic gifts he had, he was going to use them to piss in the lemonade.

But *Hostel* was not made in a vacuum. World events, particularly in the countrywide hell that is Iraq, seemed to rush to Roth's aide, rapidly cobbling together a context for his movie from the shrapnel-ridden bodies of the Iraq war.

"With *Hostel*, it's my fears of what's happening in the world and where I see America going," Roth says. "It's people who go in and kind of piss on another culture and take advantage of it and then realize how out of their element they are. Then they turn to that culture for help but they've already spurned them."

It takes some doing to miss the parallels in today's headlines. Yet detractors have proven stubbornly immune to any meaningful analysis of Roth's work, seemingly incapable of moving past blowtorch face-offs, cranial soccer games and eerily beautiful snuff set pieces.

It calls to mind the reaction America's self-appointed guardians of decency had to stand-up comic **Lenny Bruce** back in the '60s. Rapping out discourses on race relations, politics and explaining "what is" as opposed to "what should be," Bruce peppered his commentary

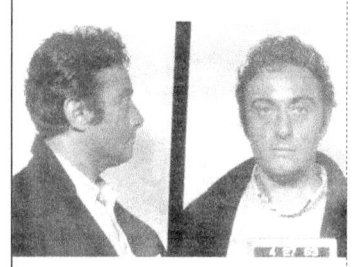

Lenny Bruce
When Roth learned this chapter was titled *"The Lenny Bruce of Bloodshed,"* he admitted Bruce is a hero of his. "When I was being put through the ringer on *Hostel 2*, I thought of him a lot. I also thought about how sad his life became, and how the powers of 'decency' destroyed a brilliant man."

with the idiom of the day, including the same dozen words that every generation uses behind closed doors. Continuously dragged into court for using objectionable language in front of nightclubs full of adults, the Powers That Be never acknowledged the value of the underlying insights in Bruce's routines. The disparities between blacks and whites in society were fine, but God forbid you should use the word "motherfucker" when describing them.

But is Eli Roth some sort of crusading Michael Moore of splatter, an overenthusiastic fanboy with a camera and the ear of a generation, or one of the most level-headed filmmakers in horror? To understand his work, you have to go back to the Roth family home in the Boston suburbs of the 1970s, and a child who was more Baudelaire than Beavis or Butthead.

'ALWAYS DRAWN TO THOSE COLORS'

Born April 18, 1972, Roth grew up in the Boston bedroom community of Newton, Mass., 10 miles to the east. Among other distinctions, it is the city from which the Fig Newton gets its name.

It's "a wonderful city, the safest city in America," Roth says. "But it's really doctors, lawyers, bankers, businessmen. If you want to do anything in the arts there, arts are considered a hobby. They're not a profession."

Yet in the Roth household, the arts were taken very seriously. Although parents Cora and Sheldon grew up in working-class Brooklyn—Bensonhust and **Brownsville**, respectively—they also grew up going to New York's museums and theaters. Sheldon, though a psychoanalyst and assistant clinical professor of psychiatry at Harvard Medical School today, had gone to the High School for Performing Arts in New York City (yes, the *Fame* school), intent on becoming an actor right up until college. Meanwhile, Cora had a deep connection with painting, though she didn't pick up a paintbrush until she was 40.

ART IMITATES LIFE IMITATES ART

Fox News' **Neil Cavuto** wasn't having any of it when, on the March 12, 2007 episode of Cavuto's program, Roth told him flat out he thought the success of *Hostel* and its kin was best explained by a populace that, having seen the horrors of the Iraq war and government bungling of Hurricane Katrina in 2005, simply wanted a venue in which to scream.

"Thanks to George Bush and Dick Cheney and Donald Rumsfeld, there's a whole new wave of horror movies," he said. "Everybody's clicked on the Internet and seen those videos of people being decapitated and it's really terrifying."

Cavuto wasn't willing to concede the point. However, to his credit, after reporting that *Hostel* made $70 million with a budget of only $5 million, he muttered, "If this guy were a stock, you'd buy him."

Brownsville

"Bensonhurst was a working class neighborhood, but Brownsville was the projects," Roth says. "That's one of the poorest, most dangerous areas of Brooklyn, where my Dad grew up. Mike Tyson's from there, as is RZA from Wu-Tang Clan. When my Dad met RZA, they talked about going to the same school and swimming at the same public pool in the projects as kids."

"My mother gave my two brothers and me easels and art supplies," Roth recalls. "Equally as important as sports or school or anything else was that we all had our own easel to create whatever we wanted."

While growing up, the boys were exposed to the great artists. In fact, it may be here that Roth's disconnect with critics first began.

"We would look at the **paintings of Goya** and Hieronymus Bosch, and there are a lot of paintings that I saw that had very violent imagery, but also were very, very beautiful," he says. "Any time I saw an image that was created in a film or photograph or painting, I knew that it was an artist's creation. I never saw it as real violence, I saw it as a representation of violence, and I was always drawn to those colors."

One only has to take in the spectacle of the festival scene in *Hostel Part II* to see the Bosch influence. "I used a lot of Bosch's paintings for the style and design and colors, and for the puppet show stage we used little pieces of Bosch paintings in the actual design," Roth says.

Paintings of Goya
Though a painter for the Spanish court, Francisco de Goya (1746-1828) is probably best known today for works that depicted the horrors of war and man's general inhumanity to man. The most famous of these include "The Third of May 1808" which depicts death by firing squad and "The Disasters of War" (above).

This is a trademark dynamic of many films in the New Horror tradition: what this book calls the "beautiful bruise." It is an at-times nauseating imagery rendered in stark, beautiful colors and expert compositions, daring you to look away and to take it all in simultaneously. Greg McLean does this brilliantly with his horrors in the Australian outback in *Wolf Creek* (see p. 44). Spain's Nacho Cerdà reached the apex—or perhaps scraped the bottom of the grave—with his 1994 short *Aftermath*.

Though inspired by his mother's artistic leanings as a child, Roth was no stranger to the baser pleasures of life. His basement was ground zero for every slashing and scream moviedom could come up with, thanks to the home video revolution. So long as the pizza held out, he was content—more than content—to experience the worlds of *The Texas Chainsaw Massacre* and *Motel Hell, Mother's Day* and *The Evil Dead*. The aspiring gorehound—at 12 already

determined to be a director—absorbed it all.

"All I wanted to do was go to the video store and load up on as many movies as I could," he remembers. "To me, that was the most fun thing in the world; everything else was secondary."

It is this unabashed devotion to grindhouse cinema upon which so many critics have sharpened their blades, using his animated interviews and wide-eyed explanation of his craft to paint him as an overgrown child obsessed with things nice grown-ups don't discuss.

Many horror fans, however, recognize in him a kindred spirit. He is someone who enjoys what they enjoy, and not only has become successful enough to be able to proclaim his love of this much-abused genre, but also has been successful in that very medium,

"Right from the get-go, I was always in this because I loved it, and that love for movies has never gone away," Roth says.

giving a double birdflip to the naysayers.

"The key thing is that, right from the get-go, I was always in this because I loved it, and that love for movies has never gone away," he says. "I think my eyes have been opened to a lot of things, and you certainly become more jaded in certain areas. I'm not naïve the way I was five years ago, but I think the key is that you have to genuinely love it."

OUT OF THE BASEMENT

You can't stay in the basement forever. As high school drew to a close, Roth still knew he wanted to be a director. He recalls his friend's parents telling him, "What you need is a good liberal arts education, then go to grad school if that's really what you want to do." Other people were telling him the same thing—don't gamble your future on a pipe dream.

One day he took this collected wisdom to his parents.

"I remember my dad going, 'These idiots have no fucking idea what they're talking about! You want to be a filmmaker? You go to film school 'cause when you're 18, you're gonna want to work on movies!'"

Dr. Roth also set him straight on the whole idea of waiting around until he had a degree in his hand before getting his feet wet. His advice? "If there's a movie that's shooting, go work on it for free. The stuff you're willing to do at 18, you'll never do when you're 22 and have a college degree," Roth remembers him saying. "And he was right."

At last, the teenager saw a path out of the basement and into the film world.

Not that the two were mutually exclusive. When he was 8, he made his first film on Super 8—*A Clickwork Orange*—down there. As he got older, the films took a decidedly more violent turn with ketchup often standing in for the red stuff he could never quite get enough of on screen.

A week after he began film school at New York University, he met someone in the elevator who was looking for help in the art department for a Russian feature film called *Black and White*. "It cost probably $100,000," he says, "but they were shooting on 35 [millimeter], and I thought that was the coolest thing ever."

After classes and whenever he could rustle up some free time, Roth would go down to the Lower East Side to dress sets, carry couches up and down stairs, and tackle many of the other tasks nobody ever thinks about going on behind the scenes. It was hard work, but it wasn't without its perks. For instance, he rubbed shoulders with Teamsters who had worked on *Basket Case* and *Frankenhooker* among other horror classics.

Later that year, he landed his first proper film job when his Super 8 film class instructor mentioned that director **Milos Forman** was helping some grad students at Columbia with a $100,000 feature and could use some help. It wasn't quite the opportunity he'd dreamed of; the filmmakers needed someone to help reconstitute film in the editing room. But every moment he could spare, Roth reported to sort through the trim bin. In the process, he not only got his hands on 35 mm film equipment, but also he learned how an editing room works. He was 18.

"My whole freshman year, people are out going to parties and all I wanted to do was work on films, and I did it every weekend," he says. "I skipped my spring breaks. Everyone else is partying in Fort Lauderdale and I was in the editing room sorting trims." And on his wall hung a reminder of why the hell he was doing all this in the first place: a poster for the 1982 cult classic *Pieces*.

Yet, spending nearly every waking moment learning film theory in the classroom and the craft on real film sets, Roth was getting the itch that every son of celluloid is all too acquainted with.

Call it cabin fever.

Basket Case (1982) and *Frankenhooker* (1990) are two classic horror/black comedy flicks from low-budget horror master Frank Henenlotter.

Milos Forman
Czechoslovakian-born American filmmaker Milos Forman is best known for the movies *One Flew Over the Cuckoo's Nest, Hair, Amadeus,* and the Andy Kaufman biopic *Man on the Moon.*

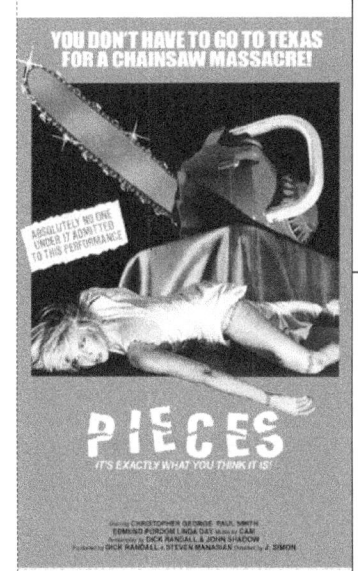

Cabin Fever carried with it an undercurrent of black humor that raised it above the level of the usual schlock that fans were used to. Here Roth acts and directs.

'EVERYTHING'S DISSOLVING'

In 1995, after moving to Los Angeles and working on dozens of movie sets—covering every base from assistant editor to production assistant—Roth and former NYU roommate Randy Pearlstein wrote the script for *Cabin Fever*.

For the most part, the story was an unremarkable one. Five young adults celebrate their college graduation by partying at a cabin in the woods. A man out walking his dog succumbs to a mysterious, flesh-eating disease and brings it to the partiers' door, infecting them in the process. Yet the script had an undercurrent of daring black humor and interesting character dynamics that raised it above the usual schlock that horror fans were used to.

The germ of the story literally came up with the stroke of a razor one morning when Roth was 19, working on a horse farm in Iceland. The day before, he'd been cleaning out a barn filled with 20-year-old hay and contracted a bizarre skin condition for his troubles. Upon shaving, his skin came away with the stubble. That experience melded with an article about flesh-eating bacteria he came across later to form the basis of *Cabin Fever*.

However, it would be another six years before he finally found the funding to put it in front of a camera. In the meantime, horror had all but disappeared at the corner cinema.

"By the '90s, R-rated horror had completely died," Roth recalls. "Everything was PG-13 after *The Ring*, *The Others* and *The Sixth Sense*—all great films, but all ghost movies. Hollywood tried to apply that formula to every horror movie, so you had these terrible PG-13 movies with no sex and violence."

When *Cabin Fever* finally began filming, Roth was asked by investors to shoot a PG-13 as well as an R-rated version, he says. They argued there was no way a truly adult horror flick would ever be welcome in theaters. He refused. "My point was that the sex and violence would be the very thing that brought people out to see it," he says. "It was very validating to have Peter Jackson and Fran Walsh [the director and co-writer/co-producer of the *Lord of the Rings* films, respectively] tell me they cheered when they saw Cerina Vincent's breasts, because they never thought they'd see nudity in an American horror film again."

In October 2001, when Roth and cinematographer Scott Kevan finally began work on *Cabin Fever* in North Carolina, they were still struggling to raise the cash, "which was a nightmare," Roth recalls. The film's main bankrollers had pulled out and the filmmakers had already spent $700,000. When the union shut the whole operation down halfway through the shoot demanding back pay, "I was like, 'Well, at least I got to shoot for 12 days,'" he says.

But Roth's father lent him $110,000 from his retirement savings, and several other private investors came through, as well. Even so, returning to LA, the filmmaker desperately needed another $800,000

"Everything was PG-13 after *The Ring*, *The Others* and *The Sixth Sense*...Hollywood tried to apply that formula to every horror movie, so you had these terrible PG-13 movies..."
— ELI ROTH

Rider Strong takes himself to the river in *Cabin Fever*.

to shoot another two days, mix the sound and finish cutting it all together. The film was edited on a borrowed Avid machine for deferred payment.

Forming a limited liability corporation, he sold shares raising $1.5 million, and ended up with a 9 percent stake in the film himself.

Had he thought *Cabin Fever* was just another in a long line of pointless splatter flicks, he wouldn't have bothered. But Roth was determined to make a film that horror fans would recognize as the work of one of their own, and Kevan, who had studied at the American Film Institute, was anxious to pull out the stops cinematically. Aside from the film's much-publicized nods to *Evil Dead* and *Texas Chainsaw* were subtler moves designed to maximize *Cabin Fever*'s overall impact.

"Scott and I wanted the lenses to get tighter and tighter and tighter," he explains. "They start very, very wide, with the guy walking through the woods; it's all shot with super-wide lenses. Whoever's sick gets shot in single and everyone else as a group, so you feel like the group is against them. The lenses get tighter and tighter so you start to feel the claustrophobia of being stuck in that cabin. We went through it with the production designer, too. We talked about how the cabin would look beautiful during the day, and dark and evil at night."

It went far beyond the lenses. The pair subjected the footage to what is called a bleach bypass, which had the effect of making the film grow progressively darker from reel to reel. "By the time [Rider Strong's character] is at that campfire at night, it really has that look and feel—you can almost see the grain," Roth says. "It feels more like a '70s film."

Following a suggestion by George Folsey Jr. (father of *Cabin Fever* editor Ryan Folsey and editor of *Hostel* and *Hostel Part II*), the filmmakers shot on Super 35. This format records a larger image on 35 mm stock by using the space normally set aside for the sound track. "It's a great way to make it look big budget," Roth explains. "I knew Carpenter had done that on *Halloween*."

What Carpenter probably hadn't done was have his artist mother and psychoanalyst father lend a hand on set.

"We were shooting the scene where Cerina [Vincent, "Marcy"] ends up shaving her legs off, and it was the first time [my parents were] on set seeing me with the crew," Roth remembers. "There she is, naked in the tub, like, 'Hi Dr. Roth, hi Mrs. Roth,' and they're waving 'hi' to her."

Ever the analytical one, Dr. Roth began peeling away the layers of meaning as his son contemplated stripping the meat from Marcy's bones. "My father says, 'Now, if you look at the rot underneath the surface, the way her flesh is dissolving is the way her relationships are dissolving, everything's dissolving,'" the director says in his father's authoritative tones. "'It's the rot, the worst part of a human's personality being brought to the surface that's represented through the disease. The body is a metaphor for the darkest part of human personalities and their selfish nature.'"

A rare shot of Tommy smothering Dennis from the director's cut, which has only screened at film festivals.

Cerina Vincent (Marcy) takes matters into her own hands in *Cabin Fever*.

Not to be outdone, his mother becomes one of the first people to dissect the aesthetics of her son's film. "My mother's going, 'Look at the beautiful colors of the red, the way that blood mixes with the white...it's like a beautiful painting,'" Roth says, laughing. "And I'm just going, 'Look at her tits! You guys are missing the best part!'"

But it wasn't all tits and giggles. A great deal of *Cabin Fever*, as Dr. Roth pointed out, is about the dissolution of relationships, which necessitated a fair amount of tears on the parts of the actors.

Roth was trying to get the tears flowing for Jordan Ladd (the doomed "Karen" who winds up locked in the shed), he remembers. "While they were lighting the shot, I was trying to direct Jordan to get her all prepared emotionally. She just looked at me and said, 'Can you just get your dad?'"

He thought about it a second and then called for the "set psychiatrist." A minute later, Dr. Roth sat down with Ladd.

"My dad says, 'Tell me about your mother,' and Jordan just starts talking and talking and crying and crying, and then he walks away and I'm like, 'Roll camera!' My little brother Gabe [who shot the *Beneath the Skin* making-of documentary] turns to my dad and says, 'How does it feel to use your powers for evil?'"

Quoth the good doctor: "I've never done that before. It's great!"

'OH MY GOD, IT WORKED'

The film was shot and everyone was in debt. "If you looked back at the risks we took on *Cabin Fever*, it was insane," Roth says. "We literally had risked everything…and people had put up their houses. If I had known what I would have to go through and what I risked and what was going to happen, I don't think I—I don't think any of us would've done it." »26

Director of photography Scott Kevan and Roth discuss a shot for *Cabin Fever*.

POSTMORTEM

The year 2002 was a horrible one for horror. Unable to find another profitable franchise like the *Scream* series, studios were throwing everything at the wall to see what stuck. Nothing did. Series retreads? *Friday the 13th's Jason X* and *Halloween: Resurrection.* Shitty remake? All aboard *Ghost Ship.* Computer game? *Resident Evil.* Crappy Stephen King flick? *Rose Red.* Then there was *Darkness, Queen of the Damned, The Mothman Prophecies, Skinwalkers,* it just went on and on. The only genuinely horrific flick to hit screens was Gore Verbinski's *The Ring*, and that was a remake of Hideo Nakata's Japanese sensation, *Ringu*.

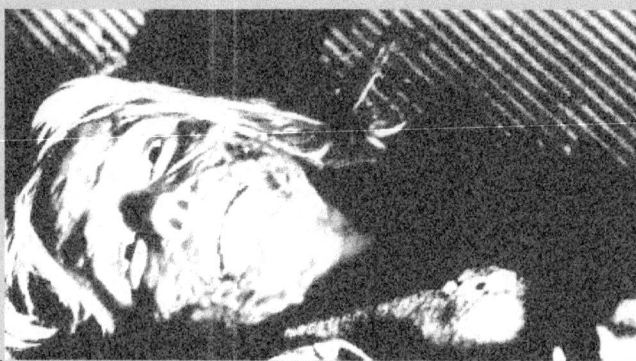

The horror climate was so awful, in fact, it seemed to spur several filmmakers to show the rest of the world how it's done. Sure, there was *Darkness Falls, Dreamcatcher* and *Gothika* in 2003, but we also wound up with a host of foreign greats like *Haute Tension, Ju-On: The Grudge* and *Oldboy*. In the States, there was *Open Water*, a pretty decent *Texas Chainsaw Massacre* remake…and *Cabin Fever.* ✛

The beauty of Eli Roth's feature film debut is the director's willingness to experiment with the line between humor and fear. Unlike self-referential films like *Scream*, the chuckles in *Cabin Fever* —who can ever forget pancake-loving Dennis?— devolve into a sinking feeling of utter alienation.

✛ Technically the spate of horrible 2002 films didn't directly drive *Cabin Fever* as shooting was completed on that movie in April of that year.

Roth set out to follow in the footsteps of Sam Raimi's *Evil Dead*, and in some ways he surpassed it. There are no evil spell books or entities here—all of the carnage that befalls the five college kids in this film is down to a flesh-eating disease, and is uncomfortably close to life as we know it. (Ebola, anyone?)

Paul (Rider Strong) Karen (Jordan Ladd), Jeff (Joey Kern), Marcy (Cerina Vincent) and Bert (James DeBello) slip off to a cabin in the woods in some hick town to celebrate graduation. The locals are creepy, but these teens are far too interested in drinking and fooling around to notice. It's not long, however, before a transient with a nasty case of something awful comes to their door. When the kids turn him away, he tries to steal their truck, prompting his accidental death. Once his body lands in the water supply, we can see where this is all going to end.

But not entirely. Though the makeup effects are all appropriately nauseating, *Cabin Fever* spends as much time focusing on the dissolution of the bonds between the friends as it does on the physical effects of the illness. In the process, it becomes something greater than the sum of its parts.

Disease-ridden as it was, *Cabin Fever* was the shot-in-the-arm horror films needed in 2003, and its effects can still be seen to this day.

«23   But they *had* done it, and now something damn well had to be done with it because there wasn't a dime available to do anything else.

In September 2002, *Cabin Fever* premiered at the Toronto International Film Festival, which also had seen international or North American launches of such films as *American Beauty*, *Sideways* and *Crash*.

"The buyers typically play it cool," Roth says of that cinematic meat market. "They don't give you any reaction." If they don't like a film, they will usually leave after 5 or 10 minutes. If you're a beginning filmmaker, this is usually where you start measuring the evening in cigarettes and alcohol.

"I will never forget the lights going down and people starting to applaud *Cabin Fever* and the way that audience reacted," he says. There was "a line out the door all the way down the block to get in, and the people who got in were going insane, screaming, laughing, and even applauding!

"I remember I walked out of that theater and I was surrounded by eight different people: Revolution, New Line, Miramax, and they were all grabbing me saying, 'We're buying it,' 'We're buying it,' 'We're buying it.' And I just thought, 'Oh my God, it worked!'"

This wasn't supposed to happen. *Cabin Fever* was just one of *those* kinds of movies, and was pretty much treated that way.

"It was the last movie; they wouldn't even put it in competition," he says. "It was the throwaway and then it stole the festival. It was all people were talking about, and all of a sudden everyone in town wants to meet me."

In the end, Lionsgate bought *Cabin Fever* for $3.5 million, earning itself a tidy $30.5 million the following year. "And what *Cabin Fever* did to their stock prices," Roth says. "It went from $1.98 to $6 from the time they bought *Cabin Fever* until it was on DVD. Which is what I was saying all along. Just because you make a low-budget movie doesn't mean it has to be low quality. It

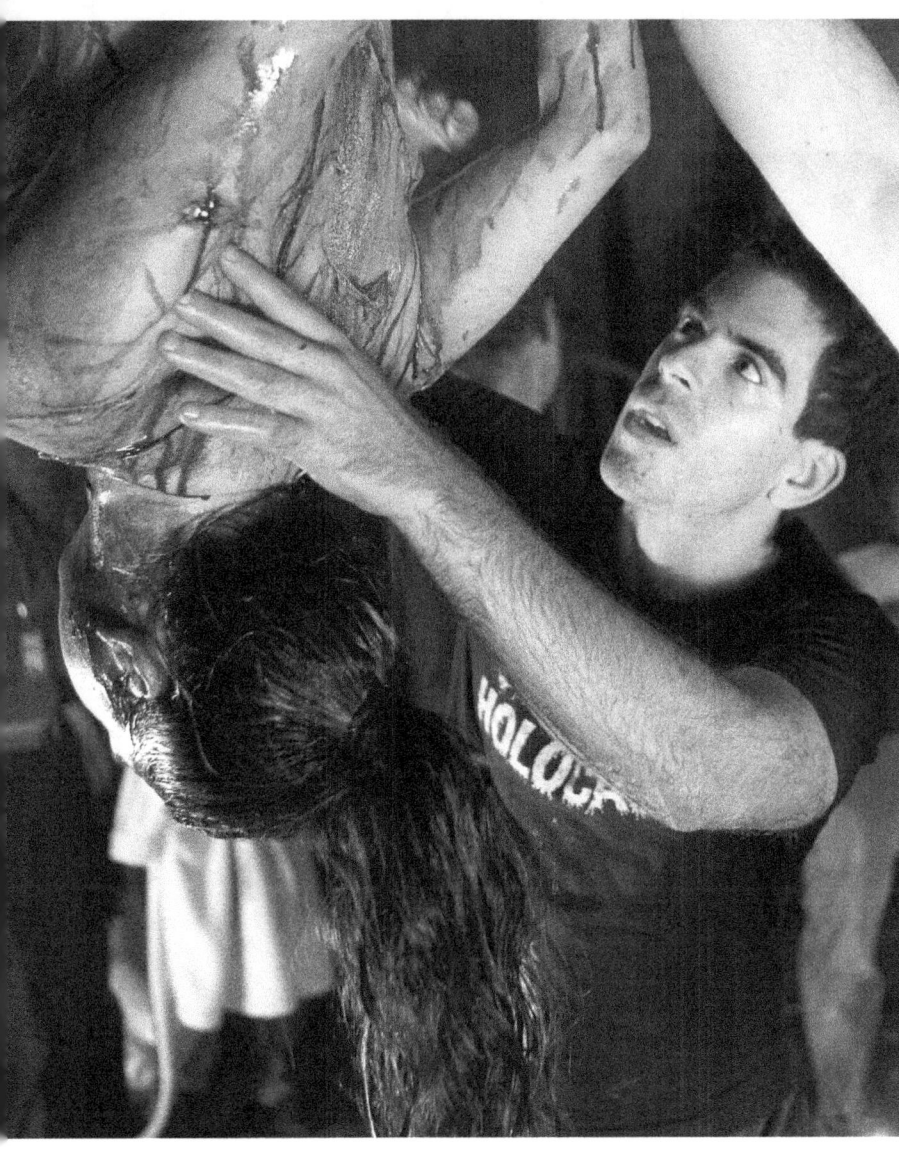

Roth helps Heather Matarazzo prepare to meet her maker in *Hostel Part II*.

can be a high-quality movie made on a low budget, and it can go into every multiplex in America."

HOSTEL TERRITORY

While *Cabin Fever* got the usual critical drubbing reserved for any film not about a historical figure, the latest Jane Austen relacing, or testament to the human spirit, the horror community greeted it and its director with open arms.

Takashi Miike
Though his back catalog is extremely uneven (covering everything from children's movies such as *Tennen Shojo Mann Next* to classic Triad/Yakuza flick *Dead or Alive*), Japan's Takashi Miike (left) was instrumental in introducing Western audiences to that island nation's tradition of extreme horror cinema. Highlights include the my-love-done-me-real-wrong tale *Audition*, the over-the-top bloodbath *Ichi the Killer*, and *Imprint*, the only episode of Showtime's *Masters of Horror* series to be pulled from broadcast.

Harry Knowles, entertainment maven and creator of the Ain't It Cool News Web site, was one of Roth's biggest boosters. It was while the director was waiting to resolve the union dispute on *Cabin Fever* that the pair got into one of those "what's the sickest thing you've seen online" discussions. Knowles sent him a link to a site that charged clients $10,000 for the thrill of shooting someone in the head in Thailand. Perhaps even more disturbing was the rationalization that the victims' impoverished families received a cut of the take.

Whether the site was the real deal or another of the Web's many hoaxes, the concept stuck with Roth. After *Cabin Fever* took Hollywood by storm, he ended up meeting Mike Fleiss, a producer on *The Texas Chainsaw Massacre* remake, and partner Chris Briggs. Briggs had an idea for a movie called *Hostel* about backpackers, but not a clue as to what the story should be about. It didn't take the director long to see the possibilities.

He had to do *something*. Sure, he was the toast of the town now, but the only scripts he was getting were for the usual low budget, formulaic horror tripe that he had purposefully avoided making the first time around. If his second feature film was a dud, he knew a lot of those newly opened doors in Hollywood would quickly shut. *Cabin Fever* had nudged the medium forward slightly. *Saw* was out at the time, ratcheting up the acceptable level of violence in American mainstream theaters even more.

But what Roth wanted to do was something that had never played in US multiplexes before: a real balls-out assault to the senses along the lines of what has to be the ultimate bad date movie: Japanese director **Takashi Miike**'s classic *Audition*. (And for pity's sake, if you *haven't* seen this film and you're reading this book, spare us both some embarrassment and rent it this week.)

If Roth needed a catalyst, and he probably didn't, he found it in the form of fellow grindhouse enthusiast and *Cabin Fever* fan Quentin Tarantino. Encouraging him to kick over the fences and make a truly uncompromising horror flick, Tarantino ended up executive producing 2005's *Hostel*.

The result was a full-on cinematic sucker punch to the nervous system that doubtless made a whole generation of idealistic young people glare at their as-yet-unread *Lonely Planet* guidebooks with a new sense of fearful skepticism. The nauseating effects cooked up by the KNB EFX team were harrowing enough, but the sting from this film lay firmly in the tale, and its thin veneer of reality. There was also something else.

Anyone who's sampled a fair number of horror films made in the last 15 years is familiar with the tendency of some filmmakers to damn the bloodlust of their own audiences through a reflexive cinematic conceit. Michael Haneke's **Funny Games** (1997) is probably the best example of this, where a pair of young men who brutalize a family address the camera, implicating the audience in the horrors that follow. Though *Hostel* leaves the fourth wall firmly intact, a good portion of the audience probably has no problem »32

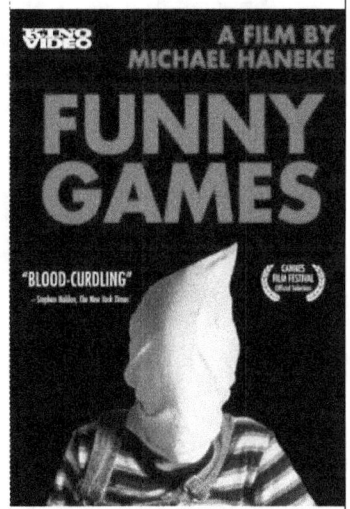

"I found *Funny Games* preachy and pretentious. I felt you could make the point of the audience as complicit in the violence in a far more subtle way, the way Hitchcock did in *The Birds* when the woman in the diner verbally attacks Tippi Hedron saying 'you brought them here! It's your fault!'"
—ROTH

POSTMORTEM

If you've never seen either of these movies, fair warning to say that they are both better, and worse, than you've been led to believe. To borrow a tagline from *Pieces*, one of the director's favorite flicks as a kid: "It's exactly what you think it is."

Hostel gets off to a rollicking start when American backpackers Paxton (Jay Hernandez) and Josh (Derek Richardson) and Icelander Óli (Eythor Gudjonsson) all leave Amsterdam for Slovakia after hearing about a hostel brimming with easy, beautiful Slovakian women. Once there, the Americans quickly gain two easy roommates (Barbara Nedeljáková and Jana Kaderabkova) but lose Óli the following morning. Soon it comes to light that the hostel is operated by an admirably entrepreneurial endeavor called Elite Hunting, which sells backpackers to sadists around the world to do with what they will in the privacy of a nearby factory.

"I wanted the audience to agree with every decision the characters make until the moment they're in the chair, when they realize that maybe it was wrong to take advantage of these girls and think you could buy and sell them just because you're an American in a country with less money," Roth says.

HOSTEL + HOSTEL PART II

> **As a film, *Part II* is far more accomplished in terms of visual style than its predecessor. We have here an excellent example of the "beautiful bruise"— the images are as gorgeous as their content is upsetting.**

What follows is an upsetting, visually stunning, and occasionally amusing descent into a nightmare world made all the more devastating by seeming to confirm the existence of people evil beyond measure. It might just be a movie, but the killing techniques on display, from blowtorches to chainsaws, doubtless have been perfected off screen in dozens of countries around the world.

By film's end, Paxton escapes the situation and hits the rails for *Hostel Part II*. The sequel promptly ties up that one loose end by dispatching him in the first few minutes. The speedy end meted out to the only person resembling a hero in the first movie sets the pace for *Part II*, which proves a far grimmer ordeal than the original. With Quentin Tarantino as executive producer, there's every temptation to compare the films to the two *Kill Bill* flicks, which followed a similar dual tonality.

This time around, students Whitney (Bijou Phillips), Beth (Lauren German) and Lorna (Heather Matarazzo) are lured to Slovakia by Axelle (Vera Jordanova), where they check into that Roach Motel for nubile young 'uns. Roth throws us a new curve here as the hostel clerk uploads their passport photos to an online auction site —Elite Hunting has embraced e-commerce. Getting into the party mood, the girls attend a village festival from which Lorna disappears. Nastiness ensues. We've definitely been here before.

Or have we? While the story remains the same, the tone is darker and carries with it the faintest hint of a director holding up a mirror to his audience. "Thought this was all a cool idea the first time around when it was a group of horny guys getting bumped off," he seems to say. "Now that it's young girls looking for a good time, you're not feeling so good, are ya?"

"I wanted the audience for just a moment to feel guilty, but then to feel redeemed by the end," he says. "They are paying to torture someone just as the clients are. [But] you just can't make people feel bad about it for too long. A minute or two's enough."

Hostel Part II is far more accomplished in terms of visual style than its predecessor. We have here an excellent example of the "beautiful bruise"— the images are as gorgeous as their content is upsetting. Roth has said that he was aiming for an operatic aesthetic for the death of Lorna specifically. That is precisely what he accomplishes, though not just in that memorable scene, but also in the movie throughout.

That said, there are a handful of films in our beloved horror genre that require the viewer to immediately take a walk, pet a puppy, or otherwise rediscover the joys of life immediately after viewing, lest they remain in a dark gloom for the rest of the day. *Hostel Part II* is one of those.

"I'm never abusive and shouting, nor am I ever derogatory," Roth says of his directing style. "But you have to show that you're in charge and that you're the leader."

«29 living vicariously through the bed-hopping backpackers who are looking to take advantage of the allegedly loose morals of Slovakian women, until the tables are turned.

When critics start laying on the frat boy references, this is the film they're usually referring to. Occasionally they go farther, confusing the director with his characters.

"This stereotype has always bothered me," Roth admits. "I went to art school. I went to one—and I mean literally *one*—fraternity party in the entire four years I was in college. I went with a girl who had been invited, and as soon as we got there, two guys cornered me while their friend who had invited her, took her to his room. After about five minutes, I shoved my way past these guys and got her the hell out of there. I never set foot at a fraternity party at NYU again. I'm not saying that all frat guys were like this, but this was my experience, so I'm going to write about it."

Frat boy stereotypes aside, *Hostel* also presents a classic caricature of the "ugly American" abroad. Yet there was another dynamic at work when it first hit theaters in 2005. Large numbers of civilian deaths in the Iraq war and Afghanistan, combined with allegedly brutal treatment of foreigners by the US military at the Guantanamo Bay naval base and secret CIA prisons around the world, suggested that American attitudes toward some foreigners wasn't that far removed from those of the backpackers in the film. It's not a perfect comparison. For all of the carnage brought about by the US military's pursuit of insurgents, their ostensible purpose—to safeguard American lives against terrorists—is far nobler than a few hikers looking to get lucky. (Though there are plenty who suggest the sweetheart deals for the American military industrial complex and oil companies brought about by these conflicts without end amount to the same thing.)

What happened next seems inevitable in hindsight. Like a handful of other films and books in the last century, from *Atlas Shrugged* to *Catch-22*, *Hostel* became a type of shorthand for an emerging facet of American culture: the spectacle of torture as pornography.

Controversy swirled around *Hostel*, but it positively consumed *Hostel Part II*, which came out in 2007. The **British government**, which has never been able to maintain a healthy adult relationship with horror films beyond the Universal monsters variety, went so far as to ask questions in Parliament about the *Hostel* sequel in »36

British Government
A British panic touched off by everything from *The Evil Dead* to *Cannibal Holocaust* resulted in the banning of dozens of films in the 1980s, and the arrest of hundreds of video shop owners. Pick up a copy of *See No Evil* by David Kerekes and David Slater (if you can find one) for a gripping, detailed account of this weird time in British history, as well as lengthy reviews of each of the verboten films.

TORTURE PORN

Hostel Part II

Not since the term "slasher" gained traction in the late '70s/early '80s has a phrase been used in horror circles simultaneously as a smear and a selling point. A slippery term to get hold of, "torture porn" originally was meant to describe a type of film in which torture was depicted in a borderline erotic fashion, with the killing stroke replacing the moment of climax in more traditional pornographic fare.

The phrase entered the lexicon via a January 2006 piece in *New York* magazine by resident film critic David Edelstein. Torture porn may have been co-opted by the genre's most unforgiving critics, but Edelstein's piece is far more searching than scornful.

In it, he makes an enthusiastic grab for the third rail straight away when he lumps in Mel Gibson's gorefest *The Passion of the Christ* with *Saw, Wolf Creek* and other genre successes. While this clearly earns him no sympathies in the eyes of the self-righteous, it does demonstrate a certain intellectual honesty that leaves the reader feeling more confident that he is willing to follow the evidence wherever it leads, rather than dragging it along toward a preconceived conclusion.

Even at the time this article was published, Americans were playing semantic games with the word "torture" as it applied to captives at Guantanamo Bay.

Edelstein saw a certain desensitization going on, not so much with the *Hostels* and *Wolf Creeks* playing at the local cinema, but with television shows like *24* penetrating homes on a weekly basis. That drama devoted a whole season "to justifying torture in the name of an imminent threat: a nuclear missile en route to a major city," he pointed out. Whatever faults can be attributed to the horrors of *Hostel* and its ilk, there's usually very little question about who the bad guys are.

Since Edelstein's piece, "torture porn" has been quickly adopted by thousands worldwide.

> "There's really something going on [in *Hostel Part II*] that's interesting on an artistic basis...Sure, it makes you uncomfortable, but good art should make you uncomfortable." — **STEPHEN KING**, *Los Angeles Times*

Since the phenomenon is clearly in the eye of the beholder, you also have normally intelligent people giving film favorites a pass while castigating others as torture porn. Take a *Los Angeles Times* interview with Stephen King published in June 2007 in which the novelist said, "I'm very uneasy about this film coming out with Elisha Cuthbert, *Captivity*."

Yet, King didn't see Roth's *Hostel Part II* as torture porn at all. His distinction? Because we get to know the victims on a personal level, we don't want them to be killed. Torture porn, on the other hand, lures us into the theater with the prospect of seeing a girl killed, which is a fascinating argument. Presumably the people who go to see *Hostel Part II* do so for that very reason. Yet, because Roth has made the characters likable, the audience doesn't want to see anything happen to them. In other words, the film rehabilitates the audience that came to see it, thus robbing itself of "torture porn" status. Film criticism can be a slippery business.

TORTURE AS CATHARSIS

While opinion is understandably divided over the ubiquitous eviscerations found in Eli Roth's work, cinematic torture has been used to astonishing effect in recent years. From Douglas Buck's *Cutting Moments* to 2008's French spectacle *Martyrs*, the infliction of on-screen suffering becomes the catalyst that transforms our feelings into those of the victim, to give us some "skin in the game." What follows is an almost religious catharsis – quite literally a purification that brings about a release from tension.

Hostel

«33 October of that year. While debating a crime bill, Member of Parliament Charles Walker castigated the film, *"which I have not seen* but has been reported on by a number of people I trust. From beginning to end it depicts obscene, misogynistic acts of brutality against women—an hour and a half of brutality—yet that film has been passed by the British Board of Film Classification for public release to people aged 18 and over."

"It was surreal," Roth admits. "It's great when the movies come out [in theaters] and you have members of Parliament rallying against it the week before the DVD comes out. That's exactly what you want because that's just a big commercial for the DVD. People that didn't see it are like, 'Now I've gotta see what it is.'"

But there were other countries that effectively cut *Hostel Part II* off at the knees. New Zealand censors demanded that Roth remove the film's main set piece in which a naked Heather Matarazzo is hung upside down and repeatedly slashed with a scythe by another woman who bathes in the resulting hemoglobinous downpour.

"You can make the argument that no, this is based on a histori-

"It's Heather Matarazzo's performance that makes that scene scary," Roth says. "It's not the gore or the violence, it's the look on her face."

cal figure and we're doing a tamer version of what she actually did," Roth says. "You see very little actual slashing."

(The historical figure in question, **Countess Elizabeth Báthory** of Hungary, is thought to have tortured and murdered hundreds of young women before she was imprisoned in 1610. A legend, unproven for the most part, holds that she bathed in the girls' blood in hopes of retaining her youth and beauty.)

"I said, 'Look, it's Heather Matarazzo's performance that makes that scene scary,'" Roth says. "'It's not the gore or the violence, it's the look on her face. If I hired a bad actor, you guys wouldn't care.' This one censor said, 'Nope,' and they wouldn't allow it on theatrical [release] and they wouldn't allow it on DVD. And the fans really suffered. New Zealand was a big territory for me—it really hurts me when the film doesn't come out."

The *coup de grace*, however, came when Germany's censor cut the scene where children are playing soccer with a person's head. "I guess because that probably really happened in Germany," Roth says wryly. So incensed was the filmmaker that when he was interviewed by a roomful of German reporters, he asked them if this was the same country that had turned "my ancestors into furniture."

"They said, 'How could you do this, how could you make something so violent?'" Roth recalls. "There is no *violence* in my movies, it's magic tricks! That's my argument with the DVD and the censor in New Zealand, and I didn't get to speak to him. It's not like I get to talk to this one person. I was saying to Sony it's a DVD where you have a 10-minute featurette on how we did the effects and we're talking about it in the commentary. Who's going to think this is real? Actually banning it makes it seem more like it's real."

Perhaps the most surprising reception any *Hostel* film received came from Japan, the land that brought us the stomach-churning excesses of Miike's *Ichi The Killer* and many, many others.

"There are different things that offend people culturally," he

Countess Elizabeth Báthory
The Hungarian noblewoman, known to history as the "Blood Countess," died under house arrest in 1614 after she was accused of murdering more than 80 people.

THE CENSOR SHUFFLE
Roth's battles with international film censors is reminiscent of EC Comics publisher Bill Gaines' wrangling with the US Senate in 1954. At one point, a senator asked him if a cover of *Crime SuspenStories* was in good taste. Replied Gaines, "Yes, sir...for the cover of a *horror* comic."

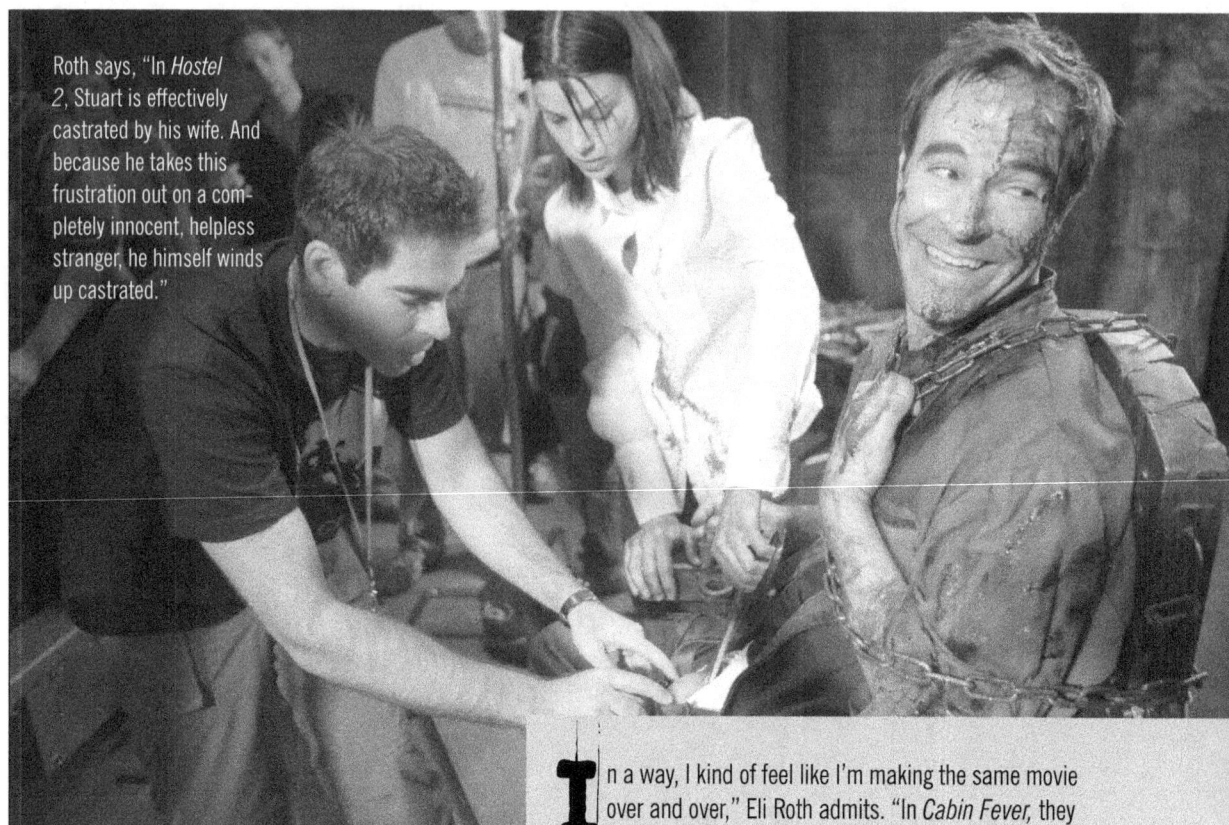

Roth says, "In *Hostel 2*, Stuart is effectively castrated by his wife. And because he takes this frustration out on a completely innocent, helpless stranger, he himself winds up castrated."

GETTING THE MESSAGE?

"In a way, I kind of feel like I'm making the same movie over and over," Eli Roth admits. "In *Cabin Fever*, they light the hermit on fire and then they themselves wind up burned by the local sheriffs. In *Hostel*, the guys pay to go into a room and do whatever they want to the hookers, and then they themselves wind up in a room with some stranger paying to do whatever they want to them.

"In *Hostel 2*, Stuart [Roger Bart, above] is effectively castrated by his wife, and because he takes this frustration out on a completely innocent, helpless stranger, he himself winds up castrated. In essence, he fulfills his own destiny.

"So there's two basic themes of leaving your home to go on a trip for fun and having it turn into your worst nightmare, but also the moral lesson of 'do unto others as you would want done to you.' If everyone — in any of my films — had just behaved like a human being and treated someone with any amount of decency or respect, they never would have gone through what they did. They bring the tragedy upon themselves."

says. "In Japan, one of the worst things you can do is disfigure someone's face. There's great shame and dishonor with your face being disfigured. In this scene [in the first *Hostel*], it's an American disfiguring a Japanese girl's face with a blowtorch. So it wasn't just specifically that it was violence, it was this specific act of an American man disfiguring a Japanese woman's face that was too much for them. And there's only like four different theater owners. If they don't want it, it's not going out in theaters. It's a whole different system over there."

Which is not to say that Roth hasn't encountered his share of negativity Stateside. Overseas it's censors; in the US, **critics**.

"Even on [*At the Movies*], Roeper said, 'I wouldn't watch these films because I don't find it entertaining to torture a woman.' Well great, thank you. I don't think anybody does."

NIGHTMARES IN A HYPERFOCUSED BRAIN

Again we return to the question of just what kind of person makes movies that rile governments thousands of miles away.

Thanks to the wonders of the World Wide Web, anyone the slightest bit interested in Eli Roth's work can check out his blog on his MySpace page: *www.myspace.com/eliroth*. A close reading of some of his more personal entries reveals that, in addition to talking to himself frequently (a creative quirk he shares with Tarantino, he says), he finds himself growing more obsessive-compulsive as he gets older. Could these traits be tied to the density of detail found in his films?

"I've talked about this with my friends and my brothers and in my relationships, how the very traits that have made me successful can also make me difficult to be around at times," Roth says. "I think that I have this obsessive, driving nature that, when it gets channeled towards a project, it's an incredibly healthy use of that energy."

His obsession with detail is a great asset to him when it comes

Critics
Film critics have never been very consistent when it comes to the horror films they review. Writer and television personality Roger Ebert, for example, is often singled out for his contemporaneous praise of 1972's *The Last House on the Left*. He called it "a tough, bitter little sleeper of a movie that's about four times as good as you'd expect," while later dismissing similar fare such as 1980's *I Spit on Your Grave* as "a vile bag of garbage."

to solving problems during the filmmaking process, but it also can leave him unable to sleep and thoroughly stressed out. "I think that getting older and having more experience is the only way I'll ever be able to not let these things completely cripple me."

However, this same problem-solving obsession leaves him ill disposed to suffering fools gladly, he admits. "If I feel like there's something that's not being done correctly or someone's not doing their job or someone's being lazy or someone's trying to fuck me over, there's a side of my personality that is this domineering lion that will just come out and pounce and go for the jugular. I'm never abusive and shouting, nor am I ever derogatory. I've spent so much time on sets around people who are abusive and screaming. I've said I'll never be that kind of director. But you have to show that you're in charge and that you're the leader."

Take the time the team was trying to get a Steadycam shot in *Hostel Part II* in which Lauren German is running through a crowded street.

"She has to take a giant coat off, she's in her sweater and now it's about 20 degrees out, she's freezing," Roth says. It's at this moment one of the camera operators decides to switch lenses. "So I'm sitting at the monitor and I don't understand why we can't reset quickly because Lauren's freezing, and this guy decided he didn't like the lens. He's a great camera operator, but I had to remind him that he was working for me."

But even before *Cabin Fever*, **David Lynch** passed on a bit of wisdom to Roth about all of the behind-the-scenes nonsense that transpires during a film shoot. Lynch's words: "Keep your eye on the doughnut, not the hole."

"The doughnut is the movie," Roth says. "The only thing that matters is the information recorded on those 24 squares per second. All the other bullshit, all the fighting between the actors, all the crew bitching about you going into overtime, about everyone being cold,

David Lynch
"Keep your eye on the doughnut, not the hole"... At 20, Roth met director David Lynch while working for film producer Fred Zollo (*Mississippi Burning, Quiz Show*). In addition to conducting some research for Lynch during the production of *Mulholland Dr.*, he helped the eccentric director with some of the material on davidlynch.com.

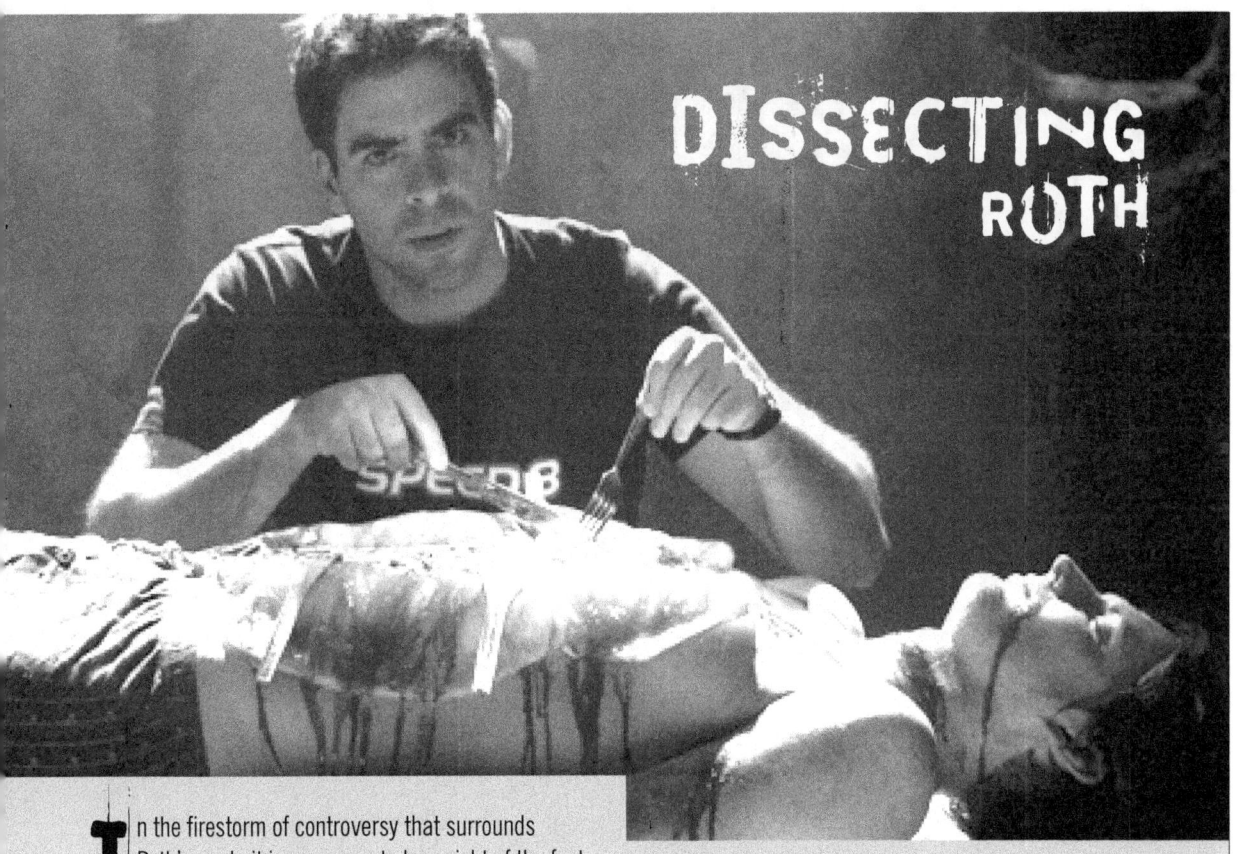

DISSECTING ROTH

In the firestorm of controversy that surrounds Roth's work, it is very easy to lose sight of the fact that it also has garnered an impressive number of accolades and champions over the years.

Jean-Francois Rauger, head programmer of the film museum Cinémathèque Française, hailed *Hostel* as an ironic indictment of America's rampant consumerism in France's *Le Monde* newspaper in 2006. That same year, *Hostel* appeared in music and video retailer HMV's annual Top 50 Scariest Movies survey alongside such classics as *The Shining* (Kubrick's, of course) and *Rosemary's Baby*. Even *The New York Times*, which has given Roth a bit of guff from time to time, has used the director's name as an answer in its Sunday magazine crossword. Whether this last fact is a validation of his overall importance in the movie world or an indication of the scarcity of good three-letter words that can be worked into crosswords remains open to interpretation.

ON NEGATIVE REVIEWS
"I was talking with film critic Elvis Mitchell just yesterday about this, because Elvis wrote a piece in *Interview* magazine which talks about how [horror] films never get good reviews. He said one of the things that made him want to be a critic was reading these terrible reviews of *Night of the Living Dead*. People were saying George Romero should be brought up on charges. Generally it's these middle-class people with children and they're so blinded by the violence that the movies themselves threaten their safety.

"Look at the reviews for all these movies.... You just look at what these guys went through and you realize that nothing changes. If a horror movie is effective, it upsets people and it threatens them."

Roth brothers Gabriel, Adam and Eli on the set of *Cabin Fever*.

about the food being crappy, all that other bullshit is the hole, and you can get sucked right into it."

He doesn't take the Hitchcock approach of regarding his cast as cattle, but he does occasionally equate handling those on set with the three summers he spent at The Meadowbrook Day Camp looking after a large group of 10- and 11-year-old boys many years ago.

"All those skills of keeping kids from fighting and crying are exactly the same skills that come into play when making a film," he says. But he also realizes, "You're hiring people who are artists and are talented and have their creative vision. But it has to line up with yours."

There was the designer on *Hostel Part II*, for instance, who patiently listened to the director's ideas about what a certain set should look like, and then went ahead and did something completely different.

"I had to tell a superbly talented designer who I greatly respect that his idea didn't work and that it all had to be redone," Roth says. "But if it's not going to work in the scene, I'm the one who has to answer for it....It's human nature to want to add your own creative touch. Whether it works or not is up to the director, and often in a time crunch, things just get added that you never asked for."

Yet through all of this tug-of-war with the cast and crew around him, Roth knows that he will never reproduce the images he sees in his mind exactly—it just doesn't work that way.

"You can get it close but you're never going to exactly replicate it," he says. "If you try to do that, you get into a danger area where you miss what's actually in front of you."

He says it was David Lynch, he of the doughnut hole theory, who taught him about "the happy accident."

"He planned something and suddenly something goes completely wrong," Roth says. "But instead of seeing that as a bad thing, he sees it as an opportunity for new ideas he never saw before. Eventually you forget what was originally in your mind."

One of the best examples of this is the alternative universe of the deleted scene. "Whenever we have to pull deleted scenes for a DVD, I forget I even shot those scenes," he says. "Once I cut it out of a film, my brain literally deletes that stuff. Suddenly, this is the way it is and you can't even remember what the old way was."

Certainly if Roth took it all extremely seriously 24/7, he would miss the joy of the journey, something his parents taught him to value above all things.

Naturally, there are still things that piss him off. The bootleg copies of *Hostel Part II* that were making the rounds on the Internet around the time of its official theatrical release remain a sore point. All of that aside, he knows just how lucky he's been.

"Having studied all those painters, you see how many people are never recognized in their own lifetimes," he says. "It's a very rare and special thing to be an artist and appreciated in the time when you're alive. No matter how mad I get about certain things like piracy—doing all that work on *Hostel 2* and having millions of people just taking it for free—there's always a part of me that's going, 'Well, at least I'm in the game and I'm getting to do what I love.' Believe me, I know plenty of people that are so successful and so rich and have everything, and they're just miserable, unhappy people." [NHH]

> "I don't think there's any more value to a film that is strictly entertaining versus a film that is entertaining and has social relevance; it's all in whether you've made a good movie or not."
>
> — ROTH

PAINTER OF SAVAGE BEAUTY

GREG MCLEAN

JUST AS THE UNIVERSE IS THOUGHT TO EXPAND AND CONTRACT OVER THE EONS, THE HORROR FILM GOES THROUGH ITS OWN VIOLENT GYRATIONS, MUCH TO THE ANNOYANCE OF FANS WHO ARE ALL TOO OFTEN AFFLICTED WITH A FORM OF ZEITGEIST WHIPLASH FOR THEIR LOYALTIES....

The current century got off to a fairly strong start with the likes of *Ginger Snaps* (2000), *Cabin Fever* (2002) and *Saw* (2004). Yet by 2005, the trend toward watered-down, teenybopper horror that started in the late '90s with franchises like *I Know What You Did Last Summer* was fast becoming the rule. One could choose from Uwe Boll's *Alone in the Dark*, jump-scares-by-the-numbers with *The Amityville Horror* remake, or its carbon-copy twin, *Boogeyman*. *Saw II* offered a fair compromise between balls-to-the-wall shock and multiplex-friendly fare, and *White Noise*, try as it might, failed to introduce any scares into the by-now anemic ghost story.

If you were really after a cinematic fix guaranteed to get the adrenaline flowing that year, it all came down to just two films: Rob Zombie's grindhouse tribute *The Devil's Rejects*, and a little something out of koala country called *Wolf Creek*.

Zombie, of course, was a known quantity thanks to countless interviews and 2003's *House of 1,000 Corpses*, a dress rehearsal for much of what would come later from him.

But *Wolf Creek*, the desperate tale of three young tourists (Kestie Morassi [cover image], Cassandra Magrath and Nathan Phillips) trying to escape the clutches of the savage Mick Taylor (John Jarratt) in his native Outback, was a particularly transgressive piece of work. Not only did it circumvent horror conventions of the last 20 years by offering up victims that audiences had absolutely no desire to see harmed, but also it cast the whole grisly spectacle against a backdrop of astonishing beauty.

The question quickly became "Who the hell is *Wolf Creek* director Greg McLean, and when did Australia become a go-to place for cruel shockers?"

Ironically, New Zealand, usually overshadowed by its Aussie twin in many areas of world exposure, had been where horror fans looked for frights at the time.

That's not to say Australia hadn't exported some genuine classics back in the day. The man vs. nature romp *Long Weekend* (1978) holds up pretty well, and even inspired a recent remake directed by Melbourne's Jamie Blanks (*Urban Legend, Storm Warning, Valentine*). And Peter Weir's *The Cars That Ate Paris* (1974) and *Picnic at Hanging Rock* (1975) are still must-sees of the genre.

But neither these nor even the 2003 zombie-comedy *Undead* captured the imaginations of gorehounds throughout North America and Europe quite like the anarchic works of a low-budget New Zealand director called Peter Jackson. Before his epic *Lord of the Rings* trilogy, he was known to every horror lover as the genius behind 1992's *Dead Alive* (aka *Braindead*) and *Bad Taste* (1987). Full stop.

Yet Australia has something going for it that New Zealand simply can't rival when it comes to generating authentic, nail-biting fear: uncharted territory. Where some 4.3 million Kiwis get along on two main islands with a landmass of about 104,000 square miles, more than 21 million Aussies live on nearly 3 million square miles of land, much of it uninhabited.

Like their counterparts in Alberta and other parts of the Canadian North (*see* Ginger Snaps *case study, p. 96*), many Australians live on the outskirts of a wilderness that can still intimidate with its sheer size and mystery. That's before you start adding serial killers to the mix.

To really get where McLean was coming from with *Wolf Creek*, you have to understand the series of events that led him deep into the dark heart of bush country.

FROM KILLER CROC TO SAVAGE *WOLF*

It seems fair to say that Greg McLean would be more of a household name today worldwide had his feature debut been a traditional drama rather than the gutsy niche nightmare he unleashed. His cinematic meditations on the beauty and detachment of nature have more in common with American Academy-Award winner Terrence

> "I think horror films and scary stories are really necessary for people psychologically. At the same time though, I'm sure I'm going to make films that strive to convince people of the goodness in the world as opposed to just showing the absolute dark face of horror."
>
> — GREG McLEAN

> "You don't necessarily always need to bash the audience to death to communicate something."
>
> —— McLEAN

Malick's *The New World*, for example, than with anything you're likely to find in the oeuvre of Hooper, Romero or the rest.

Though blessed with the good fortune to work with cinematographer Will Gibson on his first two features, McLean himself is no stranger to the creation of arresting images, moving or otherwise.

Born April 10, 1971 in Bendigo in central Victoria, McLean's early appreciation for everything from fine art to comic books led him to a five year stay at art school before he realized that moving pictures were a great deal more interesting to him than static ones.

Experimentation with Super 8 shorts gave way to a crash course in directing theater actors at Sydney's National Institute of Dramatic

Arts. From there, he fell in with director **Baz Luhrmann** (*Moulin Rouge, Strictly Ballroom*), helping him with several projects including preproduction on 1996's Leonardo DiCaprio/Claire Danes Shakespearian spectacle *Romeo + Juliet*.

With that experience under his belt, McLean realized that it was time to sink his teeth into the finer technical points of capturing life on film. Reasonably well financed film projects are extremely rare, which is why the then-24-year-old turned his camera instead to that far more ubiquitous beast, the television commercial. His first was for a discount suit warehouse, which "was one of those stores that was constantly closing down and having sales," he says. "It sounds pretty cheesy, but they did actually allow me to do whatever I wanted in a number of different commercials, and I got a lot of experience directing different things."

This was experience that he intended to put to good use on one of the first feature scripts he ever wrote: an old-fashioned monster movie about an enormous man-eating crocodile wreaking havoc in the waters of Australia's Northern Territory. At 25, he'd been so surprised that he'd actually sold a script, he hadn't foreseen what was to come.

"I spent a number of years working on that, and I actually got kicked off the film because the company decided that they wanted the script but didn't want me attached to it," he says.

There had been a clause in his contract with Beyond, the production company, that allowed them to replace McLean as director if they failed to raise the money to make the movie within six weeks. Sure, he received a relatively healthy sum in way of compensation, but it wasn't enough to ease the sting of being booted off his own movie.

"It was a bad experience at one level, but it did teach me how *not* to make films," he says, "which is to make them by committee and do things where you remove the central elements to a film."

Baz Luhrmann
The Sydney-born director first hit it big with his 1992 paean to ballroom dancing, *Strictly Ballroom*, paving the way for several less-artistically inspired dance flicks (*Save the Last Dance,* anyone?). His star rose with the Leonardo DiCaprio/Claire Danes Shakespearian flick *Romeo + Juliet* in 1996, followed by the Nicole Kidman/Ewan McGregor spectacle *Moulin Rouge* in 2001. His most recent film, 2008's *Australia* starring Kidman and Hugh Jackman, was a hit in Australia but failed to set the rest of the world alight.

Wolf Creek's Mick Taylor, actor John Jarratt, appeared in Peter Weir's *Picnic at Hanging Rock*.

Some 10 years later, he would get another crack at making his killer crocodile movie, *Rogue*. But at the time, all he saw was that his idea had been hijacked, leaving him right back where he'd started from. Meanwhile, the movie showed no signs of actually getting off the ground.

"I was getting frustrated," he says, "and out of desperation went back to an earlier idea I had about a serial killer in the Outback."

Over the next six years, he would crank out six drafts of the film treatment for what would become *Wolf Creek*, evolving the concept of Mick Taylor from rugged antihero to reprehensible murderer, all the while preserving the killer's tongue-in-cheek charm. This wasn't the cartoonish, smart ass Freddy Krueger quipping his way through impossible kills, nor a tomb-silent killing machine in the Jason/Michael Myers mold, but a simple blue collar guy who got up to God knows what behind closed doors. Above all, he was distinctly Australian.

"Mick is a pretty iconic looking guy," McLean says. "He's got his hat, his shirt, his jeans, a knife and a gun. Even though he's kind of close to reality in some ways, he's actually quite weird in lots of other ways. He's the Australian equivalent of an American cowboy, and a cowboy serial killer is an interesting idea."

A friend who was as keen to get into film as McLean knew someone who was looking to invest in a film project at the time.

"I said, 'Look, I've got the scripts, I'm going to do it really cheaply, and we're going to do it as fast as we can and get it done,'" he says. Cheap and fast: beautiful words to any investor's ears.

His benefactor put up some cash of his own, raised some more, and they proceeded to hit up the Film Finance Corp., Australia's film body, for the remainder of the $1 million budget. (The corporation was rolled into a new body, Screen Australia, in 2008.)

"It was easier to get financed because we had a pretty good crew and a great bunch of people making this very small film, so it made it very difficult for them to say no," McLean says." We were very conscious of that because none of us wanted to be in a situation again where we had a film ready to go and then got it turned down."

Frequently when you talk to directors about what went on during the making of their first breakout hit, at some point they will tell you that everyone involved in the project *needed* for it to succeed. McLean is no exception.

"I was pretty desperate because I'd spent so long trying to get a film off," he admits. "I was thinking if this one doesn't get off, I'm pretty much going to go crazy."

> "Wolf Creek was largely an experiment in what images an audience can take without turning off. It was really about playing with the audience and where they think a story's going to go, and how they think the story's going to end."
> —— McLEAN

CREATING *CREEK*

Oddly, for people who enjoy submerging themselves in fantasy worlds, horror fans are the first to glom on to a film's slightest convergence with reality. Recall that key selling points for both *Psycho* and *The Texas Chainsaw Massacre* were their tangential connections with the 1950s-era killer Ed Gein, never mind the fact that the Wisconsin farmer neither dressed up as his mother nor pursued the locals with a chainsaw.

Right out of the gate, *Wolf Creek* tells the audience that it's based on true events. However, it quickly became apparent that the film was inspired by a few different events, most notably the case of the so-called "backpacker murderer," Ivan Milat.

One of 14 children of Yugoslavian immigrants, Milat was handed seven life sentences in 1996 for the murders of seven backpackers in Belanglo State Forest in New South Wales, Australia.

Yet Milat is only the most prolific of Australia's predators. In July 2001, British tourist Peter Falconio was shot to death at night in the Outback after a stranger waved him and girlfriend Joanne Lees off the road. Abducted by their assailant, Lees later managed to escape from his pickup truck and hide in the woods. Bradley Murdoch, a 47-year-old drug dealer, was sentenced to life in prison for the attacks, though he would be eligible for parole after serving 28 years of his sentence. In 2006, Lees published a book about her life, including her Australian ordeal, called *No Turning Back*.

"Growing up here, you're always hearing stories about **people getting in trouble** in the Outback," McLean says. "I think it's part of the Australian culture. There's even a story this morning in the newspaper about a couple who's car broke down in the Outback. They died because they were out there too long. You can pretty much die in a couple of hours. There's also the real stories of people getting in trouble with bad characters. It's very easy to mythologize the Outback in that way."

Make no mistake, mythologize was what McLean set out to do. He picked the wilderness surrounding Wolfe Creek Crater National Park in Western Australia as the film's setting, not simply for its remote location, but for its supernatural reputation. Weird lights and

People getting in trouble
McLean, like Eli Roth, depicts situations in which his characters to some degree are done in by their own attitudes and behaviors. In *Wolf Creek*, there is a sense that it is the giggles at Mick Taylor's expense that doom the backpackers. In *Rogue*, the riverboat is only attacked when it wanders into sacred territory, making it, rather than the crocodile, the rogue element.

POSTMORTEM

McLean's 2005 tale of three young people who are brutalized during a backpacking excursion through Australia's Outback is that brand of film best compared to *Audition* director Takashi Miike's work: While you may have to admire the artistry involved, its intensity makes it a difficult movie to sit through.

This is odd when you consider there is very little in the way of actual gore in this movie. Nearly all of the violence is strongly implied by stomach-turning sound design (including the famous "head on a stick" scene) and far away shots rather than in-your-face visuals, and it's the stronger for it.

On a trip Down Under, British tourists Kristy Earl (Kestie Morassi) and Liz Hunter (Cassandra Magrath) hook up with Australian Ben Mitchell (Nathan Phillips). The three decide to set out for Australia's Wolfe Creek Crater National Park. When their car strands them in the middle of nowhere, they fear the worst. Fortunately, a country character called Mick Taylor (John Jarratt) happens along and offers to tow them back to his camp, where he says he has the tools to fix their car. After accepting some water there, all three pass out, and their real problems begin.

It's hard to know where to start with this movie. From sweeping views of the crater and the surrounding Outback wilderness to the awkward campfire chat between Taylor and his guests, Will Gibson's cinematography ranks favorably with just about any film you'd care to name. Add to that the expert cooperation between actors and script and you come away with a near perfect chiller.

Jarratt is frequently praised for stealing every scene, and to some extent that's true. Yet the supporting cast each play their parts to the hilt. The payoff is extraordinary for the genre: a slasher film that inspires its audience to hope the bright young things will escape the maniac, and heartbreak when some do not.

Finally, the viewer is made all the more uneasy by being left with the single question that the horrific events provoke: At what point was the trio doomed? When did Mick decide they wouldn't be leaving the Outback alive? It is a tribute to McLean's storytelling ability that we even bother to ask.

WOLF CREEK

> "We were very conscious of wanting to make the landscape into a very beautiful and powerful character."
> —— McLEAN

Cinematographer Will Gibson
Will Gibson, who brought an unrivaled beauty to the horror genre with his cinematography on *Wolf Creek* and *Rogue*, took his own life in March 2007 after a long battle with depression. *Rogue*, which premiered at Spain's Sitges International Festival of Fantastic and Horror Cinema in October of that year, stands as a lasting testament to Gibson's mastery of his craft.

UFO sightings are just a couple of the phenomena whispered about around this area where a meteor slammed into the Outback some 300,000 years ago. McLean himself has never been to the area. "I'm too scared to go," he says. "It's a very scary place, apparently. It's literally 13 hours into the desert."

The movie actually was shot in South Australia, about two hours north of Adelaide, and about 1,500 miles from the crater. Still, the nearest petrol station was at least an hour away. "We had radios and telephones and stuff," the director recalls, "but it was pretty rugged."

Cinematographer Will Gibson and his assistant traveled to Western Australia and took a helicopter ride over the national landmark. "They shot all the point of views of the characters looking at the crater, and also the aerial material of the crater," the director says.

Though *Wolf Creek* and *Rogue* are frequently praised for their top-notch cinematography, its is McLean's use of these images as foils for his well-developed characters that make his films truly stand out. Like a painter at his easel, the director adds subtle brushstrokes to a story, one detail at a time, gradually creating what at first seems a simple snapshot of his characters' lives. It is only when he adds a final, slightly sinister stroke that we come to realize we are now in nightmare country. No two-dimensional ciphers these, which makes their victimization all the more unsettling when it finally occurs.

That this make-believe carnage usually is juxtaposed against some of the finest landscapes captured on film only seems to heighten the terror. Nowhere is this more evident than in *Wolf Creek*.

"We were very conscious of wanting to make the landscape into a very beautiful and powerful character," the director says. "I think there's a kind of poetic power in that landscape, and we wanted to have that as a force in the story. You have these very small and very human characters enveloped in this vast primordial landscape. Once the landscape changes, it becomes very terrifying."

This is really where the director's extensive history in the fine arts ratchets up the effect of the film's horror, appealing to the audience's **aesthetic sense** while simultaneously assaulting the mind with some truly terrible images.

Not surprisingly, McLean storyboarded nearly every shot. "We spent a lot of time thinking about how to create that illusion of it being a documentary experience," he says, "when in fact it's a very tightly wound, manipulative experience."

UP THE CREEK + AFTER

Even by 2008 standards, the down-and-dirty violence of *Wolf Creek* sails pretty close to the wind. Many are amazed that the Australian government underwrote such a flick, especially considering how federal subsidies of far less extreme works around the world have

Aesthetic sense
Aesthetically appealing horror films are certainly nothing new. Italy's Mario Bava was very much a "painter of light" with classics like *Black Sunday* (1960) and *Blood and Black Lace* (1964). Dario Argento built an entire career on films such as *Suspiria* (1977) and *Deep Red* (1975) that are 75% visual artistry and 25% tired plot.

been met with public backlashes. *(See the Telefilm Canada sidebar on p. 108 for a textbook example.)*

"When we got the film financed, the film industry here was in such a terrible state," McLean explains. Australia was funding several different films but nothing was making any money. "I think it was a bit of a happy accident whereby we happened to come in with a really radical project while they were thinking to themselves we have to do something differently. Also, to be honest, in terms of the project going through the funding body, I'm sure not a lot of people looked at it and thought about it. That was great because if the people had actually looked at the script, they would've turned it down."

That's not to say that public funding of *Wolf Creek* sailed through without comment, he hastens to add. "When it came out, there was a little bit of controversy about what is the government doing funding this sadistic film? But I think when people saw that it was actually successful and people wanted to see it, they kind of thought we better shut up because it's a film people actually want to see."

That want arose from a word-of-mouth buzz generated after its premiere at the Sundance Film Festival in January 2005. Not since the death of the priests in *The Exorcist* had a movie so blatantly contravened cinematic conventions. Two female characters were set up as potential **Final Girls**, only to be hunted down and slaughtered by merciless Mick, with his "head on a stick" trick quickly entering the canon of ghastly dispatchings. Only the male victim survives, just, and ends up being suspected of the crimes himself before being exonerated. Only the killer experiences anything approaching a happy ending, walking off into the sunset, presumably returning to the dark heart of the natural world, and to what he does best.

"Part of the fun of the film, if you can call it fun, is watching the audiences having their expectations played with about what's right and wrong and what's justice," McLean says. "What you realize

Final Girls
Coined by Carol Clover in her study of the genre, *Men, Women and Chainsaws: Gender in the Modern Horror Film*, the Final Girl is the last character to confront the killer or other supernatural entity in a film. Think Laurie Strode in *Halloween*.

Greg McLean on location shooting *Wolf Creek*.

with a film like *Wolf Creek* is how amazingly ingrained certain narrative ideas are in an audience, particularly of horror films. They're meant to be a radical form where people can play with ideas of form and structure. But what you realize is they're so standardized and so infrequently played with. *Wolf Creek*, for me, revealed how conservative most horror films actually are in terms of notions of taboo and what you can and can't do on screen."

While the film quickly became a hit in horror circles, McLean says it did very well with mainstream Australian audiences, too. "They related to it from the point of view of this being a warning film," he says. "This kind of thing has happened in Australia before and the message is be very careful when you're traveling in the Outback."

His next time out, McLean would deliver a similar message about the Northern Territory.

ROGUE: THE CROC WITH TWO LIVES

With *Wolf Creek*, McLean had hit one out of the park. The $1 million flick earned nearly $5 million in the US on its opening weekend, grossing more than $16 million in that country alone. Naturally talk turned to a sequel, but the director wasn't about to go that route, at least not yet. First there was the little matter of his killer croc story.

By the time *Wolf Creek* hit it big, Beyond had taken a few passes at producing *Rogue* without success. Eventually, the rights reverted back to its author. With a healthy influx of capital from Dimension Films and a final budget of about $25 million, McLean set out to bring to life the deadly crocodile that had lurked in the swamp of his subconscious for more than 10 years.

"*Rogue* was around for so long, I did storyboard most of the main sequences a long time ago, and had other people come in and do adaptations of my storyboards," he says.

Set in the northernmost part of Australia, the 2007 film chronicles the plight of a group of tourists marooned on a small strip of land after their river boat is attacked by the aforementioned enormous, man-eating crocodile.

Filming, which took place in Kakadu, Katherine and Victoria, was a bit less dramatic than all that. Still, McLean gleefully observes, "The area we were shooting in up there was infested with crocodiles, so any time somebody could've been killed, which would've been a bit sad." Protection came courtesy of the national park in the form of rifle-toting wranglers, he explains. "There's always a danger of a crocodile jumping up and grabbing someone, so we had them making sure no one was getting eaten."

Though there was no way around using some CGI in chronicling the carnage unleashed by the giant croc, the filmmaker and his team kept it to a minimum. Two large animatronic beasts were used for close-up shots of the actors confronting the crocodile, while most of the action sequences were digitally enhanced.

> "Essentially, drawing is my first language, so it's much easier for me to draw a scene and then describe it in words than the other way around."
>
> —— **McLEAN** *on the value of storyboarding*

"The good part about having the mechanical parts on set were that people could interact with them really solidly," he says. "But what you see in the final film, a lot of it is **primarily digital** because of the complexity of what the crocodile is actually doing."

The crazy part of it all was realizing that the film's creature was not even supernaturally enormous by real-world standards, McLean says. "We had a wildlife cinematographer with us, and we were talking about what the biggest crocodile that people have seen was. He said he'd actually seen one that was 7-and-a-half meters [nearly 25 feet] long in this very remote part of the world." The *Rogue* croc is supposed to be about 8 meters.

Horror fans may remember actress Radha Mitchell (riverboat pilot Kate Ryan) from her performance in *Silent Hill*. It's less likely that John Jarratt (passenger Russell) would've been so easily recognized if the media hadn't publicized the fact that he'd also played the role of *Wolf Creek*'s devil of the Outback, Mick Taylor.

It had never occurred to the director to cast Jarratt because the »62

Primarily digital
The "making of" documentary on the *Rogue* DVD is highly recommended, not only for some beautiful footage of the Northern Territory, but also for a detailed look at just how much care was taken in painstakingly blending practical and CGI effects.

Actor John Jarratt swapped Mick Taylor's wicked ways for those of a sweet widower fighting for his life in *Rogue*.

POSTMORTEM

ROGUE

Let me start by saying I am *not* likely to be organizing the man vs. nature film festival at my local second-run cinema anytime soon. From *The Birds* to *Jaws*, the virtues of this subgenre have so far eluded me. Some of that probably has to do with my own natural propensity to side with the critters. We have more than 6 billion people wandering around, many of them pretty crabby most of the time. My response to these types of flicks usually is "Be my guest—dig in."

That said, *Rogue*, Greg McLean's second feature film, pretty much dares you not to like it.

While on assignment in Australia's Northern Territory, American travel writer Pete McKell (Michael Vartan) catches a tour boat piloted by NT native Kate Ryan (Radha Mitchell). On board is an entertaining assortment of tourists, including Russell, a soft-spoken, middle-age widower played by John Jarratt, the man behind *Wolf Creek's* Outback assassin. When a killer crocodile attacks their boat and forces the group onto a small landmass quickly being reclaimed by the rising tide, things get desperate. On paper it's nothing special; the joy of *Rogue* lies purely in the cinematic experience.

Will Gibson's cinematography alone is worth the price of admission. Sweeping overhead views of the virgin Northern Territory and close-up studies of insects and other wildlife are not just there to demonstrate Gibson's proficiency with the camera, but actually underscore key themes in this movie, just as they did in *Wolf Creek*.

And like that film, here McLean once again sidesteps the temptation to populate his world with two-dimensional characters that serve merely as grist for the horrors to come—a laziness many rival filmmakers have succumbed to in recent years. Strangely, the two lead characters are overshadowed personalitywise by their fellow passengers. These positively shine as little character quirks glimpsed early on give way to greater complexities when things get hairy. An asshole becomes a hero, an annoyance an ally.

> "*Rogue* is one of the best killer animal movies I've ever seen, and just one film like that can totally stoke your interest in a subgenre again. Now I want to go back and watch *Day of the Animals*."
>
> —— **DAVE ALEXANDER**, *managing editor,* Rue Morgue *magazine*

The ending feels a bit too conventional for a film made by the director of *Wolf Creek*, with the climactic set piece slipping a toe across the line of belief. Not so coincidentally, this also is when the film's beast seems the least convincing. This probably has less to do with the quality of the effects and more with how unlikely crocodiles actually look in the cold light of day.

However, *Rogue's* greatest flaw has nothing to do with its making and everything to do with distribution. In a move all too common today, Dimension Films sidestepped that whole messy, costly annoyance that is wide theater release, opting instead for low-key DVD distribution.

Getting upset with studio executives for being piss-poor judges of artistic merit is ridiculous—people in such positions have never been very good dealing with such things. However, it's entirely appropriate to take bean counters to task when they shoot themselves in the foot by forking over millions in production costs without following it through to distribution.

The tragedy is that *Rogue* is a film that truly needs to be seen on the big screen to be fully appreciated—its cinematography easily could put many of those IMAX nature flicks to shame.

To put this all in perspective, Dimension also is the company responsible for placing installments of the *Scary Movie* franchise in theaters. Does it really have to be pointed out that bad jokes do not get funnier when those who deliver them are made larger?

Enough of my grousing. Pony up the few dollars for the DVD—you'll end up rewatching it, if only for the detailed "Making of" featurette. Who knows, this may be the flick that convinces you to spring for that jumbo plasma screen. (And they wonder why no one goes to the theater anymore...)

Rogue character was so different. However, the actor rang him one day and said, "'All my mates are trying out, why can't I have a go,'" McLean recalls. "I said, 'Well, I just don't think you're right for it, but what do ya got?' So he sent me a photograph of himself in character. I just looked at this and thought it's perfect.

"Part of the fun was saying, 'Wouldn't it be great for you to be in this film and for people not to realize it's you,'" McLean says. "I thought let's break the trend early by just putting John in here being completely different and showing people what he can do."

Once again the director brought his artist's eye to setting up some truly breathtaking shots, which attracted the attentions of many, including Tourism NT, the area's tourism board.

Its Web site (en.travelnt.com/experience/nature/the-crocodile.aspx) proudly promoted the fact that *Rogue* had been shot there, and even offered a slick, two-page "*Rogue* Adventure" itinerary for those wanting to cavort with the area's toothy reptiles.

"To put it in context, the film is very different to *Wolf Creek*," McLean says. "It's not saying come and see where the serial killers are. It's more about the beauty of the landscape, the beauty of the wildlife up there. But tourists get excited about the concept of controlled danger, of going on an adventure tour where there might be the possibility of something dramatic actually happening. It sounds really strange but apparently there's been a 20 percent jump in tourism every time there's been a widely publicized crocodile attack."

Though *Rogue* boasts plenty of edge-of-your-seat moments, some *Wolf Creek* fans have accused McLean of going soft with his sophomore effort. This might've been a fair charge had he set out to be a horror director exclusively, he argues, but that was never really his plan.

"*Rogue* is much more of an adventure story," he says. "It's interesting that people have that expectation that you stay in the darkness of [the horror] realm."

At press time, McLean is working on a script for New Regency

> "Financiers + sales agents think even if they make a half-decent horror film, they can still sell it and make some money. It's not really the place you start if you're going to make something great."
>
> —— **McLean** *on why so many horror films are so bad*

"*Rogue* is much more of an adventure story," McLean says.

that also promises to cross genre lines—a supernatural war flick tantalizingly titled *Dark Forces: Secret Battles of WWII*.

"What's interesting is jumping around and playing with different ways to talk about different ideas," he says. "You don't necessarily always need to bash the audience to death to communicate something."

In fact, some of the true classics of the genre have been made by mainstream directors who decided to tell a good story by employing dark elements, he points out. *The Shining*, *Alien* and *The Exorcist* are three good examples. "I think we could do with more of the great minds of filmmaking coming in and saying, 'OK, if my goal was to tell a story that completely transforms the audience with pure terror, what kind of story would I tell and how would I tell it?' As opposed to someone saying, 'Let's make a horror story, let's make a buck, let's make it gory without actually challenging the concepts of what fear is all about.'"

From your lips to Hollywood's ears. [NHH]

GIVING VAMPIRES BACK THEIR BITE.

STEVE NILES

YOU WON'T FIND MANY WRITERS INTERVIEWED IN THE *HANDBOOK*. THIS IS NOT BECAUSE THEY'RE TANGENTIAL TO THE WHOLE MOVIEMAKING PROCESS—FAR FROM IT. RATHER, THEIR INPUT OFTEN IS ECLIPSED BY THE IDIOSYNCRASIES OF THE DIRECTOR AND WHATEVER ARTISTIC TOUCHES THE DIRECTOR OF PHOTOGRAPHY IS PERMITTED TO GET AWAY WITH...

Yet when Columbia Pictures released *30 Days of Night* in 2007, it was apparent that someone somewhere had taken it upon themselves to completely reimagine one of the longest-lived yet least-menacing monsters in cinematic history: the vampire. Of course fans of the comic book miniseries upon which it was based knew exactly who that someone was: writer Steve Niles. For once, a horror fan and relative newcomer to the Hollywood system had slipped in, laid the foundations for an original idea, and slipped out again, all before the concept had the chance to be focus grouped into oblivion.

JAMS, SCARES N' *EXORCIST* STAIRS

Like most creative types lured into horror's embrace, Niles developed a healthy love-hate relationship with fright at an early age. Born in Jackson, NJ, June 21, 1965, he quickly discovered horror movies on television. But "I didn't react well," he admits. "I'd want to watch them during the day, and then at night I'd be standing by my parents' bed, absolutely freaking out."

By the time he was in fourth grade, he'd moved to Reston, Va., with his mother and two older sisters. A planned community 20 miles outside of Washington DC, Reston was still very much under construction when the Niles family arrived. With nothing else around to hold his attention, he started noticing copies of *Creepy* and *Eerie* on the newsstands. Poring over their polished pages, he found himself mesmerized by the frightening fever dreams they contained. With that, he says, a corner was turned. "It was literally what I was most afraid of became my biggest obsession overnight."

Thus indoctrinated, he decided to approach horror films with fresh eyes. On Friday and Saturday nights, Washington DC's Channel 20 regularly aired such fare hosted by **Count Gore de Vol, aka Dick Dyszel**—Channel 20's omnipresent TV personality.

It was the Count's program that introduced Niles to George Romero's *Night of the Living Dead*. "It was almost like a *War of the*

Count Gore de Vol (Dick Dyszel)
Children such as your's truly who grew up watching Channel 20 in Washington DC were never quite sure who Dick Dyszel was. That's because he played various roles on camera including Bozo the Clown, Captain 20 (who talked to children about eating right between commercials), and horror movie host Count Gore de Vol. In 2004, Dyszel wrote the introduction to Steve Niles' graphic novel *Aleister Arcane*—the tale of a horror movie host—signed, naturally, Count Gore de Vol. You can still catch the Count online today (www.countgore.com), and in a forthcoming biopic about Dyszel called *Every Other Day is Halloween* (everyotherdayishalloween.wordpress.com).

Worlds experience," he remembers. "Me and my friend were like, 'Is this the news....is this *happening*?' We'd never seen anything like it. I remember really enjoying watching it, and then my friend went home and I just got scared out of my mind. It was the first movie that really made we want to live horror. And [Richard Matheson's novel] *I Am Legend* not only made me want to read, it made me want to write."

When he wasn't reading Matheson, **Creepy** or **Eerie**, Niles spent much of his time writing stories, putting together little magazines that he would try to sell for 50 cents each. By 13, he graduated to shooting Super 8 movies.

"That's what I would spend most of my time doing, reading *Starlog*, *Cinemagic* and *Fangoria*, doing my own little stick-people storyboards, and trying to get my friends to act," he says. "In a lot of ways, that led to me wanting to do comic books because I remember how easy it was when I was doing the storyboards. It was, 'You know, I don't have to deal with all my drunk-ass friends if I just do comics.'"

Still, while Reston remained a nice place for urban professionals to cool their heels, it offered little excitement to a teen looking for creative stimulation. At 17, Niles left home to live in the northwestern part of DC, hanging out around the vibrant Adams Morgan area. Working at a comic shop during the day, he hit the area's burgeoning punk rock scene at night, wailing on his guitar with anyone who would share the stage. Occasionally this meant playing around a DC landmark familiar to most film fans—the "*Exorcist* stairs."

"We used to play punk shows at a hall at the top of those stairs, but the liquor store was at the bottom, so we used to have to lug cases of beer up and down them. They really lost their appeal after a while."

While his music opportunities were on the rise with the formation of his first major punk band, Gray Matters, things were picking up at the local comic store he worked at, too. It was 1986 and the

Creepy and Eerie
In the wake of the self-censorship that stifled comics following the establishment of the Comics Code Authority, *Famous Monsters of Filmland* publisher Jim Warren expanded his line to include black and white, magazine-size horror comics including *Creepy* (1964-1983) *Eerie* (1966-1983) and *Vampirella* (1969-1983).

> "I grew up on the Marvel Comics stuff, so I always wanted to do Marvel. But I could never break down that door. It was in the oddest way that Marvel closing its doors helped me out so much. Most creators do 10 books and they maybe own one. Except for *Batman*, I own everything I do."
>
> — STEVE NILES

The imposing **stone staircase** that plays such a pivotal role in William Friedkin's 1973 masterpiece *The Exorcist* is located at the end of M Street in Georgetown, and still attracts a fair amount of attention today.

comics boom was in full swing, led by the likes of *The Dark Knight Returns*, *Watchmen* and others.

"I was just reaching this point of frustration," he recalls. "I'm literally reading *The Dark Knight* or something like that and thinking, 'Oh my God, why don't I just do comics?'"

The only thing he had no question about was the subject matter. It had to be horror.

In 1988, he formed his own comic publishing company, Arcane Comix, adapting the works of Clive Barker (including *Rawhead Rex* and *Dread*), Richard Matheson (*I Am Legend*) and others for Eclipse Comics.

Had he been tempted to contribute any art to these early projects? "Oh God no," he laughs. "Just scripting. I can't draw at all."

GOT TEETH?

Blurt out the words "horror comics" in a small group and a good number of people will lapse into a Pavlovian fit, banging on about *Tales from the Crypt* and other contributions from the 1950s-era **EC Comics** company.

"Everybody always assumes that I'm this massive EC fan," Niles says. "I'm a fan of the EC artists, sure. Johnny Craig and Jack Davis and the art in those books was astounding. The stories? Ehh. They were a formula and you knew what was going to happen. Somebody did something bad to somebody else, and that somebody else rose from the dead and got their revenge. That's what we got locked into."

Even when comic series like Bruce Jones' *Twisted Tales* came along in the 1980s, it was really more of the same. Not that Niles has any reason to complain, he says. "It worked out really good because everybody thought what I was doing was really shockingly new, when all I was doing was what I had grown up on. I wanted to do comics that were like the horror movies I saw."

By 1994, Niles had his own short run series, *King of the Dead*, published by **FantaCo Enterprises** with art by Brian Clark. The writer was now living in Minnesota, trying to adjust to the area's harsh winters, when he happened to catch a piece in the local newspaper about a place far colder than his new home.

"They had this human interest piece that was basically, 'You

EC Comics
Starting in 1949, publisher William Gaines transformed his late father's Educational Comics line of "good for you" publications for children into the trendsetting Entertaining Comics. With titles such as *Tales from the Crypt*, *The Vault of Horror* and *Crime SuspenStories*, it was a major force in the realm of modern horror comics anthologies. Though it employed some of the greatest comic artists of its day, EC was driven out of business by public and political pressures that objected to its extreme depictions of violence.

FantaCo Enterprises
Formed in 1978 as a comic book store and mail-order service, the upstate New York company expanded into publishing independent comics and several landmark books about horror including John McCarty's *Splatter Movies: Breaking the Last Taboo*. It also published several titles by *Deep Red* fanzine creator Chas Balun including *Horror Holocaust*, *The Deep Red Horror Handbook* and *The Gore Score*.

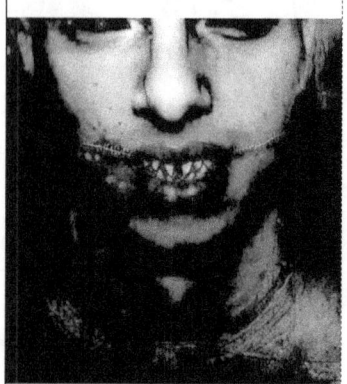

Ben Templesmith
Perth, Australia-born comic book phenom Ben Templesmith has redefined horror comics for the 21st century with his work on IDW's *Wormwood: Gentleman Corpse*, Image Comics' *Fell*, and is perhaps best known for his collaboration with Steve Niles on *30 Days of Night*. He also may be one of the most entertaining people on Twitter (twitter.com/Templesmith).

Barrow, Alaska
Located about 300 miles north of the Arctic Circle, the real Barrow experiences about 65 days of darkness—characterized by decreasing amounts of twilight each day—starting around the last week of November. It also had a population of more than 4,000 as of 2007, compared with the few hundred in *30 Days of Night*.

think *your* winters suck,' talking about this place in Alaska that went dark for a period of time," he says. "Alcohol was illegal because the depression rate was so high. It caught my attention immediately. I remember right away just writing 'vampires' in the margin."

About five years later, Niles found himself in LA. Surely someone in a town that could hang a movie on amusement park attractions and one-line cocktail napkin scenarios would recognize the potential of a vampire film set in a land of perpetual darkness.

"I pitched it as a comic, I pitched it as a movie, I pitched it every way I could," Niles says. "I was always so stunned they didn't go for the high concept. To this day I don't understand why. It was almost five years of pitching that thing to blank faces. Maybe it was the way I was pitching it. When I was describing the scene where they look out and they see the vampires coming across the tundra, maybe these people were picturing a hundred Bela Lugosis..."

Finally, IDW Publishing greenlit the idea in 2002 for a three-issue limited series, teaming Niles up with one of the great artists of modern horror—Australian **Ben Templesmith**.

The duo collaborated on the series via e-mail and AOL Instant Messenger for more than a year before they ever met in person, Niles says. "We not only had the problem of the hours and the time difference, but we also were both night owls, so we had these completely screwed up schedules we were trying to sync up."

Although collaborations are always fraught with a little nervous anticipation for Niles, "I remember that thing with that opening page—a very simple three-panel fade in to **Barrow**," he says. Templesmith "did it and it was exactly what I pictured in my head. I still have that page, too. Right from then I loved working with Ben."

To say that *30 Days'* success was immediate once it hit IDW is, if anything, an understatement. Sales didn't skyrocket with publication of the first issue, but with the publication of the *advertisement* for the first issue, three months before it was even finished. "That ad,

WORKING WITH ROB ZOMBIE

Starting in 2004, Steve Niles and horrorbilly-rocker-cum-director Rob Zombie (*The Devil's Rejects*, *Halloween* remake) shared writing duties on two horror comics: *The Nail* (Dark Horse Comics) and *Bigfoot* (IDW).

"Somebody literally threw us in a room together and said you guys would love each other," Niles says. "Then we sat there and talked and were like, 'Hey, what do ya know, we like each other.'"

Niles says Zombie is one of the easiest people he's ever worked with. "He's from the East Coast and grew up around Boston and the New York music scene, and we were exactly the same age. And I was in the DC music scene and into horror and all that, and we knew a lot of the same people."

Since Zombie came up with the concept behind *The Nail*, and *Bigfoot* was Niles' baby, "We set up a rule where whoever originated the material had final say," Niles says. "So if we ever got into a little bit of a snag, we could get out of it."

Niles hopes to see their *Bigfoot* ultimately find a place on film screens. "We have to undo the sins of *Harry and the Hendersons*," he says. "We need a good, scary bigfoot movie!"

which had that first image that Ben did of the teeth that is now the trade cover—unbelievable."

When the movie version of *30 Days of Night* hit theaters in 2007, Niles saw his idea come full circle.

"Now every time I turn around, someone's doing a comic in order to try to sell a movie," Niles laughs. "Everybody says, 'That's what *you* do.' No, that's what *happened*."

POSTMORTEM

If you've at all had it with your fellow man—and if you haven't, you really aren't getting out enough—your first glimpses of Barrow, Alaska, in David Slade's *30 Days of Night* adaptation are visions of paradise. During the Arctic city's annual plunge into a month's darkness, its already miniscule population diminishes to a little more than 100 souls.

In a scene reminiscent of Dracula's surreptitious English landfall in Bram Stoker's original novel, a strange man slips into Barrow from a large ship and proceeds to wreak havoc on its infrastructure. Sled dogs are killed, cell phones burned and utilities sabotaged, all to pave the way for what is to come.

And what comes is a frightening assault on the senses, from blood-spattered vampires that dart menacingly out of sight until it's too late, to an eerie, industrial soundscape punctuated by vampire cries that fill the night. Influenced heavily by Steve Niles' expert pacing and Ben Templesmith's nightmarish comic illustrations, the film still manages to inject enough realism into each frame to make you buy what is going on.

Several touches make these toothy terrors truly terrifying. One of the most important: the way the creatures communicate with one another in a guttural language that must be translated via subtitles. This, combined with their bestial movements and inhuman cries, sell the conceit that there is nothing human, and certainly nothing romantic, about these bloodsuckers.

If the movie version of *30 Days of Night* suffers from anything, it's an overabundance of perfectly white teeth (but only for the heroes, mind) and a final scene that, while faithful to its source material, feels a tad schmaltzy compared with all that's gone before.

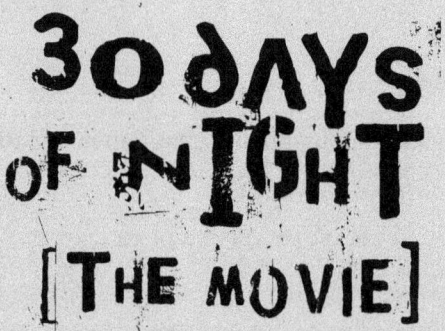

HORRORWOOD TODAY

What **David Slade** did with *30 Days of Night* is a model for how every adaptation should be handled, but rarely is.

The British director came up through the ranks of advertising and shooting music videos for artists such as Stone Temple Pilots, System of a Down and Tori Amos. With the 2005 release of the Internet-stalking suspense flick *Hard Candy*, genre fans rejoiced over this new filmmaker who quite clearly "got it."

Just a few days after Slade finished up the sound mixing for that film, Sony pitched him on the $32 million, Sam Raimi-produced *30 Days of Night*. *Hard Candy* writer Brian Nelson came on board, too, a move Slade has credited with giving *30 Days* that extra air of reality, especially in its dialogue.

Shot mostly in the snowy South Islands of New Zealand, the movie, starring Josh Hartnett, Melissa George and Danny Huston as lead vampire Marlowe, was the first truly fearsome vampire film to hit theaters in decades. Prior to its release, vampires had ranged from suave-but-cranky creatures such as Lugosi's Count Dracula and Anne Rice's legion of homoerotovamps to supernatural assholes epitomized in the *Blade* movies and the *Buffy the Vampire Slayer* TV series. While nearly all showed little hesitation in dispatching human prey, none demonstrated the vicious, animalistic savagery of *30 Days'* hordes. This quality sprang directly from the comic series.

"I love the movie," Niles says. "I think any author is always going to want a little more of their original story in there, but overall I think David Slade made a great movie."

As amazing as it was to see his story on the big screen, Niles was even more blown away by everything that went along with it.

"It was absolutely bizarre," he says. "They had a 14-story billboard on the Figaro Hotel. I look up there and just the words 'Based on a graphic novel' were taller than me. We would be driving around, cracking up."

David Slade
One of the hardest parts of putting together the *Handbook* was the small number of directors we wanted to include, but for reasons of timing or opportunity, could not. One of those is **David Slade**. With a mastery of the medium and an eager willingness to experiment, he succeeded in making **Hard Candy**, a claustrophobic two-hander starring Ellen Page and Patrick Wilson, into one of the greatest horror/suspense flicks of the last 10 years. Next time, David?

ALL BARK... + BITE!

David Slade's 2007 film adaptation of the Niles/Templesmith comic series *30 Days of Night* not only preserved the vampires' savage, animalistic manner, but actually intensified it with some hackle-raising sound design and a chilling performance by Danny Huston (above left) as lead vampire Marlowe.

At one point he was watching the guest hosts on *At the Movies* discussing the movie, "and they're kind of saying they didn't really like it, and I'm like, 'Oh well, I guess we have to listen to bad reviews, too.' Then one of the guys says, 'What's really surprising was the comic was so complex,' and they start talking about the comic. That was the moment where I understood, 'OK, the comic's one thing and the movie's another.'"

Though a big fan of horror films, Niles admits that the ones he enjoys these days are few and far between, "especially since brutality has taken over creativity."

Neil Marshall's *The Descent* is about the only movie that comes

> It shows that people were willing to go to the theater just to see Will Smith, so they could've been more respectful to Mr. Matheson's novel and shown the world what a great book this is. It has this unbelievably incredible ending, and [movies] have skipped it now three times.
>
> — **NILES** *on the 2007 movie* I Am Legend

to mind when asked to name a good one he's seen in the last five years. "When I first saw the movie, it was, 'Oh my God, it's all female characters. How soon until they all get so hot they have to take their shirts off?' And they never did. They stuck to their situation, they were strong characters, and they just got through it. I love that."

What really drives him crazy is the whole torture porn trend, he says. "Watching somebody tortured, it always seems like cheating. It's like a comedian farting on stage. I guarantee you **if I film a needle moving slowly toward an eye**, it's going to freak people out every single time. But it's lazy."

And why is it that women are so often the victims, he asks. "I've spent my whole life being called a queer by my friends and things like that because I have these views. I was raised by two older sisters and my mom, and I'm just sick and fucking tired of the way women are treated in film. I watched one recently and every slasher scene, somehow the shirt became ripped off and all these rape scenes, and I'm like how is this horror again? It's like we've lost our way in some ways.

"It's so funny because I remember in the '80s, I wasn't really fond of the slasher trend. And now with torture porn, I actually look back fondly on those slasher movies." [NHH]

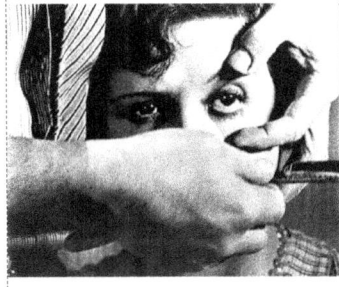

"…If I film a needle moving slowly toward an eye…" Something similar was done by pioneering Spanish filmmaker Luis Buñuel in *Un chien andalou* (1929), a 16-minute short co-produced by surrealist painter Salvador Dalí. The infamous close-up of a woman having her eyeball sliced by a razor (in reality the eye of a dead calf) in the opening scene can still bring chills to audiences today.

PART TWO

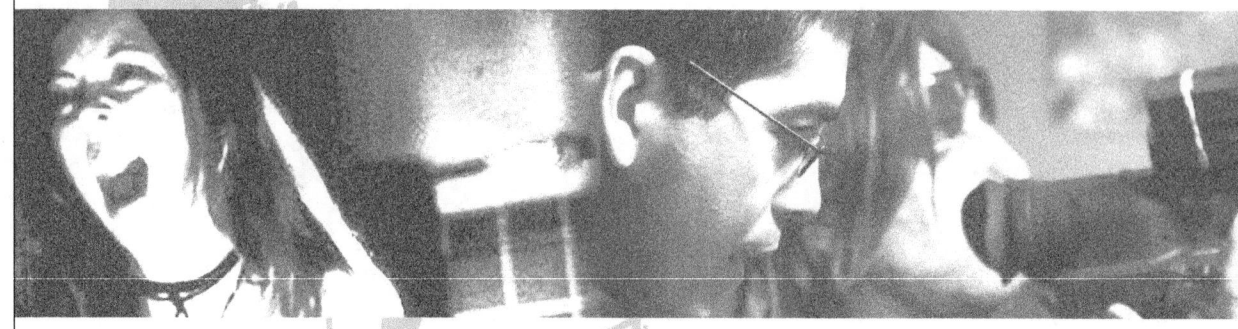

GOT SOMETHING YOU WANNA SAY?

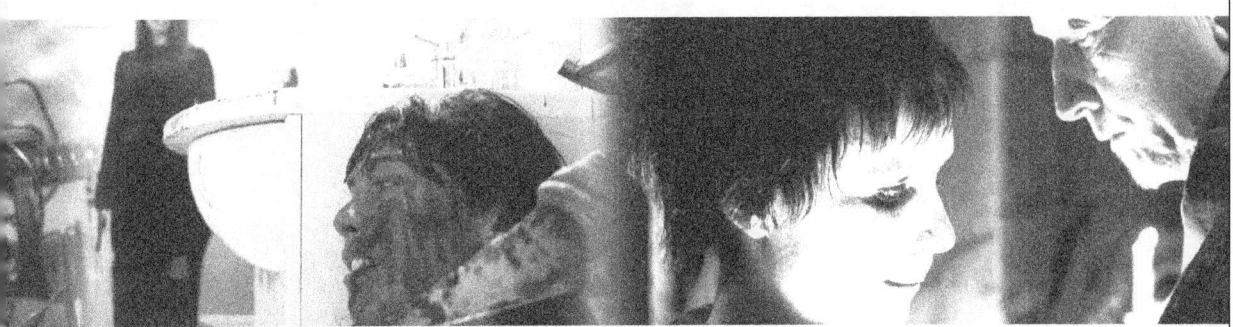

To the uninitiated, horror films appear to be all carnage, devoid of any meaning. While no one's going to be comparing gems of the genre to Nabokov any time soon, several entries in the New Horror pantheon attempt to do more than boost their gore score, and often succeed.

Canada's **Vincenzo Natali** (p. 78) burst onto the scene in 1997 with *Cube*, an exploration of human worth and the oppression of faceless bureaucracies.

A few years later, that country unleashed *Ginger Snaps* (p. 96), an anarchic horror comedy that still managed to wear its heart very much on its furry sleeve. In the process, it played with gender stereotypes the way a house cat entertains a field mouse, with much the same results.

In 2007, **Alexandre Bustillo + Julien Maury** (p. 128) brought us *Inside* (*À l'intérieur*), a kinetic bloodbath that pit a nameless psycho against a pregnant woman, all against the backdrop of the recent Paris riots.

Finally, one of the biggest surprises came from a director who received his big break directing sequels. **Darren Bousman** (p. 142) helmed *Saw II-IV*, infusing the series with a gritty pathos and signature shots that upped the creepiness quotient considerably. By decade's end, he threw his considerable directorial skill behind a rock opera that skewered Hollywood's cosmetic surgery addiction on screen, and its distribution system off.

Horror films weren't the only media with something to say. Toronto's **Rue Morgue magazine** (p. 164) grew into the official voice of the New Horror in the 2000s. Where competing publications rarely gave awful films a drubbing, *Rue Morgue* let slip the dogs of criticism, albeit with humor and imagination—a dangerous practice in an industry rife with excrement.

Kafka For The Modern Age

VINCENZO NATALI

Like a recent college graduate emerging from a life of predictable order and weekly keggers into a cold, uncaring world, the English-language horror film had no idea what it was or what it wanted to be in the 1990s...

THE '90S: HORROR HELL

A perfect storm of studio greed and stale imaginations came together in the 1990s to all but cripple modern horror cinema. In addition to seeing some of the worst entries in preexisting horror franchises such as *A Nightmare on Elm Street* and *Prom Night*, it brought us Wes Craven's *Scream* in 1996. Though reasonably well done by mainstream standards, *Scream* seemingly ushered in a type of institutionalized cynicism that led to such groaningly self-aware flicks as the *I Know What You Did Last Summer* remake, *Halloween: H2O* and *The Mummy*. Ironically, 1999 brought us *The Blair Witch Project*, perhaps one of the only truly scary films in horror film history.

The '80s had offered a cornucopia of fang-tickling fare, from the truly awe-inspiring (John Carpenter's 1982 opus *The Thing* and David Cronenberg's *The Fly* and *Dead Ringers*) to the stupid-but-fun (*The Lost Boys*, Stuart Gordon's *Re-Animator*). A decade later, what was there to get excited about?

The *Alien*, *Child's Play* and *Texas Chainsaw* franchises all continued to dribble out sequels, as did a legion of straight-to-video series, from *Hellraiser* to *Troll*. Only the Stephen King adaptation *Misery*, *Jacob's Ladder* and the groundbreaking *Blair Witch Project* contributed anything of note. There was *Prom Night III*, *Psycho IV* and *Freddy's Dead*. Leslie Nielsen and Linda Blair seemed to drive a stake through the very heart of the genre in 1990's atrocious *Exorcist* parody *Repossessed*.

What the genre needed was another *Fly*, another Cronenberg to blow in from Canada, that magical land where the casts usually speak English and their directors are far enough away from Hollywood to be immune to its Midas touch of mediocrity.

Horror fans genuflected to Beelzebub on a nightly basis, praying to see something they hadn't seen a dozen times before. In 1996, along came the too-stuck-on-itself-by-half *Scream*, proving once again the need for specific details when requesting favors from the infernal depths. Wes Craven's juggernaut managed to pull in more than $103 million in the States alone before spawning two sequels. Whatever goodwill the gentleman had built over the years with horror classics like *The Hills Have Eyes* and *A Nightmare on Elm Street* was instantly squandered. For many, it was like watching the vicar who'd spent years organizing charity events make off with the cash box.

A year later, while American audiences were trying to make do with *Scream 2*, a small independent film out of Canada began making the film festival rounds.

Though its science-fiction trappings confused many, director Vincenzo Natali's *Cube* was a straight-up horror flick that offered audiences that rarest movie commodity: a glimpse of something new. This at-times bloody but always thought-provoking tale of six characters trapped within a giant, deadly maze of cubes not only delivered imaginative kills, its Kafkaesque themes and general air of mystery kept itself top-of-mind long after viewing.

With *Splice*, a feature film about the perils of DNA manipulation, poised for a 2009 release, Natali seems to be the answer to those infernal prayers. The land of Cronenberg has brought forth another director to stir things up.

AMERICAN-BORN, CANADIAN-BRED
Natali was born in Detroit Jan. 6, 1969, but moved to Toronto with his mother when he was still an infant after his parents split up.

PENNILESSNESS IS THE MOTHER OF INVENTION

While Ontario-born James Cameron was busy shoveling some $200 million from the coffers of 20th Century Fox and Paramount into the super hit *Titanic*, Vincenzo Natali was at Wallace Avenue Studios in Toronto, trying desperately to make a single 14-by-14-foot enclosure come across as an entire world on film.

Like the best films, *Cube* stakes its entire existence on an ostensibly simple premise. Six strangers—four men, two women—each awakens to find themselves imprisoned inside a single chamber, part of an enormous, cube-like structure. They don't know how they got there, but without food or water, all realize they will die if they can't make good their escape. Thanks to a cheeky pre-title set piece in which a lone prisoner is, quite literally, cubed by a wire-mesh trap elsewhere in the structure, the audience realizes that hunger and thirst are the least of these people's problems.

What follows is a 90-minute exercise in suspense as the group moves from one room to another. All use their special skills and talents to determine which rooms to enter and which contain deadly traps. The fact that not everyone survives is as much down to petty squabbles that spiral wildly out of control as to the deadliness of the cube itself.

Canadian Film Centre
Founded in 1988 by filmmaker Norman Jewison (*In the Heat of the Night, Fiddler on the Roof*), the Canadian Film Centre is that country's largest training ground for professionals in film and television. CFC alumni include Natali, John Fawcett and Karen Walton (*Ginger Snaps*), and Sarah Polley (co-star of the *Dawn of the Dead* remake and *Splice*, and director of *Away from Her* starring Julie Christie).

My Dinner with Andre
What amounts to a two-hour conversation about life in the 20th century, Louis Malle's *My Dinner with Andre* (1981) starred Andre Gregory and Wallace Shawn.

It was an ambitious story, and the idea of telling it on Natali's miniscule budget would've been laughable had he not talked his way into the project in the first place.

What the hell was he doing trying to direct a movie, anyway? He had been a storyboard artist at a Toronto animation studio, working on everything from the *Beetlejuice* cartoon to *The Adventures of Tintin*. When you needed different backgrounds in that business, you just drew them.

But storyboarding wasn't enough for the then-26-year-old who was enrolled in the country's prestigious **Canadian Film Centre** at the time. He'd made several short films since he was a kid. Most recently he'd been using the money he made storyboarding Saturday morning children's programming to finance them.

It had taken a lot of hard work to even get this far. He and roommate André Bijelic had written the script for *Cube* about the time Natali had applied to the CFC for its director program. Once there, Natali says, "I sort of hammered them with *Cube*" until, after several rejections, they let him enter their Feature Film Project.

"Because of the nature of the Film Centre and their relationship to the industry here, there was a lot of material and equipment that was given to us in the form of deferrals," he says. Though *Cube*'s cash budget was about $350,000 Canadian, "I think if everything had actually been paid for, it would be a million dollar movie."

Even $1 million Canadian didn't get a filmmaker very far at the tail end of the 1990s. "I knew I didn't want to make a small personal drama like **My Dinner with Andre**," he says, and those are usually the types of movies that get made on such anemic budgets.

Cube was different. At its heart, it was an idea movie, a character study. Lavish settings were secondary.

"My little flash of inspiration was that I realized that one set could substitute for many," Natali says. "That led me to think of this maze of identical cube-like rooms, a symmetrical maze. That got me

With the humblest of materials and a few color gels, Natali and his *Cube* crew created an entire world that consisted almost entirely of a single 14-by-14-foot set.

very excited because I was a big fan of MC Escher. It just opened up this whole world."

It *was* a whole world, albeit one that was constructed in a dilapidated warehouse. The entire set consisted of a six-sided cube and another partial cube that consisted of just three walls. "We'd change color gels in each room to simulate transition from room to room," Natali says. When the characters are seen inside a room, they are usually standing in the six-sided set, dubbed the "hero cube" by the filmmakers. "Whenever you see the characters looking from one room into the other, they're always looking at the same room," he says—the three-sided half-cube.

A brilliant plan having one set double for many, but one always ends up paying the piper one way or another, as the director quickly discovered.

"It was a really horrible set to work in," he says. "The whole idea of this thing was to make life as simple as possible for myself as a first-time filmmaker. But actually shooting in a box is one of the most difficult things to do. The cube itself really became an instance of life imitating art because we all started to go insane in this room, being in the same place every day all day, working under tremendous strain and pressure because we had a very limited schedule and budget."

Twenty days was all the project was allotted. For comparison's sake, the French gorefest *Inside* took 35 days *(see p. 128)*.

Forget building the set and shooting actors inside it—lighting the box was one of the greatest challenges the crew faced. Doing it correctly ended up turning the cube into an enormous cooker. "We used to call it the EZ Bake oven," Natali says. "And we were the Betty Crocker mix slowly being baked."

KAFKA CUBED

"I try not to be too self-conscious but I'm definitely interested in stories about entrapment," Natali admits. "I think one of the inspirations for me initially making *Cube* was that I wanted to create a 20th century vision of hell. I wanted to pull it away from the Gothic or Dante image of what hell might be and put it into something that was more contemporary and a little more existential."

While the *Cube* prequel, Ernie Barbarash's *Cube Zero*, pulled back the curtain a little in 2004 by revealing some of the people involved behind the cube, Natali deliberately kept that aspect of the story veiled in mystery.

"To me, the notion that there is no one there running this machine is very terrifying," he says. "That the technology had a life of

Cube Zero
Directed by Ernie Barbarash (co-producer of *American Psycho* and director of 2007's *They Wait*), 2004's *Cube Zero* is the third entry in what became a *Cube* trilogy, but its events take place before the first film. Though it cannot really be considered part of the *Cube* cannon, it does have a lot to offer as a standalone movie. In it, Eric Wynn (Zachary Bennett), one of the people charged with operating the cube, is stricken with a sudden sense of compassion over the fate of those who enter it. In the process, he himself falls victim to the uncaring bureaucracy that keeps the whole mechanism going.

its own, independent of its creators, and that it had swallowed these people up. That was much more frightening than if someone were actually watching them. There's even a line in the movie that says that 'Big Brother is *not* watching you.' There's no God, not a bad one or a good one. There's just nothing. It's that idea of nothingness or emptiness that is truly horrifying."

The adjective often used to describe the *Cube* universe is Kafkaesque, after Prague writer **Franz Kafka**'s fiction, which frequently depicted everyday people caught in the jaws of bureaucracy and other malignant mechanisms beyond their control or understanding. *Cube* ratchets the threat up significantly through the implementation of technology.

Natali insists that there is no backstory for *Cube*, "there never could be." Yet this wasn't always the case.

In early drafts of the script, the characters were actually prisoners, he says. "They were people who had committed crimes and had been executed and woke up in this place, so there was a little more sense of it being an experiment. But the nature of the experiment was never made clear. At some point I decided that it was more interesting to just have normal people in this place who hadn't committed a crime, who had no reason to be punished. But André and I quickly realized that there was no explanation for this that would ever be satisfying. More importantly, not having an explanation made it all the more frightening. That's why I really resisted being involved with the sequels."

Just as he erased character backstories, he obliterated every vestige of the world outside his futuristic hell. Rumors of footage depicting the cube's surroundings have dogged *Cube* since it first screened. "I think for years I denied that [footage] even existed because truly it's not even worth looking at," Natali says. "It was a mistake to even attempt it."

The scene, an epilogue of sorts, was not shot by the director

Franz Kafka
Though the literary merits of Prague-born author Franz Kafka (1883-1924) are certainly debatable, he captured perfectly that sense of being caught up in something larger than yourself, most notably in works such as *The Trial* and *The Castle*. For those unwilling to read his fiction, the 1991 Steven Soderbergh (*Traffic, Solaris* remake) thriller *Kafka* starring Jeremy Irons is an excellent primer on the man and his twisted imagination.

himself but by his second unit, he says. "It came out of one of those bad development notes that filmmakers frequently have to vet when they're making movies, and somehow it ended up on the screen. It was never in the early drafts that André and I wrote together. I really think it came out of the producers' nervousness that *Cube* takes place entirely in one environment. Honestly, it will never see the light of day. Hopefully it's been lost. It didn't work.

"It was very clear that our story ended with Kazan walking out into the light. Anything that followed that was going to detract from this fantastic world we had spent a lot of time trying to create."

Natali has never seen nor had any involvement with the two sequels to his film—*Cube²: Hypercube* and *Cube Zero*—but feels for his successors.

"I don't know exactly what the natures of the sequels are, but I can only assume you would have to start answering questions," he says. "We barely got away with not answering them in one movie; by the time you have three, you've got to answer something."

In 2002's *Cube²: Hypercube*, we do get an answer of sorts— however predictable—depending on which ending you watch. More intriguing, though, is the nature of the cube itself. No longer a piece of improbable-yet-believable machinery, the structure in the sequel is one whose deadliest aspects lie in its ability to reverse the flow of gravity, bend time and bleed between dimensions.

Cube Zero, on the other hand, retains the original device and opts for a more Kafkaesque explanation of the forces behind the killing machine. Of the two sequels, it is more faithful to Natali's original vision, and serves up an ending that delivers a mostly crowd pleasing "Aha!" moment.

"*Cube* was a one-off," Natali says. "We always felt that there was one film to be made in that cube and God help anyone else who had to make another one."

Because the Canadian Film Centre owned the rights to the

POSTMORTEM

Oh to be a *Cube* virgin again. Few pleasures can compare with going into this intellectual odyssey blind, just as the characters do, and learning the secrets of the cube right along with them.

It's not a perfect film, but then again it doesn't really need to be. In the first 10 minutes, it sets up an intriguing premise: men and women awaken inside several 14-by-14-foot, interconnecting metallic rooms, with no memory of how they wound up there. Quickly, two men—one of them a prison escape artist—attempt to move into other rooms, and are instantly done away with by booby traps.

Our group is thus whittled down to Worth (David Hewlett), cop Quentin (Maurice Wint), math whiz Leaven (Nicole de Boer), free-clinic doctor Holloway (Nicky Guadagni) and the autistic Kazan (Andrew Miller).

Early on, Leaven thinks she's discovered the secret to identifying the trap-laden rooms via a set of numbers engraved on metal strips affixed to each entranceway. Yet once her mathematical system fails her, the already precarious allegiances holding the group together disintegrate, and it's pretty much everyone for themselves.

While the gore is kept to three or four set pieces, the underlying horror of the situation will satisfy genre fans who've grown tired of the usual stalk, slash and torture flicks choking video store shelves today.

The intense heat generated by lighting the relatively small space that served as the *Cube* set led cast and crew to refer to the in-studio structure as the EZ Bake Oven.

original film, it licensed sequel-making rights to the filmmakers of *Cube²: Hypercube* and *Cube Zero* for a tidy sum, which was reinvested into the CFC, Natali says. "I'm not unhappy that the sequels exist, but I want everyone to know that I really had nothing to do with them."

CUBE UNLOCKED

Though Natali realizes he was lucky to get his first feature film made, he was the last person to expect it to gain any sort of popularity. It wasn't a "sleeper" hit, he insists, but "a comatose" one.

"I truly had no expectations beyond being able to finish it and maybe see it released in a few Canadian theaters," he says. "The fact that it actually managed to travel internationally was really extraordinary to me."

These words aren't studio spin or false modesty, but based on a vivid recollection of how he felt during the 20 days and nights he spent in that "EZ Bake oven" in December 1996.

"It was a really awful experience making the film because it should've been a great experience," he says. "I was getting to make a movie I wanted to make with people I wanted to make it with, and everything should've gone well. Nothing worked."

For all the time and energy poured into the construction of the set, it failed to live up to the image he'd carried around for so long in his mind.

"I really thought I was making a terrible film," he recalls. "That I was taking something that could've been really great and ruining it. I felt that way right until it was finished. It took other people to recognize it before I started to think that maybe it was not so bad. I think it's because my expectations were so high. In my mind, I saw this perfect movie, and I thought that, given that it was being made in such a controlled environment, it should've been perfect. I think it was the little imperfections that really drove me crazy."

Imperfections such as the doors inside the cube that refused to open and close nearly three-quarters of the way through filming, until post-production/second-unit supervisor William Phillips rigged a pulley system to get the job done.

The cult success *Cube* ultimately enjoyed happened so gradually, the director wasn't even aware of it. Though it snagged the award for Best Canadian First Feature Film at its Sept. 9, 1997 premiere at the Toronto International Film Festival, "I think the first review for it was probably one of the worst reviews I've ever read for any movie ever," he recalls. It came out during *Cube's* Toronto showing in that city's *Now Magazine*, a publication similar to *LA Weekly* that everyone attending the festival uses as a guide for what to see there,

CUBE THE MUSICAL?

"We used to joke that we should do a musical version of it—it could've used a few song and dance numbers, I think."

— VINCENZO NATALI

he says. "I thought, 'This is going to be a disaster; I'm never going to work again.'

"I also think the people at the Film Centre weren't particularly excited about it, either—I don't even want to guess why, but it just didn't catch fire right away."

Somehow *Cube* hung on and traveled from festival to festival. Along the way, the awards continued to stack up: *Sitges* (Best Film, Best Screenplay, 1998), Puchon International Fantastic Film Festival (Jury's Choice Award, 1998), and on it went.

It wasn't until the film reached French theaters about a year later that it finally had a decent theatrical showing. Says Natali, "André and I had always felt that it was the kind of movie that might have a long shelf life because it doesn't really relate to any specific time period."

MORE 'STORIES ABOUT ENTRAPMENT'

After *Cube*, Natali directed a few episodes of the television series *Earth: Final Conflict* before hitting the big screen once more with the 2002 sci-fi mystery *Cypher* starring Jeremy Northam, Lucy Liu, and *Cube* star and longtime friend **David Hewlett**. This tale of a recently laid off accountant turned corporate spy skillfully blends the best parts of *The Matrix* and Philip K Dick's "black iron prison" delusions with Natali's own inescapable rumblings about people caught up in machinations far bigger than themselves. Next came *Nothing*, an odd sci-fi comedy starring Hewlett and fellow *Cube*-mate Andrew Miller (Kazan) about two roommates who react to a series of unfortunate events by seemingly wishing the world outside their home into nothingness, and the angst that ensues. Both films earned their fair share of awards. However, for those genre fans who were intrigued by the existential horror first glimpsed in his debut effort, the director's best work clearly lay ahead of him.

From late December 2007 to February 2008, Natali went to work

David Hewlett
Though born in Surrey, England, Hewlett has carved out a healthy career acting in Canada and the US. In addition to Natali's movies *Cube, Cypher* and *Nothing*, he's probably best known Stateside as Dr. McKay on *Stargate Atlantis*. However, his best horror movie performance to date has to be in the 1989 Canadian classic *Pin*... And like Ben Templesmith, he's quite the Twitter wit (http://twitter.com/dhewlett). Hopefully you all will remember Twitter by the time this book comes out...

In his director's commentary for *Cube*, Natali cites several films as inspirations, from one of his all-time favorites, *Alien*, to the 1979 Andrei Tarkovsky (*Solaris*) thriller *Stalker* and Hitchcock's 1944 film *Lifeboat*. However, when it came to the overall style of the film, he and co-writer André Bijelic found themselves going back to classic prison escape films like *Escape From Alcatraz* and *Papillon*.

"I think the hard part of writing *Cube* was creating the dynamic between the characters and how they were being introduced, and how they would either help each other or betray each other," Natali says. "Once we had the maze figured out, once we had the technical part figured out, that's what was really difficult about constructing the story. Because we had denied ourselves access to any props or any extraneous characters or places that we could go to. The mechanism to move us from one place to another was the characters. How do you sustain the story for an hour and a half with just a few people in a room? I think that was why we spent so much time with prison pictures."

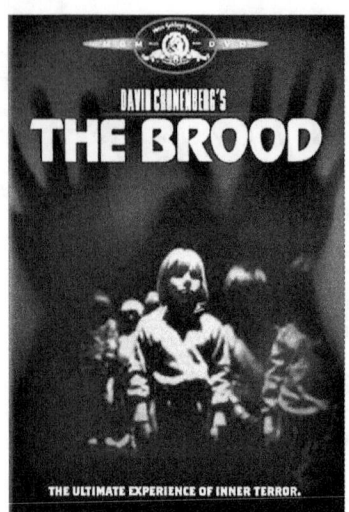

David Cronenberg
It's difficult to overestimate the impact that this Canadian auteur has had on North American cinema, especially when it comes to movies of the imagination. True, it is his "body horror" films such as The Fly, Videodrome and The Brood that receive the most discussion in horror circles today. However, his ceaseless attempts to redefine what can be shown on screen and his baffling ability to get his projects financed are what have truly served to inspire other filmmakers over the years. His movies also helped to reintroduce the rest of the world to Canadian cinema at a time when most of it consisted of dry documentaries and low-quality movies made simply because of the tax breaks offered by that country.

shooting *Splice*, a film that, at the time of this writing, has many believing that Natali has returned to that Cronenbergian path first glimpsed in *Cube*. However, whereas **David Cronenberg** has spent decades exploring the delicate relationships between flesh and the psyche, Natali seems hell bent on pursuing the far more pertinent role of technology and its impact on human relationships.

In *Splice*, two scientists played by Adrien Brody (*The Village, The Jacket*) and Sarah Polley (*Dawn of the Dead* remake and director of *Away from Her*) create an animal-human hybrid. Though the idea had been kicking around since the days of *Cube*, it was only recently that Natali was able to secure the funding—$25 million Canadian—to make *Splice* a reality. The film is being executive produced by filmmaker Guillermo del Toro (*The Devil's Backbone, Pan's Labyrinth*) and produced by Steve Hoban (*Ginger Snaps, Blood & Donuts, Black Christmas* remake).

"It has some pretty ambitious effects work in it," Natali says. "Only recently has the technology gotten to a point where we could

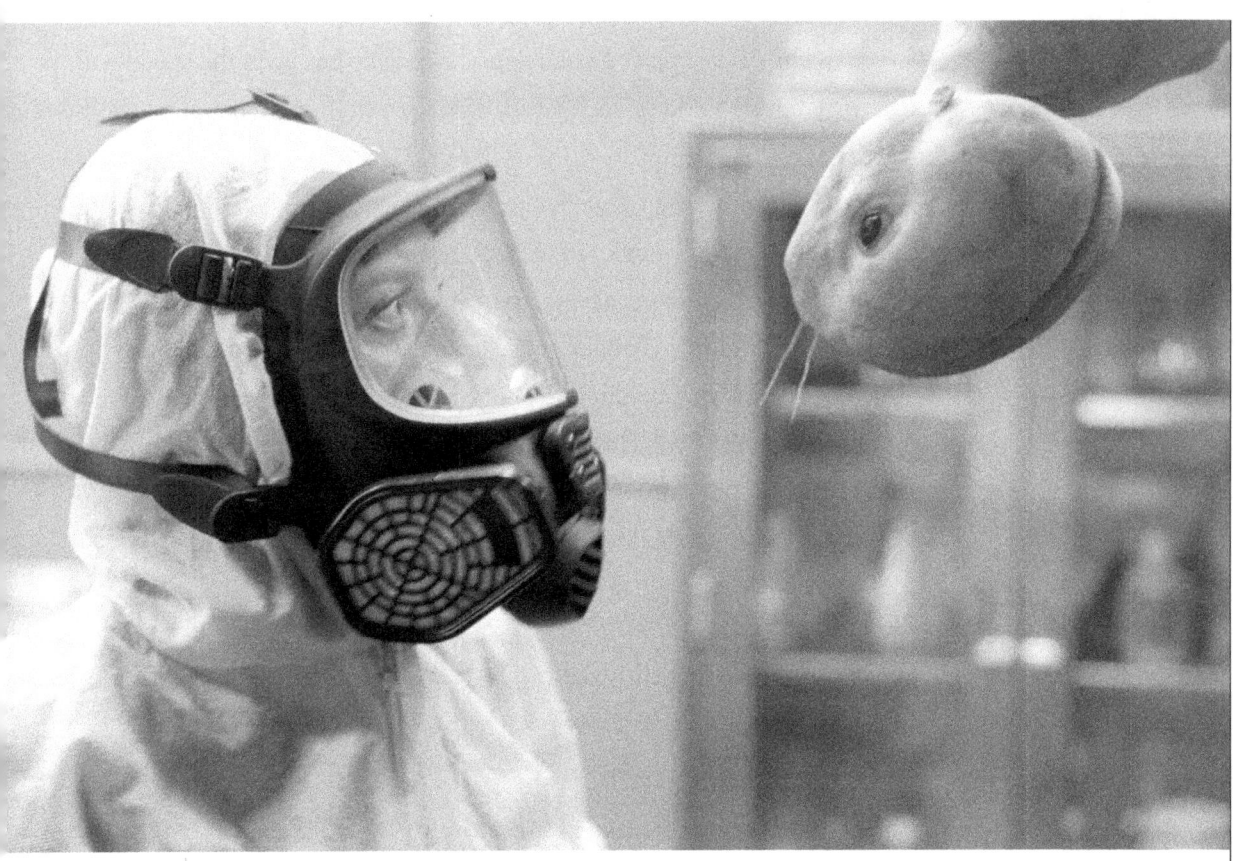

In his forthcoming film *Splice*, Natali explores the dynamics of the post-nuclear family: two married scientists (opposite) and their genetically engineered bundle of joy (above). Don't expect your typical monster flick.

really do it properly."

However, just as *Cube* is more about the characters than the giant structure in which they find themselves, *Splice*, too, leans more toward character study than B-movie spectacle.

"There are two young geneticists who, in their own way, are like outlaws," he says." They step outside the boundaries of what's acceptable in their field and do some unusual experiments, but they do it as a couple and they're very much in love. They create something that ends up turning the love affair into a triangle. That's really what's at the core of the movie, and that's what is going to separate it, I think, from a lot of other creature movies. It's very much about the relationship between the creators and the creation. It's not about the creature escaping into the world and causing havoc. It's much more insular than that."

The oddest part of the whole experience has been the speed with which real-world science has caught up with his cinematic creation, he says.

"The amazing thing is that in the time that it's taken me to write and finance this movie, they mapped the entire human genome. Technology is far outpacing my feeble ideas of what it could become. [*Splice*] is no longer science fiction, it's very much on the cusp of what could happen. With that in mind, I've tried very hard to make the technology as real as possible within the dramatic bounds of the story. Having said that, it's still a heightened reality. It's certainly not a documentary."

HIGH RISE

Though Natali is neck-deep in post-production on *Splice* when I catch up with him for this book, the shadow of yet another film falls across everything he does.

Decades ago he came across novelist JG Ballard's 1975 dystopian tale of class conflict, **High Rise**, and knew it was something he had to bring to the big screen.

"I chased the book for a number of years and I just couldn't get the rights to it," he explains. "People have been trying to make it forever. When I met Terry Gilliam, he said, 'Oh yeah, I was going to do that.'"

Finally he met Gabriella Martinelli, producer of such films as Baz Luhrmann's *Romeo + Juliet* and Clive Barker's *Nightbreed*. Martinelli was a good friend of Ballard associate Jeremy Thomas, who had produced Cronenberg's adaptation of the novelist's *Crash*. After pitching Thomas on his vision for *High Rise*, Natali ended up securing the rights.

"I hope *High Rise* is my next film," Natali says. "It's all written and ready to go. I'm pretty hopeful. It's an ambitious film. And believe me, I have not pulled back from anything in the book."

High Rise
The adaptation that Natali would like to make of JG Ballard's 1975 novel would serve as an interesting companion piece to *Cube*. In the book, tenants on each floor of a futuristic high rise square off against the rest as the building's infrastructure falls apart, and the laws of civilization slip between the cracks. Think *Towering Inferno* meets *Lord of the Flies*.

Like *Cube* and *Splice*, *High Rise* is another cautionary tale with a message tailor-made for our time. In the novel, the residents of a luxury high rise withdrawal from the rest of society and begin turning on each other, battling for access to elevators, swimming pools and other necessities of life therein.

"These people could leave any time they wanted," he points out. "There's nothing holding them where they are until things get completely out of control. It's interesting for me as a filmmaker because, unlike all my other films, there's no fantasy conceit to it. The events that occur in the film come purely out of the behavior of the characters in the movie. There's no virus or nerve gas that makes the residents of the high rise go crazy, it's just the dynamics of the society. That's why it's been so hard to write, because the Ballard novel doesn't address that directly, it just takes it for granted that those things are going to happen. I think that can work in the novel form, but in the movie, unless you want to make a surrealist film, it requires something a little more plausible.

"So it's about understanding why a vertically integrated society would suddenly, spontaneously collapse. But of course that's what also makes it fascinating. I really hope it happens, but it's the kind of movie that is that uncomfortable combination of something kind of expensive and a little bit experimental. You have to get a cast that can make the film commercial, or at least commercial in the eyes of a studio. It'll be entirely dependent on that."

Vincenzo Natali is at a fascinating stage in his career. Though appreciated by a small audience for *Cube* and his other films, he seems on the verge of trading the filmmaking freedom he has enjoyed up till now for exposure to a wider audience, possibly at the cost of some of that freedom.

"I've been lucky because with the movies I've made, I've been able to work with complete artistic control," he admits. "So you can blame me for everything that doesn't work; it's really my fault." [NHH]

> "I've been lucky because with the movies I've made, I've been able to work with complete artistic control...so you can blame me for everything that doesn't work; it's really my fault."
>
> — NATALI

CASE STUDY

BLEAK SUBURB AT THE EDGE OF NOTHING

GINGER SNAPS

IF HORROR FILMS HAVE HAD ONE OBVIOUS WEAKNESS OVER THE YEARS, IT'S BEEN A CHRONIC INABILITY TO TICKLE THE EMOTIONS. SO OFTEN THE CHARACTERS ARE NOTHING MORE THAN OVER-USED STEREOTYPES THAT, LIKE TODAY'S HITCHHIKERS, FALL DISTURBINGLY INTO TWO CAMPS: SOON-TO-BE VICTIM OR PSYCHOTIC. THE BEST ONE CAN HOPE FOR IN BOTH CASES IS A PARTICULARLY INVENTIVE DEATH...

> "Three days out of the month, I'm not much fun to be around either."
>
> —**WILLOW TO OZ**
>
> about why they should date, despite the fact that he's a werewolf, from the television series *Buffy the Vampire Slayer.* Despite being a groundbreaking show that specialized in breathing nuance and pathos into the likes of ghosts and vampires, the above quote was the highlight of its werewolf arc. Which just goes to show how hard it is to make an engaging werewolf story.

Certainly the last place one would expect to find three-dimensional characters and complex relationships is in a movie about werewolves. And genuine horror? *Pleease*.

As counterintuitive as it seems, wringing any sense of dread out of movie monsters is a fool's gamble for the simple reason that, by their very nature, these creations are utterly camp. Vampires were virtually neutered as figures of horror the moment Bela Lugosi slipped into his trademark cape in Tod Browning's 1931 classic *Dracula*. And werewolves? There have certainly been some engaging transformation scenes over the years, but the hairy mess we're left with time and time again looks far more ridiculous than frightening.

But in the year 2000, a Canadian film called *Ginger Snaps* slipped onto the world stage, deftly sidestepping the implausibility of the werewolf itself by making the long, drawn out transformation of its victim, teenager Ginger Fitzgerald (Katharine Isabelle), an allegory on a girl's traumatic transition to womanhood. Very quickly audiences forgot they were watching a film about a supernatural beast, and instead identified with Ginger's downward spiral and the wedge that ultimately separates her from her sister, Brigitte (Emily Perkins).

In the process, *Ginger Snaps* gave audiences worldwide a taste of what it's like to grow up in parts of Canada where, in director John Fawcett's words, one is forever in a "bleak suburb at the edge of nothing."

Unlike many of the films in this book, *Ginger Snaps* is less the product of a single auteur than the coming together of a phenomenal writer, director, cast and crew, into something far greater than the sum of its parts. It it for this reason that the following case study is offered.

SUBURBANOIA

In 1979, when *Ginger Snaps* writer Karen Walton was 14, the Nova Scotia-native moved with her family to Sherwood Park, Alberta—the suburbs.

It wasn't hard for *Ginger Snaps* writer Karen Walton to identify with the feelings of boredom and oppression experienced by Ginger and Brigitte. All she had to do was think back to her own adolescence growing up in the stifling suburbs of Sherwood Park, Alberta.

"It was a total culture shock," she says. "I remember moving there very clearly because I could not distinguish my house from all the other houses for the first three or four weeks, and I used to routinely end up in the wrong backyard."

Nearly 20 years later, it still makes for a good story, but at the time it was Walton's first taste of suburban life. For a young adult who wanted to see and experience life's infinite variety, it was, quite simply, hell.

One of the inspirations for Bailey Downs: the childhood home of *Ginger Snaps* writer Karen Walton in Sherwood Park, Alberta.

"To move there just when you're trying to figure out who you are and becoming curious about the world—there weren't even any trees," she says. "I was in mourning permanently because it was like moving to another country, and the values were so strange and, in my opinion at the time and to this day, rather meaningless."

That feeling of being an outsider in a place where the pressure to conform was everywhere would remain with her well into adulthood. When she met director John Fawcett in 1994, she realized that she wasn't alone.

Conformity is only part of what Fawcett found unsettling about the suburbs. Canada is the world's second largest country after Russia, yet only has about 33 million people, he points out. This leads to relatively small clusters of people being separated by huge tracts of land. "You're basically an island in the wilderness," Fawcett explains, "and I think that sense of being in this really bleak suburb at the edge of nothing is kind of how I felt growing up; I know it's how Karen Walton felt."

SHOW ME THE WAY TO BAILEY DOWNS

The Canadian suburb of Bailey Downs in which the Fitzgerald sisters live is, in fact, fictional. The author thought it might be a commentary on the dreary area itself: you would have to down some Baileys to live there. The reality turns out to be a bit more prosaic.

Karen Walton remembers, "The biggest mall closest to me out in the suburbs in the middle of nowhere was in a district called Bonny Doon. 'Doon' is Scottish for 'Downs,' right. I remember going 'Bonny Doon,' like it means 'Beautiful Downs.' So I was like, 'That is so perverse, that is so typical.' Bailey Downs probably came from Bonny Doon. It's weird how you remember the free associations a decade later.'

MEETING OF THE SUBURBAN REFUGEES

When Walton and Fawcett first met, they were at different places in their careers.

Walton had broken into the industry by talking her way onto the set of *Prom Night II* in 1987—as an apprentice stuntwoman. It was being shot on location in Edmonton, Alberta, about a half-hour from where she'd lived in Sherwood Park. At the time, she was working on her Bachelor of Arts degree in drama at the University of Alberta.

The original *Ginger Snaps* lineup: Writer Karen Walton, Katharine Isabelle, John Fawcett, Kris Lemche and Emily Perkins.

"I body doubled and got stomped on by marauding extras and worked crowd control in the mass-panic sequence," she recalls. "It was totally awesome."

It was also the first time Walton had worked with a professional film crew. It was this experience that convinced her to ditch theater in favor of film. *Prom Night II*'s stunt coordinator, Dwayne McLean, who has handled stunts on everything from *Land of the Dead* to *Silent Hill*, later lent a hand on the Canadian Film Centre film she and *Cube* director Vincenzo Natali *(see p. 78)* created: *Elevated*.

Walton says of Canada, "It's the tiniest country in the world."

Fawcett, who grew up in Calgary, moved to Toronto around the age of 22 to attend the CFC. He was in his late 20s when he met Walton, and was working on his first feature, **The Boys Club**.

In 1994, Fawcett drove to Edmonton to get one of his short films transferred to video, only to have his car break down on the way. A friend of his coaxed a bunch of mates out to entertain him, including Walton, while his car was in the shop. Walton and Fawcett had met very briefly at the Banff Television Festival a year or two before, but barely had the chance to chat then. Now they hit it off instantly. They moved to Toronto, and in together, later that same year.

"We had so much in terms of taste and drive in common, the sta-

The Boys Club
John Fawcett's 1997 feature debut *The Boys Club* is an effective coming-of-age thriller about three teen boys who befriend a psychotic—the late Chris Penn—and the effects that friendship has on their lives. Director Vincenzo Natali (*Cube, Splice*), who had met Fawcett in 1991, ended up doing all of the storyboarding for that film.

tistical probability was very high that sooner or later we'd see if we could do something together creatively, dates or not," Walton says.

By this time, Walton had recently quit her day job and started writing. Fawcett was itching to make some kind of horror film with one or two strong female leads. A horror fan going way back, he'd had it with seeing the same stock female characters screaming and running blindly through the woods. It was not only dumb, it had been *done*.

"Also, a big part of wanting to work with women was because I identified with them and because I like being around them; I like their energy," he says. "I'm just not drawn to the macho guy stories. I'm not handy, I don't own any power tools, I'm really shitty with cars."

It was more than Fawcett's ineptitude with automobiles that brought the couple together; each had a deep respect for the other's work.

In January 1995, Fawcett had an idea. Walton recalls him saying, "'I know what you have to do with me. You have to write a teenage girl werewolf movie!' And I said, 'No fucking way.' Why would I do that as my first feature—he was already *on* his first feature."

That year she was studying at the Canadian Film Centre. For a writer who had prided herself on telling stories through the complexities of her characters, horror was utterly unappealing. "I couldn't picture myself doing it because I had the attitude that all uninformed people had at the time about horror, which was, 'Don't they just run around and stab people till there's no people left?' What do you need a writer for?"

But Fawcett was having none of it. He insisted that they both take all of the conventions they detested about the dreck that came out of the studio system and toss them out the window completely. Pretty soon, Walton began to see the possibilities.

HOW THE COOKIE CRUMBLED

Not immediately, though. This was Canada, after all. Hollywood may be the cinematic equivalent of a Pablum factory, but at least there's a mechanism in place to get Pablum made. "There's no studio system in Canada," Walton says. "There's no such thing as a big company you take your things to and pitch. It's just not done that way here."

Still, they knew they were on to something. As they began outlining the story, Walton's first thought was that the two girls should be twins, a conceit quickly abandoned. However, the twin-like aspects of the characters' relationship remained. It's not surprising that Cronenberg's **Dead Ringers** influenced the creation of the weird dynamic between the sisters.

"*Dead Ringers* is an example of a really cool horror movie that is more about the people and who they are and what they mean to each other than it is about the gimmicks," she says. "That was what I was super interested in, and obviously what Mr. Cronenberg does very, very well."

Walton also hit the books, reading up on the relationships of sisters during adolescence and about the physical and psychological changes that they endure. She made two lists: one of these traits and behaviors, another of all the things she could think of that would make for a bad-ass werewolf.

"We didn't make a list of the scares first," she says. "We made a list of the things that could be going on psychologically with these two first."

The next several weeks consisted of Fawcett reading what Walton wrote, them discussing it, and Walton going back to do rewrites. "She's a very, very funny girl," Fawcett says. "Very quick, very witty, and it was always fun to jam ideas with her because she would come up with some hilarious stuff."

However, neither of them was particularly happy with the »106

Dead Ringers
Though the idea of Ginger and Brigitte being twins was quickly dropped, it's interesting to see how Walton kept some decidedly twin-like qualities for the girls. In Cronenberg's 1988 movie *Dead Ringers*, Elliot Mantle is arrogant and aggressive while his identical twin, Beverly, is shy. Both are gynecologists, cripplingly codependent, and played to wonderful effect by Jeremy Irons.

POSTMORTEM

Horror movies can be intriguing, thought provoking, even adrenaline inducing. Seldom, however, are they really, really fun.

Yet fun is what's on the cards with this tale of dour 16-year-old Ginger Fitzgerald (Katharine Isabelle), whose first period leads to her vicious attack at the claws of a werewolf. From that point on, she contends with the travails of two problems that quickly blur: her gradual transformations into both a werewolf and a young woman. Through it all, her equally gloomy younger sister Brigitte (Emily Perkins) stands by her. Once close, the two are torn apart by Ginger's twin predicament. No, that's not the fun part.

Ginger Snaps waivers between black comedy and genuine horror flick, but is most effective when it's poking fun at gender politics and suburban life.

One of Ginger's first acts following the wolf attack and subsequent awakening of her libido is to jump the bones of the jerky boy who's been lusting after her. After their aggressive, unprotected encounter, the boy discovers he's been infected with the werewolf disease; to his horror, he begins to pee blood.

Delivering news of his sexual conquest to his friends, they burst his bubble when they spot a bit of blood on the front of his pants and ask if Ginger was on the rag. "The curse" and its attendant embarrassment has been transferred to one of the boys most likely to make fun of it. Ginger's response learning that her sexual conquest's becoming a werewolf, too? "Oops."

There's plenty of gore on hand, from multiple dog carcasses left behind by the werewolf that's been stalking the Fitzgeralds' suburb to Ginger's own grisly handiwork.

> "At its heart, it was about the characters and the emotional bond between these two sisters. That was what was really going to make the movie work." —JOHN FAWCETT

GINGER SNAPS

While Mimi Rogers and Kris Lemche deliver brief but memorable performances as the girls' over-eager mom and ally Sam, respectively, the chemistry between Isabelle and Perkins is the backbone of the movie. How much that chemistry relies on Karen Walton's sparkling dialogue and John Fawcett's spot-on direction will become instantly apparent to those brave enough to sit through the franchise's third installment—*Ginger Snaps Back*.

The one thing that keeps *Ginger Snaps* from being a perfect movie is the decision to have Ginger transform completely into a werewolf in the last act. The film's main strength and primary focus is the relationship between the sisters. When one is replaced by a latex monster, no matter how convincing (a different conversation entirely), the magic disappears. Perkins does an admirable job of trying to row this two-seater herself, but with just the one oar, she can't be expected to do more than go 'round in circles.

Bruce McDonald
Indie Ontario filmmaker Bruce McDonald is the director of the 1989 oddball drama *Roadkill* and *Highway 61*. He is perhaps best known outside his homeland as a director of episodes of *Queer as Folk* and *Lexx*. That seemed all set to change in 2008 with the release of his offbeat zombie film called *Pontypool*.

Cookies
President's Choice English-Style Gingersnap Cookies and a few drinks were the culprits that gave the movie its clever name. "No genius involved," writer Karen Walton says, "just the right amount of alcohol and sugar."

«103 title they'd settled on for the film. "I think it was something bad like *Wolfer Girls*," Walton recalls. She was well into writing the story treatment when all of that changed.

After a few drinks and a night on the town with Canadian filmmaker **Bruce McDonald,** the couple lay around their Toronto flat eating President's Choice brand English-Style Gingersnap cookies.

"I'm eatin' gingersnaps and I say to John, 'I have an idea for the title of this film, but I'd have to change the characters' names,'" Walton says. "He goes, 'I don't care if it's good. What is it?'"

Ginger would be their werewolf chick, and naturally she "snaps." The girls' parents were hippy-dippy types who named her after Ginger Rogers, and her sister Brigitte after Brigitte Bardot.

So...cookies?

"The *best* **cookies**," Walton insists. "No genius involved, just the right amount of alcohol and sugar."

In February 1996, they finally took their film treatment to producer Steve Hoban, someone they had both worked with before. Co-founder of an animation studio for IMAX Corp., Hoban had just completed production on Holly Dale's *Blood & Donuts*. This not-quite-a-horror-movie movie about a vampire who falls for a doughnut shop waitress had two things going for it: an appearance by David Cronenberg and that it was the first product of the Canadian Film Centre's Feature Film Project, which ponied up the financing and mentoring talent needed to put out the flick. Unfortunately the finished product, with its animal-blood subsisting vampire, left horror audiences cold.

Hoban told the pair that he had no interest in getting mixed up in another horror movie, Walton recalls. Again Fawcett persisted, asking him to give the treatment a read. Hoban called back—he was in.

"It was a whole bunch of freaks going, 'Wow, this is really twisted—let's do it,'" Walton says. "Wouldn't it be great if that happened for everybody? I wonder what the movies would all look like if we did that all the time..."

Now that the characters were coming together, Fawcett was getting a better sense of just how he was going to translate Walton's humor and complex characterization into a gripping, fang-in-cheek frightfest.

There was a certain quality he wanted for their wolf girl, one he had glimpsed briefly in *Return of the Living Dead 3*'s **Julie Walker** (Melinda Clarke) after she's brought back from the dead as an alluring-yet-impossibly-pierced zombie.

"I remember seeing her as a monster and being very drawn to the strength of that," he says. "There was a real sexuality to the monster, but she was really scary at the same time."

By this point they had already overcome the first problem that nearly all werewolf films face. Rather than wolfing out right away and becoming just another inarticulate monster, Ginger would transform gradually enough that the audience would be able to relate to her as a human being, nearly to the end of the picture.

The biggest problem now was money.

By July 1996, Walton had banged out the first draft of the script, which promptly went to Telefilm Canada for financial consideration. About $12,000 Canadian was forthcoming. It was a drop in the bucket for what the project needed, but it served as the pistol shot that announced production of *Ginger Snaps* was finally under way.

'UNITED AGAINST LIFE AS WE KNOW IT'

January 1997 brought new help when Hoban introduced Walton to story editor Ken Chubb.

"It's like having a coach if you're an athlete," Walton says of their relationship on *Ginger Snaps*. "I'd be sitting there going, 'John wants a sex education scene and I can't figure out why or how I'm going to use it.' So I'd map something out and Ken and I would just bang it against the wall until it worked."

***Return of the Living Dead 3*'s Julie Walker**
Though one of those movies that people can't help calling "good" without following it up with "for what it is," 1993's *RotLD3* revived the concept of the hot-but-deadly monster chick. Reanimated when her boyfriend exposes her dead body to the series' zombification gas Trioxin, Julie Walker (Melinda Clarke) discovers that piercing her body with bits of metal, glass and other debris temporarily keeps her hunger for human meat at bay. It also has the (mostly male) crowd-pleasing effect of transforming Julie into a sort of S+M centerfold come to life.

Telefilm Canada
Originally called the Canadian Film Development Corp. from its inception in 1967 until 1984, Telefilm Canada is the government-funded organization filmmakers go to for financing. It will be remembered that, prior to the release of David Cronenberg's CFDC-funded film *Shivers* in 1975, *Saturday Night* magazine published a scathing review by journalist Robert Fulford titled "You Should Know How Bad This Film Is. After All, You Paid For It." Among other effects, the scurrilous piece convinced Cronenberg's landlady to evict him and his wife from their apartment.

The following month, **Telefilm Canada** kicked in about another $30,000 Canadian. Money was still an issue. Everybody was under the gun to see the project get off the ground.

"The job requires all of your brain and most of your time, and just trying to keep up with your personal life is a struggle," Fawcett says. "It was an incredibly important movie to me as it was to a lot of people. It was my baby. I put every bit of energy I had into it."

Though Fawcett and Walton never set out to keep their personal relationship a secret from the rest of the team, they also never mentioned it, either. "We broke up when we knew the film was greenlit," Walton says. "We held that back for a little while to avoid any panic as a result. Prep came first. We'd worked too hard to be distracted by anything as marginal as our personal lives by then."

The next year shot by in a blur of ups and downs that tried the patience of everyone involved. A new producer, Karen Lee Hall, was added; distribution deals were made with Motion International and Trimark, only to have the latter pull out at the last minute. In January 1999, Unapix and Lionsgate swooped in to pick up US and foreign distribution rights, respectively. By April, the last remaining bit of government funding came through.

Eager to proceed, the filmmakers began their search for a casting director. After the funding fiasco they had recently endured, most were guardedly optimistic that they could now finally get on with things. In the background, the TV news was as grim as ever, buzzing with reports about a high-school massacre that had taken place across the border in Littleton, Colo.

SUBURBANOIA: TAKE 2

There was a chilling irony that the Fitzgerald sisters would've appreciated in the tragedy that befell Columbine High School on April 20, 1999, and the effect it would have on *Ginger Snaps*.

While it's difficult to understand just what led teens Eric Har-

GINGER SNAPS + FEMINISM

Emily Perkins

Many may enjoy the *Ginger Snaps* saga for its dark humor and novel spin on the werewolf tale, but others can't help but see it as a modern parable on society's inability to see women's sexuality as anything less than dangerous. In the first movie, Ginger tells her sister that they should make the world's sexist attitudes work in their favor:

"No one ever thinks chicks do shit like this. A girl can only be a slut, bitch, tease or the virgin next door. We'll just coast on how the world works."

Drug-dealer hero Sam, the only male protagonist, fails to fully understand the whole Ginger-as-werewolf problem. "Your problem is physical," he tells Brigitte, "so your solution is physical." As we see throughout, only part of the problem is physical, for Brigitte still loves her sister very much.

"Obviously there are feminist elements in it," Karen Walton says. "A woman wrote it—how could there not be?"

And yet what Walton and director John Fawcett set out to do above anything else was create compelling, complex characters within a horror framework.

However, to Emily Perkins ("Brigitte"), it's very hard to miss the feminist undertones of a film that equates a woman's coming of age with a destructive, unstoppable force.

"But I don't think John sees the films in the same way I do," she says. "I was a women's studies student at the time we were making the film, and when I started talking to him about my ideas of what I was seeing in the films, he was kind of like, 'Oh, go back to college.' I think he thought I was reading too much into the script. But I think it worked out quite well in the end."

ris and Dylan Klebold to murder 12 students and a teacher that day, years of bullying and a deep dissatisfaction with suburban life were two factors that are hard to ignore.

In this post-Sept. 11th age, it's also easy to forget just how shocked North Americans were by the events of that day. A month later, for example, the *Buffy the Vampire Slayer* season finale was spiked by The WB network because the heroes of the series destroy their high school to prevent a demon from wreaking havoc on the fictional town of Sunnydale.

Eight days later, a 14-year-old boy shot and killed one student and injured another at WR Myers High School in Taber, Alberta.

"People were very uptight then and very sensitive about what was going on in the news," Fawcett recalls. Some of the Canadian casting directors who received the *Ginger Snaps* script were so morally outraged by this horror tale about high school girls, they actually tried "to band together casting directors to actually ban the film," he says.

He admits that the script making the rounds at the time "probably read a little bit more gruesomely and graphically than I had ever intended to shoot it. The script was very aggressive, but it needed to be aggressive."

The resulting fracas "was irritating because there were certain casting directors in the city (who I won't name) who took it upon themselves to make it a media show," Fawcett says. "In the end, that did hurt us for a while, but we ended up finding a great casting director [Robin Cook in Canada; Robert McGee had already signed on in LA] who believed in it. In the end, the media was great for us. By the time the movie was being released, that was all part of our publicity, that people had been so offended by it they tried to ban it."

Yet the media outcry also hampered the team's efforts to find places to actually shoot the movie.

"We had a hell of a time finding a school that would even let us step foot on the property because it had been in the news," he says. "Boy, you're doing a movie about kids killing kids—they didn't want anything to do with us. We were lucky we found a school that would actually allow us on their property, and in the end there wasn't a school anywhere that would allow us *inside* their school."

The only cooperative school, one in Etobicoke, Ont., kept everyone outside, leading to the writing of the **hockey field confrontation** scenes between popular girl Trina Sinclair (Danielle Hampton)

> "They had no issues with us putting a dead dog in their football field."
>
> — **TODD CHERNIAWSKY**, *production designer, about the school used for the high school exterior in* Ginger Snaps

Hockey field confrontation
The hockey field also was the scene of one of *Ginger Snaps'* few filming injuries. The ferocious on-screen fight between Ginger and Trina resulted in Ginger actress Katharine Isabelle accidentally breaking the nose of the stunt woman playing the bully. "I was [acting] punching her in the face and then my hood flipped over my eyes and I cracked her nose on my elbow, and she ran off," Isabelle remembers. "They wouldn't let me see her after and I felt so, so, so horrible."

and the Fitzgerald sisters.

"Fortunately we found a standing high school set we were able to use as our interior," Fawcett says. "It didn't have the scope that a real high school would give you, but at least we had something."

Unfortunately, "we went in assuming we would have a [real high school] location where you have very little control, so you don't budget a lot of money because there's very little you can build or do to a school for quick changeovers," says Todd Cherniawsky, production designer for all three films. As a result, "I don't feel the high school interior matches as well as everything else does in the rest of the film, but you do what you can."

While the *Toronto Star* stirred up some of the same controversy over the film's public funding that plagued Cronenberg's *Shivers (see sidebar p. 108)*, "I think these people would've been offended by the material regardless," Fawcett says. "It was a weird time."

WAKING THE BEAST

Six months after casting began, leads **Katharine Isabelle** and Emily Perkins were discovered when their Vancouver agency sent a tape of them auditioning together. Though Perkins was 22 and Isabelle just shy of her 18th birthday, it was the latter who would be cast as the elder sister.

"I think it was pretty clear they were looking for someone who was more sexually confident and had the body to back it up for Ginger," Perkins says, laughing. "I've never really gone out for those roles because I'm not really built that way."

While not real-life sisters, the Vancouver women knew each other pretty well before *Ginger Snaps*. In addition to being represented by the same agency, they were born in the same hospital and attended the same schools growing up.

"I remember the first time I ever spoke to her," Perkins says of her co-star. "I was like 9 or 10 and she was 6, and I had seen her in

Katharine Isabelle
Ginger Snaps fans are strongly encouraged to hunt down a 2001 Canadian family drama called *Turning Paige*. Katharine Isabelle stars as the eponymous Paige, a teen who buries herself in the short stories she writes to avoid confronting what's left of her family following her mother's death. Strong, career-defining performances from Isabelle, Nicholas Campbell, Philip DeWilde and Brendan Fletcher (doomed to death-by-werewolf in both the *Ginger Snaps* sequel and prequel) make this one a don't miss. Unfortunately, it hasn't been officially released on home video. Perhaps if enough movie lovers ask film distributor Filmoption International (www.filmoption.com) for a release, this will change.

The multidimensional *Ginger Snaps* manages to be disturbing, darkly amusing and a feminist cry against society simultaneously.

a commercial on TV. I went, 'Wow, you were great!' And she goes, 'So.' That so typifies Katie. She was kind of like a cynical little kid but she was really cute. She totally had this dark sense of humor." In other words, she was a bit like Ginger.

"We have that sort of relationship, the sister bond," Isabelle says. "We argue and nag each other and debate things for hours. We're also super tight and I guess that came through."

The Fitzgerald sisters might've been cast, but no one had been found for the role of their mother, Pamela. Without a star name, Lionsgate was reluctant to follow through on their end of the distribution deal. It wasn't until a couple of days before filming began that Mimi Rogers (best known these days as Mrs. Kensington in *Austin Powers: International Man of Mystery*) signed on to play the eccentric Mama Fitzgerald. Brampton, Ont.-born Kris Lemche (*eXistenZ*, *Final Destination 3*) rounded out the cast as drug dealer/near-hero Sam.

'OUT BY 16 OR DEAD IN THE SCENE'

Shooting began on October 25, 1999, primarily because the story takes place around Halloween, with the Toronto suburbs of Etobicoke, Scarborough and Brampton serving as the fictional Bailey Downs *(see sidebar p. 100)*. Fawcett had tapped Thom Best, a longtime friend who had shot everything from his first short to *The Boys Club*, as director of photography for *Ginger Snaps*. Scenes were shot roughly in order, Perkins recalls.

"I think the first scenes that we shot when we were just trying to establish the characters of Brigitte and Ginger were hard for me," she says. "It took me a while to sort of find out who Brigitte was."

Hardly surprising considering that some of the first material recorded were the stills taken for the Fitzgerald sisters' **staged death images** that play during the opening credits. In them, the girls take turns casting themselves in elaborate scenes of suicide: one impaled upon a white picket fence, the other gutted beneath a lawn mower, etc. Over and over these scenes—at once humorous and deeply morbid—play out like crime scene photographs against a slightly mournful theme. Distorted giggles—ostensibly those of the sisters, but easily construed as those of children everywhere—add an eerie icing to the cake.

"That opening sequence, to me, speaks very much to the tone I was really trying to establish with the movie," Fawcett says. "You look at those images and a lot of them are shocking and over the top and gory. Some of them are romantic deaths, some of them are fucking just downright funny. If you took that music track out of there, I would see that as more humorous than anything else. I like that kind of humor where you just aren't certain whether to be laughing or not."

"The death scenes are awesome," Walton says proudly. "We called it the 'suicide slide show.' It turns out in the following scene that it's a class project where they've been asked to talk about life in Bailey Downs. And their class project about life in Bailey Downs

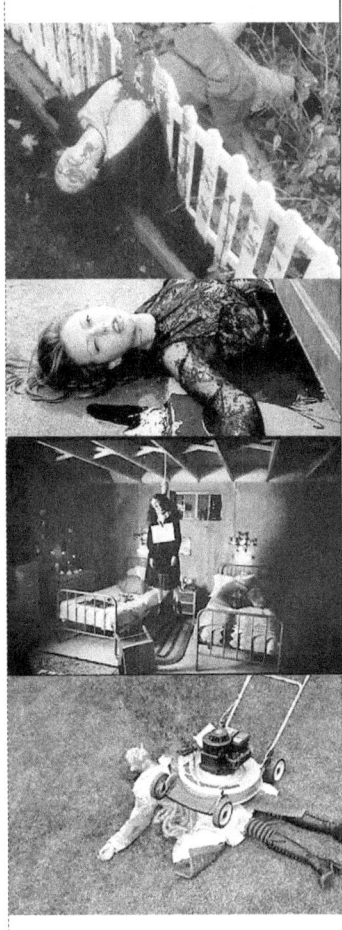

Staged death images
"You look at those images and a lot of them are shocking and over the top and gory," Fawcett says of the *Ginger Snaps* intro. "Some of them are romantic deaths, some of them are fucking downright funny."

> "It came from a dramatic necessity which was 'I'm bringing you to the suburbs but I'm going to introduce you to two young ladies in the suburbs who I am pretty sure you have never met before. They're the girls who live in the basement by choice because they're not happy here.'
>
> — KAREN WALTON *on the 'suicide slide show' that plays during the opening credits of* Ginger Snaps

is 'It's killing me. I'm impaling myself on white picket fences here!' That is their comment on life in the suburbs. It's like death.

"What I wanted to do in the first few minutes was establish a number of things about those girls' characters and their relationship," she explains.

Walton was on a Greyhound bus traveling between Alberta and Toronto when she read Jeffrey Eugenides' breakthrough novel, *The Virgin Suicides*. "It was just this wonderful story about these five sisters all deciding to kill themselves, and I was like, 'Wow, five teenage girls all killing themselves—I wonder what that looked like.'" Naturally she gave the book to Fawcett.

Later, Cherniawsky received a compilation of different suicide methods from Fawcett, he says, "but that was only about half of what we ended up doing that day."

With a list of props they had available on hand, the production designer turned to a book of crime scene photos from the Los Angeles Police Department from the 1920s to the 1960s, he recalls. "That was a really good starting point for us as far as trying to get color palette ideas and composition ideas and wacky ideas of how people do themselves in."

From there, prop master Michael Followes and the set dressers loaded their vans with all of the agreed upon implements of death, he says. "We were already starting to dress the location because it was only maybe a week before the shoot started. We had the garage already dressed and decorated. The wheelbarrow with the circular saw across Ginger's stomach, all that stuff was a little bit improvised on the day once we let everyone go on the set."

Says Perkins, "It only took a few hours to actually shoot, so it wasn't a big deal from my perspective, but I guess a lot of planning went into it. I felt like the production designer and the costume designer and the director all had so much fun coming up with the 'death shoot' as they called it. I think it was partly inspired by a

"We argue and nag each other and debate things for hours," Isabelle (left) says of her real-life relationship with Perkins (right). "We're also super tight."

Cindy Sherman show that was on at the art gallery at the same time, because I remember they had postcards of her art around the office."

The suicides were filmed outside the house that was used for the exteriors of the Fitzgerald house in the movie, Isabelle recalls. Her favorites?

"I liked the lawn mower with something hanging out of my mouth and the Wicked Witch of the West socks on," she says. "And I liked when Emily was wrapped in plastic bags in the trunk."

However, there was something of a logistical problem with the shoot, she says. "There was a little boy in the house, maybe 3 or 4, and we kept having to herd him around so he wouldn't stumble onto these horrible death scenes that were, all the sudden, everywhere."

Almost from the get-go, *Ginger Snaps* established a uniquely visceral feel with the introduction of the "Beast of Bailey Downs" in the opening minutes of the film. The unseen werewolf that terrorizes the area leaves only dead dogs and wagging tongues in its wake. The message is clear and distinctly Canadian: Beyond the suburbs, there's a wilderness waiting to devour. »118

Cindy Sherman
The Glen Ridge, NJ-born photographer frequently photographs herself as recognizable character types (e.g., film noir woman, clown, etc.) to draw attention to the stereotypes that dog women in society today.

POSTMORTEM

A straight-up horror sequel to what is essentially a black-humor extravaganza, *Unleashed* would've been much better received had it simply dropped the *Ginger Snaps* name.

This grim mood piece opens shortly after the death of Ginger and finds Brigitte (Perkins) dosing herself with monkshood regularly to stave off her own werewolf transformation. She's also on the run from another lycanthrope that's looking for a mate and fancies her as the perfect life partner.

OD'ing on the monkshood, she awakens to find herself in Happier Times, a care center for drug addicts and accident victims run by the tough but benevolent Alice (Janet Kidder, niece of actress Margot Kidder). Deprived of her medication (which was losing its efficacy anyway), she struggles to hide the changes her body is going through while fighting off the sexual advances of orderly Tyler (Eric Johnson), who frequently trades drugs for sexual favors.

In the process, she captures the imagination of an already overly-imaginative young Happier Times inmate called Ghost (Tatiana Maslany, bottom left, seen most recently in Romero's *Diary of the Dead* and the Pang Brothers' 2007 American debut, *The Messengers*). Ghost helps Brigitte escape the center, and together they flee to the home of the little girl's grandmother, a patient at Happier Times thanks to a fire that left her burned from head to toe.

The smiles are few, and usually come from the ridiculousness inherent in therapy and rehabilitation. Ginger (Isabelle), terribly underused—and yes, she's supposed to be dead—appears to Brigitte in a handful of hallucinations to tell her that there is no fighting what is about to happen to her. We are left with the image of a painfully skinny and bedraggled Brigitte, the character we rooted for throughout *Ginger Snaps*, fighting against both herself and the werewolf that hunts her—a fight that we know from the outset she cannot win.

> "I'm interested in reading about horror and what it has to say about the larger culture we live in, but I'm not all that interested in watching it. I'm more detached and clinical when I watch a horror film, which probably isn't as much fun."
>
> —EMILY PERKINS ("Brigitte")

GINGER SNAPS: UNLEASHED

Though it seems to come out of left field, the ending will intrigue many and explain why there has been some discussion by the Powers That Be over the years of resurrecting *Ginger Snaps* as a television series featuring the character of Ghost.

Though *Unleashed* is well directed and expertly shot, one would've expected a much tighter film from director Brett Sullivan, who edited *Ginger Snaps* and went on to do the same for *Saw IV*. At 94 minutes, it does drag in some places. There is a scene at the very beginning that, though effective in setting up the plot, seems tacked on merely to establish a running gag for the *Ginger Snaps* sequels in which Brendan Fletcher ("Mark" in *Freddy Vs. Jason*) is twice unceremoniously picked off by werewolves.

The film's greatest strength is clearly Perkins. With her strong performance coming a year before Ellen Page's tour de force in *Hard Candy*, one can be forgiven for thinking that the Canadians have been secretly engineering a breed of consummate super-actress behind closed doors. Now *there's* a movie.

IT'S NOT AMERICAN, IT'S CANADIAN!

Despite some extremely Canadian elements, *Ginger Snaps* is often mistaken for a product from across the border, Karen Walton says. "It's very funny because if you'd told us that in 10 years we would have to go into our own video stores and explain to the owners that they had filed *Ginger Snaps* under the wrong country, we would've laughed our asses off," she says. "It's very flattering to be mistaken for an American film. Obviously we're filmmakers because of American films. They influence us and they are what we aspire to in many, many respects. This film is a product of two kids who grew up knowing very little else but the American point of view on how to tell a story."

« 115   "I suppose that concept of something coming in from the wilderness was important because we had to make sense of where this thing came from," Fawcett says. "Where I grew up and where Karen grew up, we were in the suburbs close to the edge of the city, and beyond that there's just nothing. That's weirdly Canada."

If, like Fawcett and Walton, "you grow up in a place like Calgary or Alberta where it can go down to -40, I think you probably feel that a lot more pressingly than living in Vancouver," says Vancouver native Perkins. "It's just wet here. You don't feel like your environment is hostile to life, which it really honestly is in parts of Alberta. No matter what you're wearing, you can't stay outside for long. If you wander off and you're a couple of miles away from civilization, you could die."

'I TOTALLY BELIEVED THIS CHARACTER'

Everything had lined up perfectly for *Ginger Snaps*, and the creative team knew it. The cast was tight, the writing hit just the right balance between darkly humorous and appropriately touching. The only thing really preying on the director's mind now?

"It was the monster stuff for sure," Fawcett admits. "I was trying to make a monster movie with not a lot of dough. That was my biggest fear: that the monster was going to look like crap, that no one was going to believe it, that everyone was just going to think it was someone in a big rubber suit, and that the whole thing was never going to work because we didn't have all the money and time to throw into making that stuff look utterly fantastic."

Paul Jones, who has created makeup effects for films ranging from *Hellbound: Hellraiser II* and *Wrong Turn* to *Silent Hill*, created all of the creature effects for *Ginger Snaps*. He supervised a dozen Toronto prosthetic artists as they produced all of the ancillary bits of gore and grisliness—from severed fingers to dead dogs—that plague Bailey Downs.

For the *coup de grace*—the werewolf itself—Jones looked to a number of sketches Fawcett had made over the years and did his best to bring the creature to life. The director was determined to rely on practical effects rather than CGI.

Yet, after all the planning and preparation, the director ended up cutting 75 percent of the monster's appearances out of the film, he says. "It wasn't because it was bad effects or bad makeup or anything like that. To hang on to any shred of belief with this thing, I had to show it as little as possible."

As excited as he was to work with all of the blood and other horror genre trappings, he knew where the strengths of the film resided: the sisters' relationship.

"I remember sitting on the set, and it was practically the last day of shooting," he says, referring to the final scenes of the movie. "I remember working with Emily in the scene where she's stabbed Ginger and she's leaning against the wall, and I knew the emotion I wanted to get out of that. I knew I wanted to see her with tears rolling down her face. We were shooting that really late at night, and the tears just weren't coming. She'd go, 'John, I can't do this. I'm there emotionally, I just can't get the tears to go.'"

Between each take the two huddled together and discussed the problem and what they could do to get around it.

"I can't remember what it was that ultimately got them to go, but eventually take 6, take 7, suddenly boom, there they were," Fawcett says. "I was sitting in that chair watching her face, and I was seeing that image on the big screen. I knew at that moment that what I was getting there was one of the biggest moments in the movie.

"Immediately all those fears that I'd had all through shooting of this goddamn rubber monster completely disappeared because I realized in that moment it didn't matter that that was a latex thing lying on the ground. I totally believed this character, and I »122

> "You were supposed to be aspiring to a Cannes award, to get all critically acclaimed. 'What? A werewolf movie? That's hardly Canadian. I don't think we should be supporting that kind of nonsense.'"
> —WALTON *about bucking the trend in Canadian film*

> "For me right now, the ideal life is just having a lot of time to stay home and read novels. I just like to spend time with family and not go out much. I'm really a bit of a hermit and pretty introverted. If I don't have many opportunities for self-expression, that's OK. I'll take a painting class at my community center—that's just dandy."
> —PERKINS *on her similarities to "Brigitte"*

TODD CHERNIAWSKY: PRODUCTION DESIGNER

Each film in the *Ginger Snaps* series has a wholly different look and feel, something that has a great deal to do with the work of production designer Todd Cherniawsky.

Though he's worked on everything from *Beowulf, War of the Worlds, Armageddon* and *Sphere* to the forthcoming Vincenzo Natali film *Splice, Ginger Snaps* was where he got his start.

GINGER SNAPS

Like *Ginger Snaps* creators Karen Walton and John Fawcett, Cherniawsky grew up in Alberta, just outside of Walton's Sherwood Park. It was that shared memory of growing up in a suburban area ringed by the wilderness that greatly influenced the look of Bailey Downs—particularly our very first glimpse of it.

"It was so important that we had this shot where we started with the open, untouched field and panned over to see the 7,000th suburban development going up in the neighborhood, and just how cheap it was," he says.

To capture the feel of Sherwood Park, he printed out a large map of that area and hand drew what would become Bailey Downs over it, he says. "It was just about trying to establish the geography and the world, and it helped everybody get a sense of how contained it was and what a small story it was in the sense of it taking place in a specific community."

GINGER SNAPS: UNLEASHED

Although Cherniawsky knew little about the lay of the land in Ontario where they shot the first film, the sequel, shot around Edmonton, Alberta, was another matter. Not only had he worked on a movie for CTV there called *A Hundred Days in the Jungle,* the cabin setting where the climax takes place was only about 10 minutes from where he'd grown up.

The location crew must've scouted more than 1,000 homes in the area before finding that cabin, he recalls. Even so, they ended up reworking the exterior of the house, complete with a false front entrance and garage. "Shooting a house on location is very difficult; that's why you build it on stage, so you can blow out walls. But when you build a complete house, the interior walls, there's no place for them to go, so you have to design a very clever system for sliding walls out or guillotining them up—using pulley systems or chain motor systems—into the rafters. All of the sudden with your low budget movie you're trying to do some pretty big budget things."

Perhaps the biggest challenge was shooting the scenes where Brigitte is locked up in the psychiatric hospital—in a vacant wing of an operating psychiatric hospital.

"It was made very clear to us, and from what I understand, part of our contract, that we did everything possible that they never saw us," he says. "Obviously we're not going to put someone halfway into the werewolf costume and have them walk around the psychiatric hospital. But we had to be very careful that we weren't disruptive to the healing environment that they were trying to provide. And film crews are not necessarily the most docile creatures."

Challenging, definitely, but not altogether unrewarding, he adds. "The creepiness factor always makes the whole experience fun. When you're location scouting in those buildings and there is no power yet and you're there even

In *Ginger Snaps Back: The Beginning*, Brigitte is the teary, cowering female, and far more dolled-up than in the previous films.

at 4 o'clock in the afternoon—when it's November in Alberta, it's pitch black. There is a nice thing about being in a place that actually did serve as what you're using it for."

GINGER SNAPS BACK: THE BEGINNING

Not surprisingly, the Ginger prequel proved to be one of the most challenging films to design. Though the bulk of the action takes place at a detail-rich 19th century trading fort, Cherniawsky and his team didn't get an approved shooting script until the last minute, he explains. "As I was wrapping on the sequel, I was starting to think about the prequel and how we would stage that. So the fact that they were shot back-to-back made the third one, which otherwise probably would've been the easiest of the three, almost the most difficult because I only had two weeks between wrapping the sequel and shooting the prequel. That's pretty tough."

At one time, the third film was set in Newfoundland, he says, squarely amongst the Scottish, Welsh and Irish settlers of the time. However, the prequel and sequel were shot back-to-back to save money, so there was no way to justify a Newfoundland location when *Unleashed* was set in Edmonton. With that reality in mind, Cherniawsky set his sights on Fort Edmonton.

"There are many, many better forts than Fort Edmonton," he says, "but they're all military forts. Fort Edmonton is by far the best trading or historical fort." Its keepers were particularly helpful, he adds. "They didn't give us the keys to the kingdom but they really supported the local productions. There's no way we could've pulled off a 10 day prep period, and I think we shot it in maybe 30 days. Very quick, very intense."

believed that *she* believed that was her sister. That was huge for me. That's what's important for the movie. At its heart, it was about the characters and the emotional bond between these two sisters. That was what was really going to make the movie work."

But what had happened to bring forth those tears?

"I hope you're not looking for a romantic answer," Perkins says. "On a low budget film, you don't have all the takes in the world to get it right. And it was probably the last few hours of shooting; I felt like there was so much pressure. So they just sprayed my eyes with irritant. After that, I felt like the pressure was off." From that point on, Perkins got her own tears flowing.

What was important to Perkins was that Brigitte be seen crying over her sister. "Too often, the Final Girl always comes across as masculinely triumphant in the end. They conquered the enemy and they achieved this masculine form of power. For me it was very important that Brigitte retain her femininity."

Fawcett's fears about the man in the werewolf suit's effect on the emotional integrity of the final product were well founded, but ultimately his instincts proved spot on.

"I think the reason why you don't completely shut off at the point that the latex monster comes out is because Emily's so captivating in that whole last sequence," Isabelle says. "Any emotion you still felt for Ginger is because Emily was so amazing at that.

"It didn't occur to me how moving that last little bit was going to be," she says. "I was there that day filming and maybe watching monitors or eating potato chips or peeking around the corner. I wasn't up close, right in Emily's face, looking at the emotion that was coming out. I probably just wanted to see the dude in the wolf suit. But you put so much effort into it, you just want to be there for all of the exciting stuff, especially if it's not you having to go through it."

'SYLVESTER THE CAT'

Katharine Isabelle, who had spent up to seven hours a day in the makeup chair having prosthetics applied to and removed from her body, had clearly earned the right to sit on the sidelines for a minute or two by filming's end.

"I had an amazing time shooting that," Isabelle says, "but I learned how to read my scripts better in terms of what all is going to be physically involved in it."

Though a self-described trooper when it comes to working because, as she puts it, "I don't have the worst job on set—ever," she has yet to encounter a part as physically demanding as Ginger.

She credits her pursuit of all things hiking and camping with toughening her up enough to make it through *Ginger Snaps*' 18-to-20 hour days of being dragged through the woods by her ankles and other grueling challenges. That love of the outdoors was fostered between the ages of 12 and 17 when she lived on Salt Spring Island—a 70-square-mile land mass off the South coast of British Columbia—where there's little else to do but hike and camp.

One thing it did not prepare her for was Ginger's fangs.

Isabelle wore a dentist-made set of upper fangs that snapped over her own teeth. Considering how subtle they were on camera, they were the cause of much laughter behind the scenes, she says. "They make you sound like Sylvester the Cat."

The lisping the **teeth** brought about forced her to loop, or rerecord during post-production, every line she delivered that contained an "s" for all three movies, she says. "In the first movie, I'm like, 'I don't know, letth athk tham, he'th the exthpertt!'"

Even by the third film, *Ginger Snaps Back: The Beginning*, the same problem marred what should've been a powerful scene. "I bust open the walls of the fort and walk up and I'm all strong and I've got my cape on and I'm all looking crazy. The bad guy walks up to me and I say, 'I've come for my thister!' And everyone just fell over laughing." »126

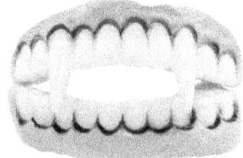

Teeth
Isabelle still has her Ginger teeth. "Halloween is so not exciting to me because my regular job is dressing up in fantasy beast outfits," she says. So when October 31st rolls around, she simply pops in her fangs and is ready to go. "They're not that apparent unless I really smile at you and you're actually looking at my teeth."

POSTMORTEM

GINGER SNAPS BACK: THE BEGINNING

If sequelization can be likened to the digestion of an idea, *Ginger Snaps Back* is the last stop in the process before seeing the light of day again. Strong words, certainly, but this belongs to that worst class of sequel: the variety that leaves you questioning the worth of the original film. When the production is as sparkling an example of the genre as *Ginger Snaps,* that is unforgivable.

Perkins and Isabelle reprise their roles as Brigitte and Ginger, this time as orphans in the Canadian wilderness of the 19th century. Happening upon an indigenous warrior, they are brought back to a settlement of fur traders who warily put them up, ever on guard against a legion of werewolves that stalk the woods come nightfall. Ginger gets bitten, Brigitte sticks by her. You know the rest.

Given a forest of wooden dialogue to stumble through with only the thinnest wisps of plot to cling to, Isabelle looks nearly as bored as the audience, and Perkins is not far behind. Facing the same hurdles, the rest of the cast nearly gels in place. Humor, one of the defining strengths of the original, is relegated to a couple of throwaway lines in the beginning and copious ladlings of the word "fuck." The question that occurs to even the most causal observer is simply, "Why was this movie made?"

Isabelle herself, though too polite to speak badly of the sequels, nevertheless has this to say. "I think there could've been some more time taken to develop the second two so that they were the same caliber as the first one. I was a little concerned that the same creative team wasn't going to be behind it. But I'm just an actor, what do I know?" In hindsight, quite a lot.

Particularly offensive is the alacrity with which *Ginger Snaps Back* embraces the genre clichés so skillfully dodged by the original: preternaturally wise indigenous people, evil holy men. And poor Brigitte. Though she may have shed a tear or two for the fate of her sister in *Ginger Snaps*, here she is the teary, cowering female, and far more dolled up than in the previous films, to add well-coiffed insult to injury.

Searching vigorously for something to praise, the author tips his hat to a 30-second segment in which a cloaked-and-hooded Ginger, clearly infected with the werewolf curse, returns to the fort to exact her revenge. It's an iconic image—think a fanged Nastassja Kinski in Polanski's *Tess*—and the only bit of sunshine in this maelstrom of disappointment.

Normally one recommends that fans of any series take in the sequels, if only for completeness' sake. There is no reason to take that kind of bullet for the sake of *Ginger Snaps*. Not even a silver one.

«123 Towards the end of filming on Dec. 6, "We were shooting in this really dirty, gross warehouse that wasn't really a studio," Fawcett remembers. "It was more of a place that we could get reasonably cheap to build our sets in."

Also by that time, illnesses were whipping through cast and crew alike. "It's the hours and no one was getting much sleep," Fawcett says. "By the end I had some vicious cough and everyone was pretty sick."

Adds Perkins, "It was a pretty grueling shoot. I was so tired at some points I was having auditory hallucinations. Like I'd hear people saying that I was doing a bad job. [*Laughs.*] I was *so* tired. But that's just what happens when you're so overworked."

FROM COOKIE TO PHENOMENON

In September 2000, after a 33-day shoot and eight weeks of editing, *Ginger Snaps* hit theaters in Canada, garnering critical praise and several awards including "best film" from the International Horror Guild and a Special Jury Citation from the Toronto International Film Festival.

"America is actually the last country to come to it," Walton says. "It did so many things for us in so many territories as it sort of bled out of the festival system and into theatrical release in England, Japan, Korea and Mexico. It had a long and healthy release life over several years because it was an indie."

Though it pulled in just $425,000 Canadian at the box office in its homeland, its subsequent home video sales worldwide convinced the Powers That Be that the tale of the Fitzgerald sisters still had some marketable life left in it, even if one of them had not actually survived the original ordeal.

In 2003, two sequels were filmed back to back, with Hoban producing and Fawcett as executive producer.

Ginger Snaps: Unleashed, written by newcomer Megan Martini,

THE OTHER GINGER

Before there was bored-chick-turned-werewolf Ginger Fitzgerald, there was Ginger…the pony.

For a long time, actress Katharine Isabelle had a pony called Ginger. "She was small and red and completely evil. Cute, cute, cute, cute, until you got right up to her and she lunged at your face with her teeth," she says. "But she was amazing."

And before the past tense bums out animal lovers, evil Ginger is still very much alive. Seeing that Ginger was getting on in years and could do with some more space, Isabelle sold her to a friend for a dollar, "so technically, if she kills some kid, she's not my responsibility," Isabelle says with a laugh. She still visits Ginger once a year. "She pins her ears at me and I'm like, 'I love you so much.'"

takes place shortly after the events of the first movie and finds Brigitte confined to a scary rehab clinic after her attempts to cure her own werewolf nature have some unintended consequences. *Ginger Snaps Back: The Beginning*, written by Christina Ray and Stephen Massicotte (who would later write the screenplay for Fawcett's *The Dark*), is more of a prequel, with the sisters dealing with werewolves in the 19th century Canadian wilderness. Special effects for both sequels were handled in part by the KNB EFX Group.

The first sequel was directed by Brett Sullivan, who edited the first film; the second by *Ginger Snaps'* second-unit director and Fawcett's film school friend, Grant Harvey.

"The process of making these three films has always been about family," explains Fawcett, who also shot second unit on *Ginger Snaps Back* and was heavily involved in the formulation of the sequels' storylines. "We've always done it with close friends. I think it shows in the work."

By the time there was any talk of sequels, Walton felt she had said all she had to say about the characters. "I liked Steve [Hoban]'s suggestion at the time when I did pass [on the sequels]: 'Maybe the thing to do is to give other new first writers a shot at monkeying with our business here.' I thought that was a great idea."

Ginger Snaps' legacy continues with the films appearing as the subjects of numerous Ph.D. theses, and rumors about a television series (discussed-but-as-yet-unmoved upon, Fawcett says) spreading across the Internet every year. Everyone concerned remains surprised by the series' longterm following.

Of course, Walton adds, "I think you'd have to be some kind of pompous ass to make a creative project expecting to make an impact on anybody beyond your audience. But on the bad days, it really helps you keep going." [NHH]

> "I had the attitude that all uninformed people had at the time about horror, which was, 'Don't they just run around and stab people till there's no people left?'
>
> What do you need a writer for?"
>
> — WALTON

OUVRE-MOI TA PORTE... QUE JE T'OUVRE LE VENTRE

À L'INTÉRIEUR

URBAN UNREST OUTSIDE, VISIONS OF HELL WITHIN

ALEXANDRE BUSTILLO + JULIEN MAURY

[INSIDE]

THE RAZOR'S EDGE BETWEEN WHAT SUCCEEDS IN EXTREME HORROR, BOTH ARTISTICALLY AND IN TERMS OF ENTERTAINMENT, AND WHAT MERELY SPIRALS INTO THE ASHCAN OF EXCESS, CAN BE A MADDENING GEOGRAPHY TO EXPLORE.

In 2007, torture porn flicks had effectively hit bottom. While *Saw IV* had done reasonably well at the box office that year (a $32 million domestic opening weekend for a $10 million outlay), *Hostel Part II* only enjoyed those types of numbers when its entire world gross was taken into account. Director Eli Roth attributed this poor showing to Internet piracy of his film, which no doubt had a considerable impact on ticket sales. Yet one still couldn't help but feel that this odd subgenre—at its height appealing only to a small segment of horror fandom—had finally worn out its welcome.

That same year, the sumptuously-shot yet profoundly disturbing adaptation of Jack Ketchum's child abuse polemic **The Girl Next Door** sailed straight to video generating far more buzz in genre circles than most DVD-only titles usually enjoy. While many rightly emphasized the production's spot-on 1950s set design, beautiful cinematography and notable performances, there was one extremely large elephant in the room.

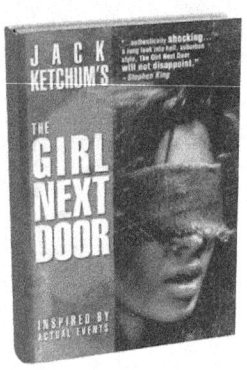

The Girl Next Door
Ketchum's 1989 novel is based on the real-life 1965 murder of 16-year-old Sylvia Likens by neighborhood children and the woman entrusted with her care. In addition to the 2007 film adaptation, the Likens case spawned another production that same year called *An American Crime* starring Ellen Page (*Hard Candy*, *Juno*).

Because of the unseemliness of its source material, *Girl Next Door* had a shaky leg planted in both the torture-porn and social-conscience camps, making it a particularly tough sell to either, and an impossible one for horror fans and the mainstream. However gorgeous it looked on screen, a movie about the systematic abuse of an innocent teenage girl—one of the most vulnerable classes of society—was simply too rough for all but the most jaded sensibilities. Even if you could bring yourself to enjoy it on some artistic level, you certainly couldn't recommend it to anybody else.

That same year at the Cannes International Film Festival, the 83-minute French shocker *Inside* (aka *À l'intérieur*) from the writer/director team of Alexandre Bustillo and Julien Maury premiered with a premise that promised to be even more off-putting than *The Girl Next Door*: A pregnant woman attacked in her own home by a crazed woman desperate to tear the unborn child from her womb.

However, when *Inside* hit North American video shops in

2008, it found an army of supporters in the genre press, and even the ink-stained legions of the mainstream one gave it passing marks for accomplishing what it set out to do. Dave Kehr in the April 15th edition of *The New York Times* called it "an accomplished, effective, hard-to-shake shocker," before cheekily adding that pairing it in a double feature with *Juno*—the previous year's Oscar-winning indie about a spunky, pregnant 16 year old (Ellen Page, again)—was "not recommended."

How had a pair of relative neophytes from a nation hardly known (until recently) for innovations in horror cinema managed to pull off a film whose subject matter should've relegated them to virtual obscurity amongst all but the most hardcore viewers?

FRANCE'S NEW NEW WAVE

When it came to fearsome flicks, the year 2005 was a real mixed bag. Though it ushered in such instant classics as Neil Marshall's *The Descent* and *The Devil's Rejects*—the first genuine indication that Rob Zombie was a director with a band rather than a rocker playing at director—by and large it was crap that was on tap at the local multiplex.

From Uwe Boll's *Alone in the Dark* (Tara Reid = scientist, what else to say?) to *The Amityville Horror* remake and *Boogeyman* (essentially the same jump-scare show reels), things were not looking good. Japanese horror, once thought the savior of the medium if only for its near limitless remake fodder, was proving to be more of a one-trick pony with a dark, seaweed-like comb-over. As it is wont to do during such creative dry spells, the genre was quickly eating itself.

When Alexandre Aja's *Haute Tension* (aka *High Tension* and *Switchblade Romance*) hit US shores that year, horror fans heaved a collective sigh of relief. Sure, the plot only hung together after a few shots of Jim Beam and the discarding of one or two key scenes, but its unrelenting pace and crowd-pleasing arterial sprays suggested that there was now a new country to look to for a much-needed artistic injection.

> "We tried to make a horror movie for women. Except for our girlfriends, all the rest of the women left the theaters. But our mothers liked the movie, too."
> —JULIEN MAURY

Ills (aka Them)
The 77 minute Ils (Them) relies on high-tension pacing, expert editing and a "Holy shit!" ending to tell the tale of a French school teacher in Bucharest and her husband who are set upon one night by shadowy figures in their isolated home.

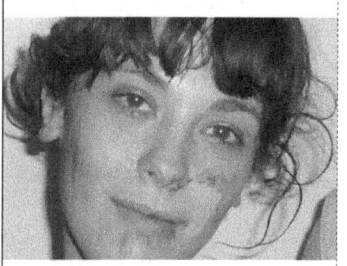

Alysson Paradis
Alysson Paradis, who had but a few films to her name at the time of Inside, is also the sister of French singer/actress Vanessa Paradis, partner of Johnny Depp.

Béatrice Dalle
Prior to Inside, Béatrice Dalle was perhaps best known for her role in 2001's Trouble Every Day, in which she played a cannibalistic femme fatale. She came to worldwide recognition for playing the unhealthily obsessed title character in 1986's Betty Blue.

Its subsequent success sent distributors scavenging for other dark Gallic productions. In 2007, the home-invasion thriller *Ils* (aka *Them*) from writer/directors David Moreau and Xavier Palud landed at the South by Southwest Film Festival and got tongues wagging. The French juggernaut chugged on into 2008, bringing similar offerings (old and new) to DVD shelves.

'WE WANTED FOR THE AUDIENCE TO BE PUSHED'

The same year that *Haute Tension* hit the States, Alexandre Bustillo, then a 30-year-old writer for the French horror and fantasy movie magazine *Mad Movies*, wrote the first draft of the script for *Inside*.

Inspired by a friend's pregnancy, he wondered what it would be like to be a pregnant woman stalked by a madman. Quickly realizing it was like every other slasher film he'd seen—hell, his very first piece for *Mad Movies* had been a 1999 feature about slasher flicks—the writer changed the woman's adversary to another woman.

In the final production, photographer and expectant-mother Sarah (**Alysson Paradis**) survives a nasty car crash that takes the life of her husband. Four months later, on Christmas Eve and the night before she is scheduled to be induced, an unnamed woman (**Béatrice Dalle**) dressed all in black breaks into her home, clearly intent on freeing her child from her womb in a violent manner. It is only in the final few minutes of the film that we discover what is fueling this madness.

Yet the motivations for Dalle's character remained completely mysterious in the first draft of the script, Bustillo says. She "was only a woman who came from the night like a demon right from hell to take the baby. She's like a [*Hellraiser*] cenobite for us. A cenobite with a human face." She had no backstory.

It is not until well into the film that we get a good look at what Dalle is wearing: an intricate dark gown that could easily have been torn off the back of a Renaissance fair serving wench.

"Dressing her in black wasn't a way to show she's bad," explains director Julien Maury. While a very utilitarian reason for doing so will be discussed later, Dalle's dress was part of a larger effort to pull off a plot reversal in the finest tradition of *Psycho* and *Audition*.

As *Inside* opens, we are thrust into the wreckage of Sarah's car—she was driving—in a scene that visually is nearly monotone, despite the massive blood loss of its passengers. From that point on, colors gradually emerge throughout the film like a photograph in one of Sarah's developing trays, adding to what we know about the characters.

When the pregnant woman first comes to blows with her attacker, she is wearing a white nightdress, while the latter sticks to the shadows. As their conflict grows increasingly more violent and third parties are offed within the house, Sarah is gradually coated in the victims' blood as well as her own, taking on the appearance of a savage, red devil. Her animalistic survival instincts take over, making her the perfect foil for Dalle and her own increasingly emotional outbursts, which also find her spending longer periods of time in the light.

Toward the movie's end, the viewer begins to weigh up several cues that have been glimpsed throughout about Sarah. Rudeness to friends and family previously chalked up to the loss of her husband now take on a new light as we're led to wonder if she was this way prior to the accident. An ornamental pitchfork affixed to her wall; a barely glimpsed house number: 666; threatening the life of her own child with a kitchen knife to her belly: the imagery is overwhelming. Expertly, the audience is primed for a reversal of sympathies. So much so that it only takes a couple of lines from Dalle to, if not win over the audience completely, at least to slide our sympathies to her side like roulette winnings after a successful spin.

"It was really important for Alex and I to not have a too simplistic vision," Maury says. "We wanted for the audience to be pushed, and not to be—how can I say—like in every other horror movie. We've

LIVID

As the *Handbook* went to press, Maury and Bustillo were set to begin work on a new film, *Livid*, this time in English. Principal photography for the estimated $8.5 million feature was scheduled to get under way in Ireland in November 2009, with the intent of finishing it in the spring of 2010.

In *Livid*, a young in-house nurse signs on to look after a comatose dance teacher in her isolated house. Learning that old Mrs. Jessel is reputed to have squirreled away a vast treasure, she and a couple of friends start turning the house inside out, trying to find the old woman's fortune. That's when the supernatural steps in to spice things up a bit. Says Maury, "It's really less gory than *Inside*... more fantastic!"

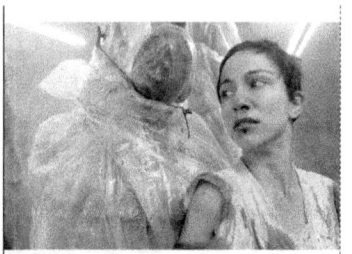

Frontière(s)
2007's *Frontière(s)* has been viewed as something of a companion piece to *Inside*. Originally intended for release as part of After Dark Films' "8 Films to Die For" series that year, an NC-17 rating bounced it to its own limited theatrical release in 2008. This tale of a group of neo-Nazi cannibals trying to bring about a bloody Fourth Reich was shot by *Inside*'s cinematographer Laurent Barès, and many members of that film's crew, and hit DVD a month after *Inside*.

Georges de La Tour
(1593-1652)
Demonstrating many influences (including that of Caravaggio), a great number of his paintings depict nighttime scenes lit only by a single candle or lamp. The resulting images are intensely moody, with inky shadows accentuating the latent mysteries of otherwise prosaic scenes.

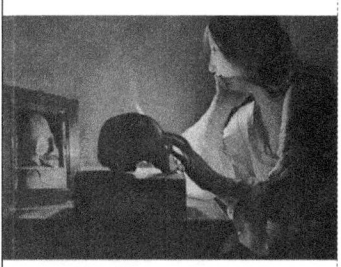

seen a hundred, a thousand, and we all know how it's going to be. So Béatrice, you cannot justify what she's doing, but maybe you can understand her."

'VISIONS OF HELL'

Like so many artistic works that deal with violence, *Inside* could easily have become an unwatchable piece of nihilism had it not been for tight direction and a painter's eye for style. Unlike Greg McLean *(see p. 44)*, neither Bustillo nor Maury are dab hands at the easel. Both, however, knew what they wanted to see on screen.

The first 30 minutes or so that we spend in Sarah's house is done so in considerable darkness, the pregnant woman usually sitting in a pool of lamp light.

The duo showed director of photography Laurent Barès (*Hitman*, *Frontière(s)*—both for writer/director Xavier Gens) paintings by 17th century Frenchman **Georges de La Tour** for inspiration, Maury says. "You have a really big painting only lightened by a single candle" in many of those. This was one of the main reasons why Dalle wore black. The first time we realize the huntress is actually inside the house, her face alone slowly, subtly emerges from the darkness behind Sarah. "It was for us a way to make her a part of the shadows in the house," Maury says.

The works of Hieronymus Bosch were also consulted for building the final 20 minutes of the film, he says, because "we wanted the ending of the movie to be a real vision of hell."

The pair didn't have to go too far to find contemporary visions of hell. When Bustillo sat down to write the first draft of *Inside*, the 2005 riots were raging throughout France. Initially sparked on Oct. 27 by the accidental deaths of two teens in the Parisian suburb of Clichy-sous-Bois, civil unrest quickly spread throughout the country. It is images from this national emergency—"the only real violent image of the movie," Bustillo insists—that Sarah is watching on television just before her own world disintegrates.

The primary reason for the riot clip, Bustillo says, searching for the appropriate English expression, "is to have a stressful ambience."

"Sort of a frightening background," Maury explains.

"It was also for us to show that the real violence is not in the cinema," Bustillo says. "The real violence is on the streets."

Remains of a burnt-out car during the French riots in 2005.

Neither man has any question of where most of the blame for that violence should be placed. In June 2005, just four months before the riots, then-Minister of the Interior Nicolas Sarkozy was widely quoted as saying he would cleanse a low-income Parisian suburb of undesirables with a "Kärcher"—a reference to a German-made high-pressure hose, and a not-too-subtle allusion to the way demonstrators were treated in France and Germany during the 1968 protests in those countries. A few days before the riots, he again angered many by referring to those living in suburban housing projects as "racaille"— basically rabble or scum. Sarkozy rose to the presidency in 2007.

"It's impossible to say that when you want to be president of a country," Bustillo says. "It was a pleasure for us to show that the riots in France were Sarkozy's fault because he told us the people who live in suburbs were like dogs. If people are violent, there are reasons for that. If you speak to someone like a dog, the dog will bite you."

Words to ponder when viewing the climax of *Inside*.

THE END + THE BEGINNING

Nearly all of the action of *Inside* was filmed in a French rental house over the course of 35 days, with the exception of the standoff in the

JULIEN, MEET ALEX. ALEX, JULIEN...

Béatrice Dalle, François Maury, director Julien Maury, Alysson Paradis and writer/director Alexandre Bustillo on the set of *Inside*.

Born in the Paris suburbs in 1975, Alexandre Bustillo and his cousin would rent horror films that he says he was much too young for such as Lucio Fulci's *Zombi 2* (known in the US as *Zombie*). Though his parents weren't too fond of the movies —he recalls hiding himself away to watch Alfred Hitchcock's *The Birds*—his aunt bought him a copy of *Mad Movies,* sort of a French-language *Fangoria*, when he was young. In 1999, he wrote his first piece (about slasher films) for that magazine.

Julien Maury was about 8-years-old when his big brother François (who later would make the behind-the-scenes documentary about *Inside* found on the DVD) began showing him horror films. "It was a sort of an epiphany," he says. The first he can remember is *The Exorcist*. "As I was really young, I was convinced it was a true story, that it was like a documentary. I remember being really scared at night in bed, and the sensation that it was forbidden because my parents weren't at home and my brother made me swear not to talk about it to them."

After reading Bustillo's work in *Mad Movies* for a while, Maury got in touch with him through a mutual friend, and the two clicked at once. By this time, Maury had made a few short films, which Bustillo enjoyed, and Maury couldn't stop praising the first draft of *Inside*.

bathroom, which was shot in studio. "So you can imagine the problems we had to shoot with the crew, and we were 35 persons," Maury says. They also only had a single camera, so there was no way to shoot second unit material.

The movie was shot pretty much in chronological order. With the dozens of injuries to character, costume and surroundings that are racked up over time, doing otherwise would've been a nightmare for even the most experienced continuity professional. However, Maury says, there was another reason why scenes were shot linearly. "It was

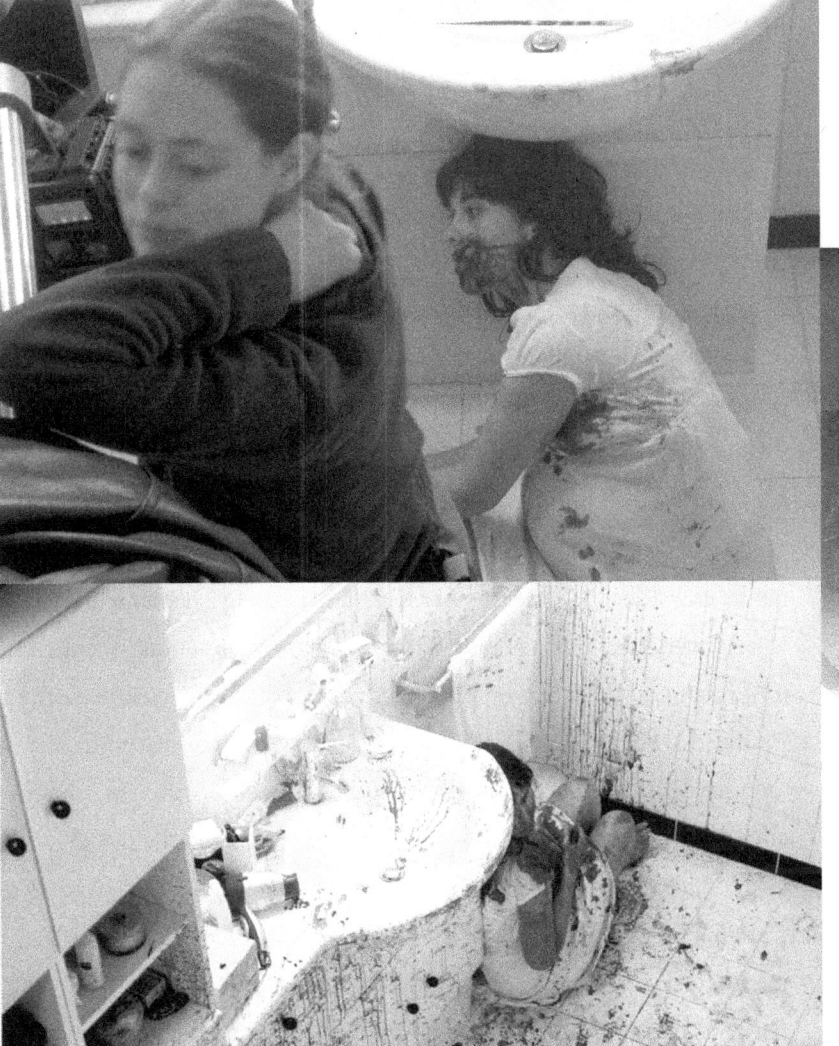

Pascale Marin (camera department) and Paradis take a bathroom break during filming of a crucial scene.

Only the bathroom scenes were shot in studio; the rest of *Inside*'s carnage was filmed with a single camera in a rented house.

> "[In *Inside*] we wanted to have the kind of ambience that you have in Argento's movies. The fact that the story takes place in a city, a house. It's in a really common place, a place you can relate to."
>
> —MAURY

Tenebre
Dario Argento's 1982 giallo stars Anthony Franciosa as a thriller writer stalked by a killer who is inspired by his works. Throw in some memorable kills and a little gender-bending and you've got yourself a good time.

really important for Alysson and Béatrice to be able to act in chronological order because it was the first time Alysson had the leading role, and it was not a piece of cake. We asked her to express really difficult feelings, so it was a way for us to make the acting easier for her."

By their own admissions, Maury and Bustillo went blood crazy with *Inside*, the rental house virtually bathed in the stuff by shooting's end. Although they told the house's owners that they were using it to shoot a horror film, "I don't think they read the script," Maury says. "I think they have discovered by seeing the movie that we put gallons of blood on their floor. But we were really cool guys and we have cleaned up everything and put a new painting on the wall. It was really a nice place after the shooting." In all, it took about a week to get everything clean again.

One of the most shocking kills in the film finds Sarah lashing out in a blind panic at her mother with a knitting needle, catching the doomed soul in the side of the neck. Cue an arterial spray that may look oddly familiar to fans of Italian director Dario Argento.

"The murder of the mother with this trail of blood on the white wall, it's like the end of *Tenebre* when he cuts the woman's arm with the ax and her blood spatters the wall everywhere," Bustillo says.

"The mother and Sarah's boss were the two persons who were able to prevent her from going mad," Maury adds. "She witnessed the murder of her boss and she killed her mother—she has nothing left after that."

At every turn, the pair aimed to flout genre expectations, the director explains. "We have tried not to cast a tall, blonde, big boobs mother for the lead character. We hired a kind of girl next door who you can identify with. She can be your girlfriend or your sister. She's not the really pretty woman screaming for her life and running in the woods."

Yet maddeningly, wherever the film has been shown—Spain, Canada, Japan, the US, even in France—the audience has completely misinterpreted one key scene. If you've seen *Inside*, chances are you know the one. A cop is mortally wounded, yet somehow pulls himself

How Inside Got Out

"We were really lucky because it's really hard to make a horror movie in France," Julien Maury says. "We don't have the culture of horror movies, and the producers don't want to produce these kinds of movies."

It was Lionel Amant, Maury and Alexandre Bustillo's representative, who introduced them to his friend Franck Ribière at the French distribution company La Fabrique de Films. Both Ribière and colleague Vérane Frédiani loved the script and signed on to produce.

The company had only *co*-produced films before, most notably the works of Spanish-born Álex de la Iglesia. "This was the first time they had wanted to produce a 100-percent Fabrique de Films movie," Maury says. "They asked us to rewrite a little bit in the beginning, but we were inexperienced and they weren't so confident to let us direct the movie."

But the other company that was chipping in for what would become the 1.7 million euro *Inside* was Canal+, the French pay TV channel that has funded a number of genre titles including David Lynch's *Mulholland Dr.* and the 2006 French horror flick *Ils (Them)*.

Recalls Maury, "They said if we co-directed the movie, they'll put the money in."

The rest, as they say, is bloody history.

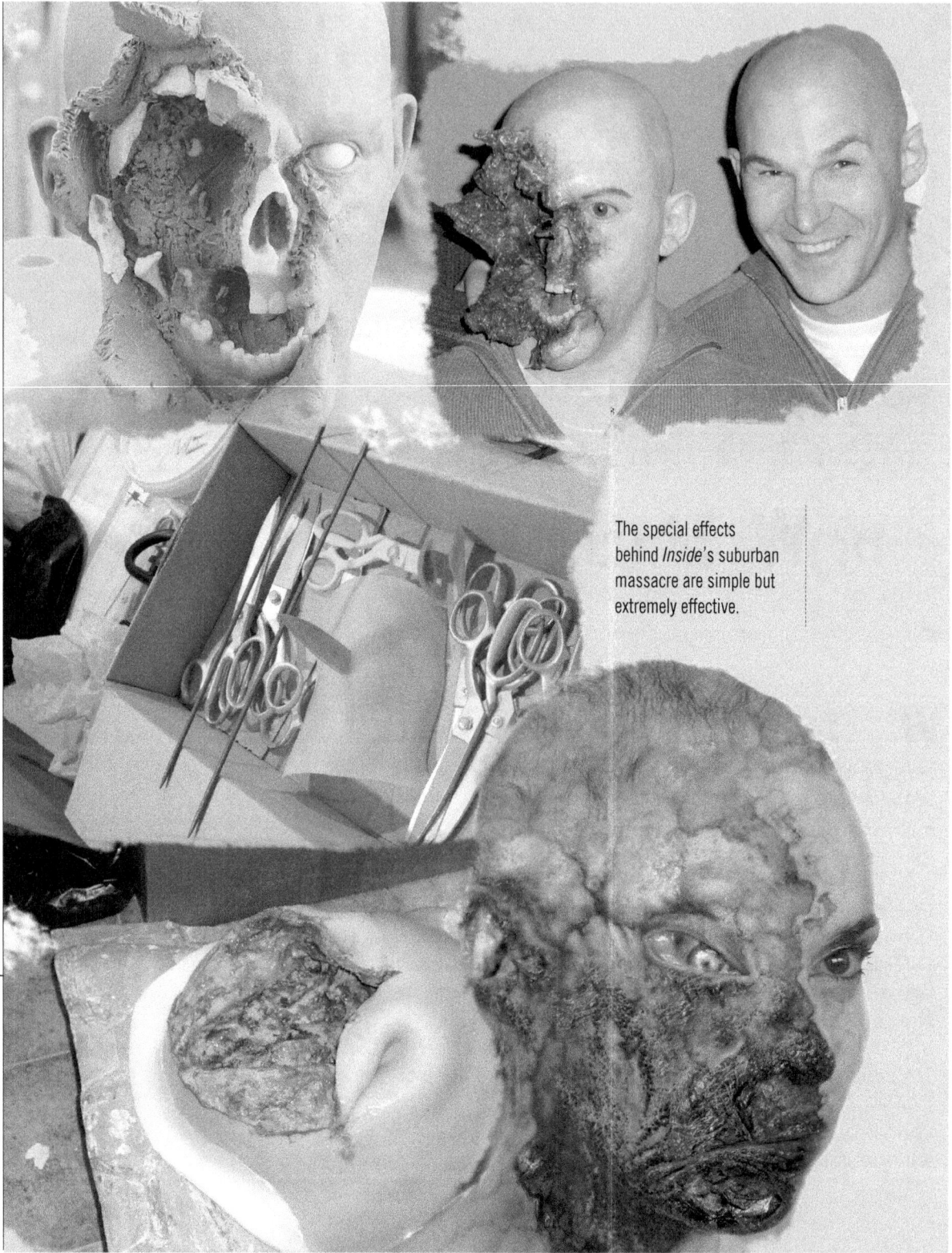

The special effects behind *Inside*'s suburban massacre are simple but extremely effective.

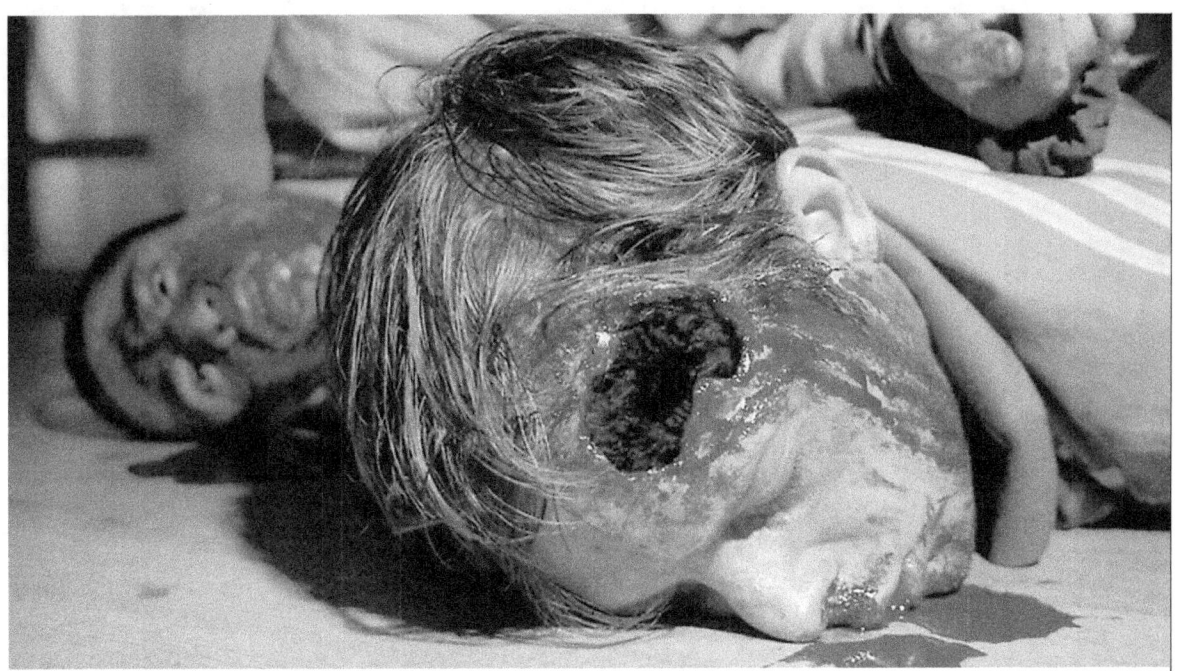

Despite audience misunderstandings to the contrary, the cop with the severe head wound does not spring to his feet because he's a zombie, Maury says. The dying man is simply acting instinctively.

to his feet and switches on the lights.

"As he has a hole in his head, people keep saying, 'He's dead, why is he coming back—that's a zombie movie, I don't understand,'" Maury says. "And we were just saying everywhere, 'No, no, no, it's just 'cause he was shot in the head and his brain is damaged and now he's acting like a zombie.' He has no memory of who he is or where he is. The two things in his mind are 'I must put back the light on' and 'I am threatened. There is a threat in the house but I can't remember what is the threat.' The first to come is the pregnant woman and, unfortunately for Sarah, she becomes a threat for him."

Today, the cop's dead-eyed face resides in Maury's home. More precisely, it's packed away, just as the burned-up face of Dalle's character is packed away in Bustillo's home. Proud of their first feature film, they had naturally wanted to display these trophies where all could see them.

"My girlfriend says, 'Fuck no,'" laughs Maury. "She said put this horror back in the basement." [NHH]

FEVER DREAMS OF THE DESPERATE

DARREN LYNN BOUSMAN

BY 2008, IT WAS LOOKING A LOT LIKE THE BEST OF TIMES AND THE WORST OF TIMES FOR HORROR. AMERICAN FILMMAKERS HAD SEEMINGLY GIVEN UP ON PUSHING THE ENVELOPE, WHICH WAS JUST AS WELL AS THEATRICAL DISTRIBUTION CHANNELS FOR THE GENRE HAD ALL BUT DRIED UP...

> "I can't tell you the last time I saw a comedy film. And I can't tell you where I was when I saw it. I liked it, I thought it was funny, but it leaves me the second I leave the theater. However, I can tell you where I was the last time I was truly scared, truly disgusted, truly frightened. That's the kind of movie I want to make."
> —DARREN LYNN BOUSMAN

Horror's own cyclic popularity combined with an internal political shake-up at Lionsgate saw the label, among other things, dropkick the highly-anticipated adaptation of Clive Barker's *The Midnight Meat Train* straight to DVD after a token theater release.

Lionsgate's about-face no doubt will be a temporary one. As Eli Roth has pointed out many times, it was horror films such as his own *Cabin Fever* that made the company what it is today. However, for anyone with the slightest interest in the genre, Lionsgate's apostasy was particularly worrisome because of its timing. It just so happened that in 2008 it was sitting on another release—far more ground-breaking in scope than *Meat Train*—that many fans were anxious to see on the big screen: Darren Lynn Bousman's *Repo! The Genetic Opera*.

Promising an experience akin to *The Rocky Horror Picture Show* in its heyday, this feature-length rock opera about a near future where people have their transplanted organs viciously repossessed by repo men struck many as just the shot in the arm the genre needed to move past years of by-the-numbers slashers. For the director who had made a name for himself expanding the world of the popular *Saw* franchise, it seemed a once-in-a-lifetime opportunity to show the world that he was so much more than a camera for hire.

BOUSMAN *THE DESPERATE*

In one of those weird class distinctions that can only happen in the cultural ghetto that is horror, Darren Bousman has spent much of the last decade as something of a socially acceptable Eli Roth. Though both directors are fun loving and extremely passionate about film, Bousman has so far escaped scapegoat status in the public eye. There are a couple of reasons for this.

For starters, he has yet to shoot a high-profile film of his own writing, so he can hardly be faulted with furthering the torture porn —or any other easily pilloried—concept. More importantly, if the

Bousman (left) setting up a scene on the set of *Saw II* with actress Shawnee Smith (Amanda).

mainstream public knows him for anything, it is for continuing the already established *Saw* franchise, itself a splatter series with a built-in defense. However gory the goings on get, they are buttressed by the conceit that series villain Jigsaw and his disciples are only out to promote an appreciation for life, never mind how many limbs need to be mangled in the process. For a major chunk of American society with such deep Puritanical roots, it's a hard message to fault, and a Get Out of Jail Free card for whatever carnage ensues. (*The Passion of the Christ* remains the gold standard for this.)

Born Jan. 11, 1979 in Overland Park, Kansas, Bousman became a slave to the horror gene early on thanks in part to the way his family pulled out all the stops for Halloween. "We decked the house out," he remembers. "We built old-school haunted houses, we went to haunted houses around the Kansas city area—the macabre always fascinated me."

As he grew up, he briefly toyed with pursuing an acting career, even starring in a national Dr Pepper commercial. Yet quickly he realized he wanted to be behind the camera rather than in front of it. "It wasn't so much I was in a Dr Pepper commercial," he explains. "It was that I was on set with all these cameras, with a director screaming at everybody. And I was like, '*I* want to scream at everybody.'"

Like most aspiring directors in America, Bousman got himself to Los Angeles, and proceeded to be disillusioned. "Nothing was happening," he says. "I was basically stuck in this void of nothingness. I hated it." He landed a small job on *The X-Files*, but was fired for spending too much time working on his own scripts. He was hired as a production assistant on 2002's *Van Wilder*, but lost that job, too.

"I saw all of these people who were directing and working that I felt I was as good as," he recalls. "I was like, 'How is it that these guys are getting to direct and do these things, yet here I am getting coffee?' You hear the story that, 'Oh, you've got to pay your dues.' Well, I'd been there at this point for years. How long do I pay my dues before I either break or give up?"

It's a desperation that every artist feels at some point, where the bills just aren't getting paid and the old line about the stage janitor not wanting to quit lest he "give up show business" hits painfully close to home. Being the writer he is, Bousman injected all of that bitterness and heartsick depression into a script called **The Desperate**.

"It was basically a last chance to prove myself as a writer," he says. *The Desperate* "was about what you would do to accomplish what you wanted in life. How far would you go? Would you kill someone? Would you rob someone?"

In *The Desperate*, 12 people who have each reached the ends of their ropes enter into a game, with the winner standing to gain whatever he or she wants most. "It was a very horrifically dark horror script," Bousman says. "It borderlined on almost being offensive. But that's why I loved it, and that's what got it noticed."

The Desperate
Despite having his hands full with *Repo* and several other projects, Bousman, at the tail end of 2008, found himself reenergized to see *The Desperate* made into a movie. "The only thing similar to *Saw II* is the character names and possibly the ending, which I would change on *The Desperate*. It's so completely different, and also I think it would be an easy marketing thing: 'The original *Saw II* as it was intended to be seen.'"

"It was basically a last chance to prove myself as a writer..."

— BOUSMAN
on his script for The Desperate, *the ending of which was borrowed for the conclusion of* Saw II.

A FOOT IN THE DOOR

It was 2004 and Lionsgate was preparing to unleash *Saw*, the first installment in a new franchise destined to be the first in years to appeal to horror fans and mainstream audiences alike.

While the writer/director team of Leigh Whannell and James Wan had their fingers crossed for the feature's debut, Bousman's script for *The Desperate* was making the rounds and, they noticed, shared many of *Saw*'s central themes, including an emphasis on an appreciation of life. The duo's production company, Twisted Pictures, rang Bousman one day to get a better sense of the man behind the script.

"I thought they were going to sue me or something," he says. Instead, they showed him *Saw*, and he instantly understood why they had contacted him. "I think at that point they wanted to do

Gregg Hoffman
Gregg Hoffman passed away Dec. 4, 2005 at the age of 42 from a bacterial infection. Co-founder of Twisted Pictures, Hoffman is credited with discovering the 8-minute short that became *Saw*.

CUBE AS INSPIRATION?
Seeing what Bousman pulled off with such limited space in his *Saw* films, one wonders if he was at all inspired by Vincenzo Natali's *Cube* (see p. 78). "It's funny, I had seen *Cube* before I'd done *Saw II*," he says. "If any of them, I'd think *Saw II* would be the most that you could really compare *Cube* to because it's all in one location, every room is trapped, and anyone's going to die if they're in a room. That being said, a lot of independent films go by the same formula, and the formula is we don't have any money—what can we do in one location without having to leave? Yet what *Cube* pulled off was amazing. They actually only had one room; we had a house."

a [*Saw*] film every year, and time was running out" to make the sequel, he says. It just so happened that *The Desperate* had a killer twist ending that would fit perfectly in the clever-but-cruel world of *Saw*. "It was this thing of the cop trying to find these people and the [video] feed wasn't live. So they had asked me if they could buy it and turn it into *Saw II*. I said no."

No?

"As my last ditch effort in Hollywood, I said I'm not giving you this movie unless I direct it," Bousman says. Until then, he hadn't directed more than a few "atrocious" shorts. At that point, he had nothing to lose.

Twisted Pictures producer **Gregg Hoffman** asked him flat out why they should let him direct *Saw II*.

"I said you *shouldn't* let me direct this movie, I'm the complete wrong choice," Bousman says. He told them, "'I've never done anything and you guys have a popular franchise about to start. That's exactly why I'm perfect.' *James Wan* was a first time director. I gave a very impassioned speech, and now here I am years later."

BUDGET, MEET THE STRETCH RACK
When producers Hoffman, Oren Koules and Mark Burg formed Twisted Pictures, it was with the goal of churning out balls-to-the-wall horror films for just a few million dollars each as an alternative to Hollywood's increasingly bland scare fare.

When Bousman began work on *Saw II*, he quickly realized just what that low budget was going to mean for him behind the camera. "I don't think anyone realizes the lack of budget" on the *Saw* films, he says. "We were in this soundstage in Toronto. Space was a problem."

To do what had to be done in the space allotted, one set would be torn down as the next was being constructed. Fortunately, because everything that was shot took place under one roof, "If I realized that something did not work, did not cut together or did

»152

SAW'S JIGSAW: TOBIN BELL

"Tobin Bell is the most eccentric, awesome person I've ever worked with," Bousman says. "Leigh [Whannell] is going to hate me for saying this, but the majority of things that Tobin did or said, Tobin wrote. Some of the coolest lines, and some of the smallest lines, Tobin wrote, because he had his own philosophy.

"For example, there was a line in *Saw III* where he is talking about Amanda, and he looks at Lynn (Bahar Soomekh) and says, 'She swims in my sea.' And that's just a weird line until you think about what he's saying. He wrote that. I knew he wanted to say it in *Saw II* but it didn't make any sense. But in *Saw III* it made complete sense, saying that they're the same type of person.

"Tobin had this book, and he still carries it with him. He writes down every line of dialogue he says. Then he will write what that line really means to him. That's why, in my mind, Jigsaw is such an awesome character, because there's never a false moment.

"Everything that Jigsaw does or Tobin Bell does, he does it with reason and meaning behind it. You'll never give Tobin a line and just have him say it, because he will look at it, he will philosophize about it, he will write a two-paragraph explanation for a three-word sentence to make it ring true to him. And if it rings true to him, he'll say it. I think that's what makes his character so cool."

Perhaps Bousman's greatest contribution to the *Saw* universe, and possibly even to horror itself, is the odd-yet-engaging bond we see develop between Jigsaw and his young protégé Amanda Young (Shawnee Smith).

"When I did *Saw III*, the first thing I said when I came in was I want to make a character study and a love story, and everyone kind of looked at me and laughed," Bousman says. "If you look at it beneath the surface of the gore and the violence and the traps, *Saw III* is a love story between Jigsaw and Amanda. Whether that be like a teacher and student or lovers or friends, they had this powerful connection.

"And when you see Amanda make the wrong choice, you see the pain in Jigsaw's eyes. You see this serial killer crying because he did not want it to get to where it came to. That was what was important to me: the relationship.

"I would say I spent more time dealing with small interactions in that movie than I ever did the violence. Little things like a scene where Shawnee appeared for the first time and goes into Tobin's lair. She picks up a glass of tea and hands it to him and he sips this tea. That one action we talked about more than Shawnee pulling a gun on somebody. I think that's what makes a good film."

JIGSAW + AMANDA: A LOVE STORY?

THE TRAPS

"I'm sure the trap would probably have something to do with what it was in the mausoleum trap [in *Saw III*], stitching my mouth shut, because I've got a big mouth and I talk a lot of shit."

—BOUSMAN *on the type of trap his film crew might devise for him*

"One of the things that we made sure of was that any of the traps had to really work," Bousman says. "You couldn't have a science fiction trap. You couldn't make a trap that was physically impossible. So David Hackl, the production designer [and b-unit director] and myself, we always went to great lengths to make sure the traps worked. They did what they said they were going to do.

"That also posed a problem because it would stunt people's creativity if they had this great idea for a trap and it didn't work, I wouldn't shoot it. So David Hackl and I were the guys who would sit there and try to figure out will this work, can we really do this? I give a lot of credit to David Hackl, who is now directing *Saw V*, because he's the guy with the daunting task of drawing the traps out and actually making sure everything worked on them."

> *"Paranormal Activity. That's probably the last time I saw a movie that I was really taken aback by and could not remember seeing another movie like it."*
>
> — BOUSMAN

« 148 not look right, we would run back to that set and do pick-ups," he says. Bousman credits his close working relationship with editor Kevin Greutert (who edited *Saw II-V* and is slated to direct *Saw VI*) for making this near guerrilla-style moviemaking possible. They kept in touch with each other around the clock so that Bousman knew exactly what footage they had in the can and what was needed. *Saw III*, arguably the best in the series and the director's personal favorite, came together at a particularly frenetic pace.

"Talk about lack of time and lack of budget," he says. The scene of Jeff (Angus Macfadyen) confronting the judge in the pig-slaughtering pit caused Bousman more than a few anxious hours. "I had this great idea that I was going to do a whole scene in one take. It was an extremely complex move where we had this crane following the guy in and up the ramp and down into the pit. It was all one shot. I thought that was a great idea until I saw it, and it was extremely boring. I wanted to fast-forward through it, but when I fast-forwarded through it, it looked like I cut, so the whole point of the crane sort of died off."

By the time he decided to reshoot the scene, "we filmed that on a Monday, and on Wednesday that set was already being torn down to build a new one."

Yet where some directors would've spent most of their time simply trying to plow through each shot to stay one step ahead of set construction, Bousman used the situation to his artistic advantage.

'LINES ARE BEGINNING TO BLUR'

In the first few minutes of *Saw II*, Bousman puts us on notice that he is out to do far more than retell the *Saw* story with new characters in the typical fashion of Hollywood sequels.

Brooding over a falling out he's had with his tearaway teenage son Daniel, Det. Eric Matthews (Donnie Wahlberg) receives a call at home from police headquarters asking him to come to the scene

SAW II

In this installment, Det. Eric Matthews (Donnie Wahlberg) matches wits with cancer-weakened John Kramer, aka Jigsaw (Tobin Bell) as he tries to locate the booby-trapped house where his son and several other victims are being held.

Bousman's expert direction—including playful uses of continuous tracking shots—as well as an end twist cribbed from his own script *The Desperate*, takes *Saw* to its next evolutionary level. However, it also continues one of the franchise's most maddening aspects—offering up the choicest plot morsel in the last few minutes of the film. In *Saw II*, we get the first big reveal of the father/daughter relationship between Jigsaw and Amanda (Shawnee Smith), which will be fully explored in *Saw III*.

SAW III

Easily the best of the Bousman-lensed *Saw* flicks (if not of them all), *Saw III* transcends the splatter-by-numbers genre conventions the series has flirted with by lending the tale of Jigsaw and his bizarre crimes a poignant emotional edge.

Several months after Det. Matthews is captured by Jigsaw's protégé, Amanda, Det. Allison Kerry (Dina Meyer) and Lt. Daniel Rigg (Lyriq Bent) discover a new pattern to Jigsaw's crimes: death traps that cannot be escaped. The real meat of the movie, however, is in the growing schism between Jigsaw and Amanda, every bit as gripping as the best Shakespearian tragedy.

POSTMORTEM

Saw III is the best work Bousman has done to date, and transforms a one-gimmick series into a three-dimensional contemplation on love, loss and forgiveness.

SAW IV

Bousman admits that his attention was already on his then-forthcoming movie *Repo* when he was putting together *Saw IV*, but that is only part of the problem. For starters, it was the first *Saw* film not to be co-written by *Saw* creators James Wan and Leigh Whannell. *Feast* co-writers Patrick Melton and Marcus Dunstan did the honors, much to the movie's detriment.

This time around, Jigsaw himself is dead, but the mayhem continues. FBI agents Peter Strahm (Scott Patterson) and Lindsey Perez (Athena Karkanis) deduce that Amanda wasn't strong enough to set some of the death traps seen in *Saw III*—there must be (yet) another Jigsaw devotee out there. Meanwhile, Lt. Rigg from *Saw II* and *III* is following messages seemingly left behind by Jigsaw as he searches for Det. Matthews.

Despite some arresting visuals, the movie quickly implodes under the weight of too many ideas, confusing time lines and an utter lack of the depth that so distinguished its predecessor. Lyriq Bent turns in a suitably intense performance as Rigg, but the rest of the cast is given little room to maneuver in a plot that is the cinematic equivalent of a No Pest Strip.

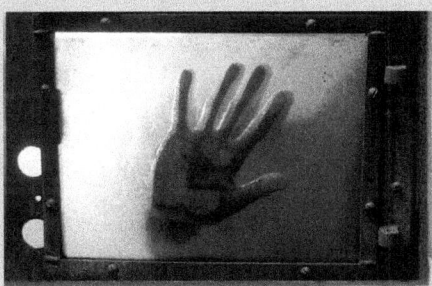

Splat Pack

Respected horror journalist Alan Jones coined the term "splat pack" in *Total Film* magazine, referring to directors Bousman, Eli Roth *(see p. 10)*, Alexandre Aja *(Haute Tension)*, Neil Marshall *(Dog Soldiers)*, Greg McLean *(see p. 44)*, Rob Zombie, James Wan and Leigh Whannell.

Showing Off?

On film techniques such as his scene transitions in *Saw II-IV*: "There's two schools of thought," Bousman says. "It's one thing if a director is basically kissing his own ass and doing shots that do not benefit the movie, but just does them to showcase himself. It's another if he's doing things that are seamless when you watch them and you realize after the fact how cool that was. I tried to do that with the transitional shots. When I watch Paul Thomas Anderson *(There Will Be Blood)* movies, I'm blown away. Not necessarily while I'm watching the movie, but after the fact."

of Jigsaw's latest crime. "I'll be right there," he says, hanging up the phone, slipping into a jacket and stepping from his room straight onto the crime scene. It's a jarring transition, and one that Bousman used to increasingly greater effect throughout his *Saw* films.

"My original intention in coming to Hollywood was not to be a horror director, a member of the '**splat pack**,'" he says. "I lucked into that, but that wasn't what I came to do. What I didn't want was for the violence in the films to overshadow me as a director.

"With the transitions, I wanted to remind people that I wasn't just a dude who threw blood up on the screen, that there was some creative thought behind things. I would say the majority of people don't realize the transitions until they've seen the movie a couple of times."

Bousman's favorite transition remains one that probably went largely unnoticed by first-time viewers of *Saw III*. Det. Allison Kerry (Dina Meyer) is examining the remains of Troy (the director's longtime friend J. LaRose), who was eviscerated by the double threat of a bomb and several chains hooked through his body. A moment after we see Kerry look down at the carnage, the camera follows her gaze, tracking along the floor, passing chunks of Troy along the way. During this pan, the bloody floor becomes a carpeted one and the camera rises to reveal Kerry in her bathtub at home, trying to unwind from the day's horrors.

"That was an extremely complex setup," Bousman says; it took a good day and a half to shoot. "There was no cutting on it. Dina Meyer was fully clothed in a cop uniform, and as the camera hit the ground, she threw her clothes off on set, ran behind the camera and jumped in a bathtub. Then the bathtub water had to be completely calmed so you didn't see that she had just jumped in, dunked her head underwater, and then came up as the camera hit."

What makes this technique so interesting is the way that it becomes increasingly more pronounced, more surreal throughout the course of the films, building to a brief but astounding visual

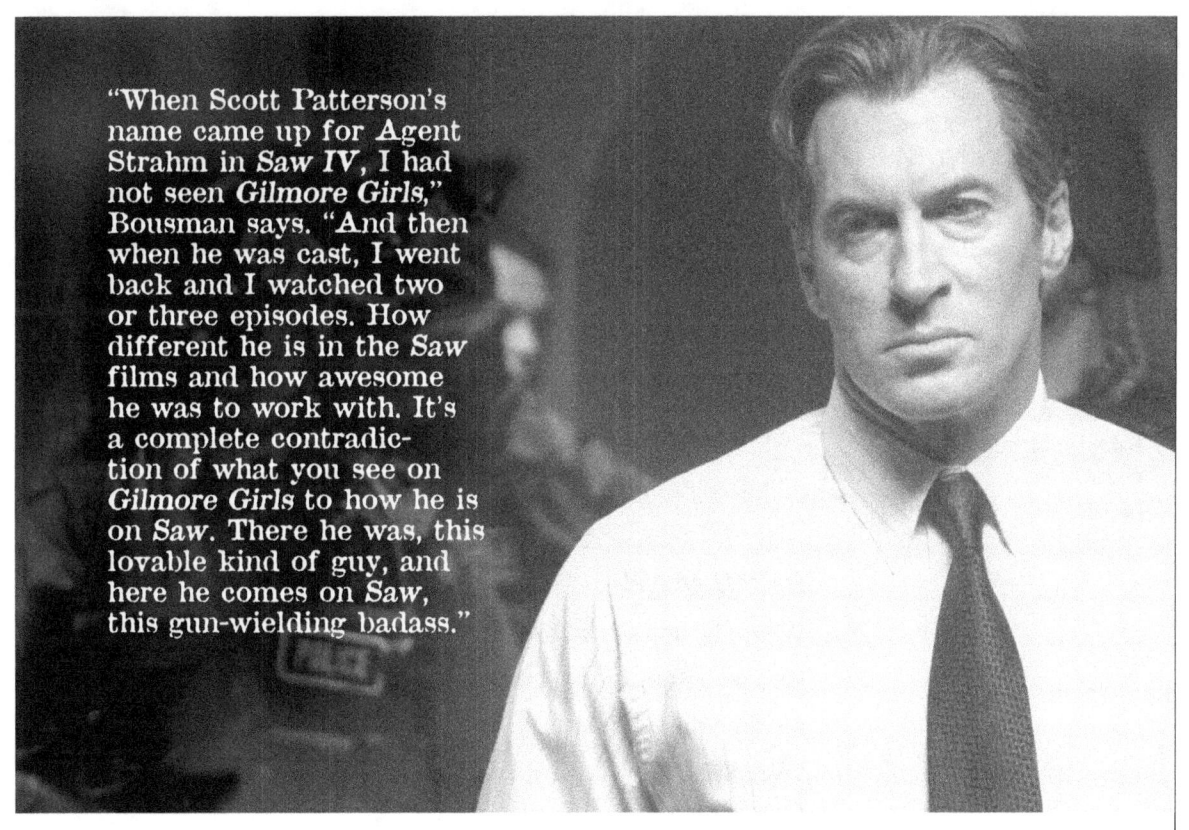

"When Scott Patterson's name came up for Agent Strahm in *Saw IV*, I had not seen *Gilmore Girls*," Bousman says. "And then when he was cast, I went back and I watched two or three episodes. How different he is in the *Saw* films and how awesome he was to work with. It's a complete contradiction of what you see on *Gilmore Girls* to how he is on *Saw*. There he was, this lovable kind of guy, and here he comes on *Saw*, this gun-wielding badass."

crescendo in *Saw IV*. This, the last Bousman entry in the *Saw* series, features a scene in which Lt. Daniel Rigg (Lyriq Bent), sliding into his own Jigsaw-induced madness, hurls a woman through a mirror and into the next scene. In essence, the audience is forced to share Rigg's madness.

"The lines are beginning to blur between different worlds," the director explains. "The world of the horrors of Jigsaw and the people who are investigating it. I wanted there not to be a comprehensive line that you could see. I wanted it to kind of flow together to see how his life was bleeding into their world."

Had the rest of *Saw IV* been as strong as this one sequence, it could well have rivaled *Saw III* as the strongest entry to date.

"When it got to *Saw IV*, it did get hard," he admits. "I mean, how many movies can you make about a guy who's dying of cancer and is a serial killer, and what else can you say? He's dead. I think

Challenge making *Saw IV*
"I did want to try something with *Saw IV* that had not been done with the *Saw* films, and try to make it intricate. You have a problem with every *Saw* film, which is that you have to one-up the audience. The audience is smart. If you go to message boards now, the majority of people guess the ends of movies. Especially when you run a marketing campaign and show images from the movie, it's harder and harder to trick people."

you have to try to make it more frenetic and more crazy and take the audience into the insanity of this world. Or you're going to be a classic story of sequels where every sequel is dying further and further."

Bousman faced yet another **challenge making *Saw IV***. In addition to orchestrating more twists for the story and working with new writers—Patrick Melton and Marcus Dunstan (co-writers of *Feast*)—he was deep in pre-production for *Repo*. After three sequels, the desperation he felt this time was to bring something never before seen to the nation's movie screens. Says Bousman, "I'll be the first to admit my attention was split."

REPO MAN

Before he entered Kansas University's film program, Bousman studied acting and found himself in nearly every play staged during his time there. It was also there that he first developed his lifelong love of musicals, having appeared in a fair number of them. When he saw *Jesus Christ Superstar* for the first time, "it blew my mind because it combined two elements that I absolutely loved—movies and music," he says.

When he had the opportunity to direct a rock opera stage play called *Repo! The Genetic Opera*, he was intrigued by the way its audience reacted night after night, dressing up as the characters and joining in on the songs. Comparisons to *The Rocky Horror Picture Show* were unavoidable. What he was witnessing was not merely performance, but an event.

Written by Terrance Zdunich (who also plays Graverobber) and Darren Smith, *Repo* is set in a near future following a worldwide epidemic of organ failures. GeneCo, a multibillion dollar biotech company, quickly steps in with expensive organ transplants that it brutally repossesses if its customers miss a payment. These repossessions are carried out by skilled assassins called repo men.

To Bousman, *Repo* had everything a film should have. It needed

Repo
Repo actually began life as a 10-minute musical performance piece called "The Necromerchant's Debt" in 1999, written and performed by Terrance Zdunich and Darren Smith at various rock clubs in California. The first full-length stage show of *Repo* was performed in 2002.

POSTMORTEM

By now, just about everybody has weighed in on this rock opera, including many who have yet to see it, I'm guessing. Much of the controversy has more to do with the circumstances of its creation than its artistic merits.

Set in the year 2056 after mankind has been devastated by an epidemic of organ failures, *Repo* tells the story of GeneCo, a firm that supplies replacement, designer organs...for a price. To those who miss a payment, it dispatches a "repo man" (Anthony Stewart Head) to messily reclaim the merchandise. The repo man has his own problems, including a rebellious teenage daughter, Shilo (Alexa Vega).

Firstly, *Repo* is a horror movie in the sense that *The Passion of the Christ* is a horror movie; it sets out to tell a story with as much bloodshed as is necessary to tell it, with no real horror elements beyond that to speak of. It boasts one or two catchy tunes, which makes it a hard sell as a musical. That leaves you with the story, which is simply too thin to sustain its 97-minute running time.

As many have already observed, congratulations must go to Bousman for prying the cash to make *Repo* from Lionsgate's hip pocket, but the plaudits end there. This is a shame because there are some impressive performances (both in acting and singing) by Head, Vega and *Repo* co-creator Terrance Zdunich as Graverobber.

Bousman and company have been blasted for setting out to purposefully (read: *cynically*) create a "cult film" in the *Rocky Horror Picture Show*/midnight movies vein, which seems an odd thing to beat up on a film for. Does anyone really think that the makers of *Rocky Horror* released a movie they thought would play opposite more mainstream Hollywood fare?

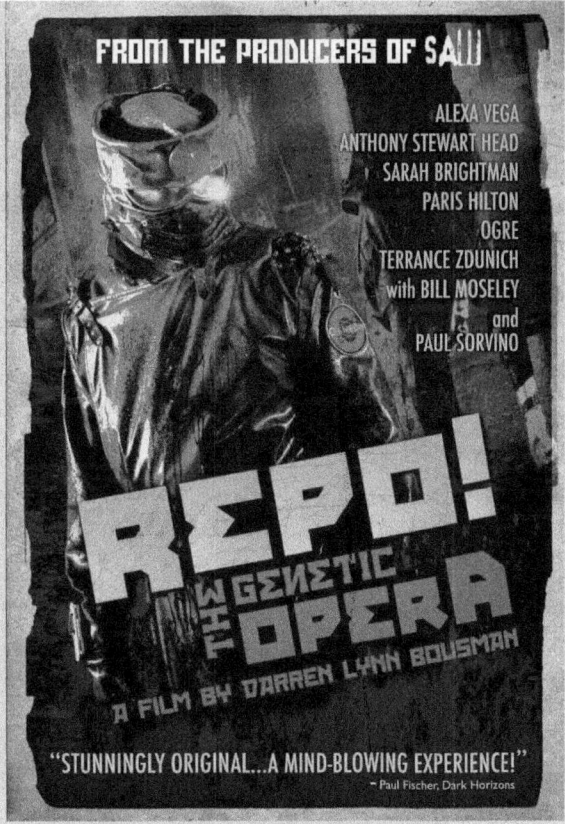

And David Lynch (*Eraserhead*, *Blue Velvet*) and John Waters (*Pink Flamingos*), to name just two, have built healthy careers doing nothing but purposefully directing cult films.

Repo is a work that could easily find an audience with the release of a tighter director's cut. For all of its faults, the movie does succeed in showing you something you probably haven't seen before. In a multiplex world of anemic remakes and workshopped-to-death originals, maybe that's enough.

Repo man Nathan (Anthony Stewart Head, right) slides into the bloodlust that earns him his daily bread in Bousman's *Repo! The Genetic Opera*.

to be on screen. It was while he was filming *Saw III* that the director started work on a short *Repo* film, he says. "It was such a hard sell, I had to do something that was kind of different to get these studios to look at it. I couldn't walk in with a script or a song, so I went out to shoot this 5- or 6-minute short film."

Fortunately for him, *Saw*'s Amanda Young, actress Shawnee Smith, was also the vocalist for metal band Fydolla Ho, with a set of pipes tailor-made for a rock opera. She was quickly cast as Amber Sweet. "She came in and recorded the song and it was great," he says. "She was amazing. But when it came down to the feature film of it, I wanted to try to work with people I hadn't worked with in the past because I didn't want this to be the *Saw* musical. That was one thing that kind of scared me."

With the exception of a cameo by *Saw III*'s Troy, J. LaRose, *Repo*'s cast was made up of actors the director had never worked with before. However, they were by no means unknowns.

Bousman had only seen a couple of episodes of *Buffy the Vampire Slayer* before Anthony Stewart Head (Giles) was cast as the repo man Nathan Wallace. Someone called the director one night to alert him to the airing of "Once More With Feeling," the musical episode of *Buffy*, he says. "When I heard it was on, I rolled my eyes but I knew I had to watch it. Five minutes into it, I was like, 'This is not only good, it's great.' And then here Tony comes in singing. Immediately after it was over, I went online, downloaded all the music, and put it on my iPod. I was extremely impressed by it."

A coup for any lover of musical theater was *Repo's* casting of Sarah Brightman in her movie debut as Blind Mag. While he hadn't seen her live appearances as Christine in Andrew Lloyd Webber's *Phantom of the Opera*, he was a fan of her cast recordings. "She was probably the easiest person for us to cast which, in retrospect,

> "My Number One thing about going to the set is if it's not fun, I don't want to be there. There's always music playing—it's fun. I've learned that I get so much out of my crew if they're having a good time. It's the crew that makes the movie, I'm just the guy that says where to point the camera."
> — BOUSMAN

Popular singer Sarah Brightman made her screen debut in Bousman's *Repo*. "It took one phone call and she said sure, I'd love to," he recalls.

Bousman and Alexa Vega walk through a shot for Repo!

is kind of ridiculous when you think about it," he says. "Her name came up and I was like, 'Whatever, like she's really going to do my movie.' Sarah Brightman did my movie. It took one phone call and she said sure, I'd love to."

Yet more casting coups came in the form of horror icon Bill Moseley (*The Devil's Rejects, Texas Chainsaw Massacre 2*) and Paris Hilton as Amber Sweet.

Considering its fish-nor-fowl nature, *Repo* and the story of how Bousman pushed it through the bland factory of Hollywood would make for a film every bit as gripping as any in the *Saw* series.

'UPHILL BATTLE'

"I don't know how much of this should actually be on the record, but I'll just say it," Bousman says. "We're not having much luck with the distributors. When I made the movie, I think it was 'the guy from *Saw* wants to do another movie and he wants to do it with this studio,'" Bousman says. "And the answer was, 'Of course, yes we'll do it.' I don't think they realized what they said yes to—a full blown, in-your-face rock opera."

Finally, he showed the film to several Lionsgate executives.

"They see the movie and then all the sudden the first question is, 'Well Darren, where's the talking,'" Bousman recalls. "I said, 'There is no talking.' It was just this kind of dumbfounded look on their faces of what do you mean there's no talking? Guys, you've just purchased a rock opera. Ever since then, it's been an uphill battle."

The $8.5 million *Repo! The Genetic Opera* beggars description—a nightmare for any distributor in a business where films are signed or scrapped based on a single-line pitch. Bousman often contends that *Repo* is not a horror movie, regardless of the gory antics that its repo men get up to. That said, it accomplishes many of the things that the best horror films do: It subverts the norms of cinema with its stylish sets and moody performances, and places before its audience spectacles seldom seen. In short, it has cult film written all over it.

Not surprisingly, Lionsgate prepared a less-than-enthusiastic launch for *Repo*, opening it on Nov. 7, 2008 in just eight cities. Like a panic-stricken mother dumping her newborn on a hospital doorstep, this tactic has obvious echoes of *Midnight Meat Train's* shabby handling. To give you some perspective, Lionsgate opened the lowest-common-denominator spoof *Disaster Movie* (from the makers of the *Scary Movie* series) in more than 2,600 theaters in America alone.

In many ways, genre star Bousman finds himself in much the same boat as beginning filmmakers like the crew behind

> "When I saw *Pineapple Express*, I liked it, I thought it was funny, but I didn't talk about it after I walked out of the theater. Not the case with *Martyrs*, not the case with movies like *Frontière(s)* or other horror films. Even if horror films aren't good, I still talk about them."
>
> — **BOUSMAN** on why he loves horror movies

Martyrs

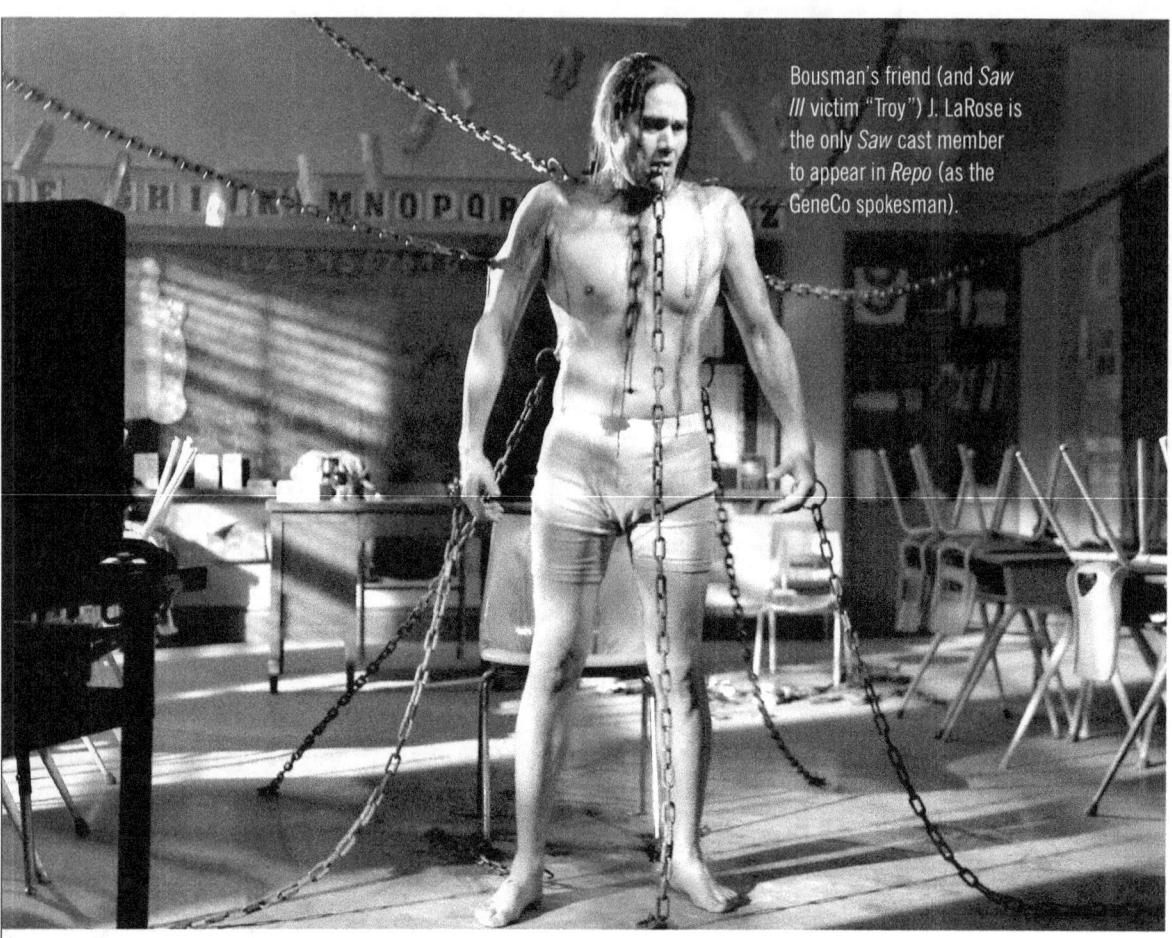

Bousman's friend (and *Saw III* victim "Troy") J. LaRose is the only *Saw* cast member to appear in *Repo* (as the GeneCo spokesman).

> "When it got to *Saw IV*, it did get hard. I mean, how many movies can you make about a guy who's dying of cancer and is a serial killer?"
> —BOUSMAN

Zombie Girl: The Movie (see p. 204). Overwhelming odds have been overcome to make a piece of cinema, only to beg the question: Now what?

Fortunately for *Repo*, Bousman and company have gone to unprecedented lengths to get their work before audiences throughout the country.

"I wish that people actually knew the depths we went to getting this movie out," Bousman says. Once it wrapped, he spent thousands renting out movie theaters for "little rogue screenings" for critics and friends in the industry, trying to generate some buzz.

"There is something extremely liberating about what we're doing," he admits. "In *Saw*, I was never involved in the marketing. I finished the movie, I did interviews when they called me, and that was it. With this movie, every single day, from the moment I wake up until the moment I go to bed, I'm on the Internet trying to set up interviews."

Throughout 2008, the director took *Repo* on the festival circuit, premiering it in July at Toronto's FanTasia (where Bousman picked up a "Ground-Breaker" award), hitting Fantastic Fest in Austin, Sitges in Spain, and Toronto After Dark. Bousman even took the movie on a seven-city road tour, including stops in Seattle, Chicago and Orlando.

The cornerstone of the film's marketing efforts has been a visually stunning Web site (www.repo-opera.com) brimming with informative behind-the-scenes videos, film clips, online karaoke contests and merchandise. More importantly, the site serves as a gathering place for the "*Repo* Army," a group of *Repo* fans—most of whom have yet to see the film—every bit as positive and persistent as the Barack Obama boosters who herded voters to the polls the same week *Repo* was released.

Without the Internet, Bousman says, there's no way *Repo* could've risen above its lack of marketing dollars. "There's actually a silver lining to all of this. The fans have found us. If you go on our message boards, there is a legion of fans. I'm talking not 10 or 20 or 100, I'm talking thousands. They're dressing up like *Repo* characters and doing stunts. And this movie hadn't even come out yet.

"The big question is why are they doing this? I think it comes down to one thing: They feel like they've discovered something. This was not something that was pushed on them, not mass-marketed to them. This was something that they found and they feel they helped create." [NHH]

> "We feel comedy, drama, we laugh, we cry. We're nervous. But to actually be terrified in our everyday life doesn't really happen. And I think that's why the horror genre has always connected with me. It's the fact that here is a chance that I can actually do something that will scare people."
> — BOUSMAN

The Rue Crew: From left, Monica S Kuebler, Jovanka Vuckovic, Rodrigo Gudiño, Audra Jacombs, Tomb Dragomir, Dave Alexander, Justin Erickson, Gary Pullin and Marco Pecota.

THE ALGONQUIN ROUNDTABLE IN HELL

RUE MORGUE MAGAZINE

IF YOU'RE GOING TO LAUNCH A RADICAL NEW MOVEMENT, YOU BETTER MAKE DAMN SURE IT HAS A VOICE TO HERALD ITS ARRIVAL...

Fangoria

In its 30 year history, *Fangoria* has made its own significant contributions to horror movie fandom. Launched in 1979 as an attempt to cover fantasy films, *Fangoria* stumbled along for a few issues before hitting its stride. Ditching fantasy and sci-fi covers for those focused on current horror flicks, editor Bob Martin transformed the publication into one that every teen and twentysomething went to for the goriest images from the latest movies. Martin left in 1986, ultimately replaced by Tony Timpone, who holds that position today. Under his leadership, *Fangoria* branched out into home video, launched its Weekend of Horrors convention, and its own channel on Sirius Satellite Radio. In 2009, the magazine underwent a radical redesign (see below).

Back in 1920s America, *The New Yorker* magazine emerged from the gatherings of some of the country's greatest wits at New York's Algonquin Hotel. While many writers such as Dorothy Parker, Robert Benchley and EB White frequented these meetings of the so-called "Algonquin Round Table," the sessions also attracted the likes of playwright/director George S Kaufman, Harpo Marx, actress Tallulah Bankhead and composer Deems Taylor. The members of this very unofficial group shared their experiences, gossip and ideas, and then went off to change American culture, often through creative collaborations.

The same phenomenon has been seen more recently in the world of horror journalism.

By the late 1990s, cinematic horror had virtually stagnated, as had the periodicals covering it. The US's *Fangoria* magazine, the No. 1 authority on the subject since its debut in 1979, continued to produce news-rich, photo-packed issues. Unfortunately, the likes of Freddy Krueger, Jason Voorhees and Michael Myers had each spiraled into self-parody, making stories about their films as tedious and uninspiring to read as the source material was to watch. A generation of filmmakers that had grown up on the exploits of same, or had been strong-armed by bean counters into aping these franchises, produced equally bland fare, which also had to be covered in horror magazines.

Fangoria's standards remained top-notch in terms of celebrating horror movies of every stripe, including those that otherwise would've slipped silently into obscurity. Yet, at the end of the day, it remained a publication geared primarily to gorehounds in their teens and early 20s who still called makeup effects pioneer Tom Savini God, and delighted in poring over every latex gash and dismemberment depicted therein. As every horror fan knew even back then, Savini is *a* god, but only one in an infernal pantheon that reaches beyond splatter effects to include literature, toys, comic books, video games, music and more.

In October 1997, a thin little zine called *Rue Morgue* climbed quietly onto store shelves in Toronto and proceeded to infect the blood of nearly every person with a penchant for the dark side who came in contact with it. Unlike *Fangoria* and its UK-based competition, *Shivers*, *Rue Morgue* cast its net beyond horror films alone to celebrate the genre in all of its variety.

More than a decade later, *Rue Morgue* has evolved into a veritable New Horror artist collective, with individual members collaborating on films, publishing books, producing art prints and hosting Internet radio shows when not opening their veins to meet a grueling 11-times-a-year magazine deadline.

ASSEMBLING THE ANGRY MOB

Every once in a while we experience a moment of clarity and glimpse, if only for a second, how every step we've taken has led us to where we are now.

The year was 1998 and the FanTasia Film Festival was, like the films it frequently screens, engaging in a little experiment. For its first two events, it stuck to Montreal, but this year it set up shop in Toronto's second-run Bloor Cinema. (Remember that name, it comes up again.) Though it would go down in FanTasia history as one of its least successful festivals, it was nevertheless instrumental in the creation of *Rue Morgue*.

Emerging from a festival screening of Douglas Buck's 23-minute visual assault **Cutting Moments**, Jen (later Jovanka) Vuckovic saw an earnest-looking man sitting at a table in the lobby with a handful of magazines "in quiet defiance," she recalls. Getting a closer look, she saw the magazines were actually back issues of *Rue Morgue*. She recalled seeing issue 3 at her local Suspect Video store a little while before, but had thought it was a heavy-metal magazine at the time. Oddly, she had just won a six-month subscription to that very magazine for answering some trivia questions at FanTasia. "This

Cutting Moments (1997)
Douglas Buck's 23-minute exploration of a family's dissolution is both simpler and more complex than the sum of its parts. It's your typical American home: Patrick (Gary Betsworth) is freezing out wife Sarah after his inappropriate advances toward their little boy could mean Joey being taken into protective care. In a last ditch effort to be heard, Sarah (Nica Ray) resorts to some brutal self-punishment. Patrick at last gets the message and sends one of his own. It's not surprising that *Rue Morgue* would later go on to champion the New York City filmmaker's low-budget efforts within its pages. Most recently, Buck wrote and directed a remake of Brian De Palma's 1973 classic *Sisters* in 2006.

Under the influence of art director Gary Pullin, *Rue Morgue* has evolved with the times. Clockwise from top left: issues 3, 32, 61, 66 and 77.

magazine just wasn't going to let me pass it by," she says.

The earnest-looking man turned out to be 30-year-old Rodrigo Gudiño, founder of the then-year-old horror magazine. Quickly they fell into a passionate conversation about the films they had seen so far at the festival. At that time, the 21-year-old Toronto woman was an award-winning visual effects artist who was not sure she was really in the right profession. Just a few years later, she would take over the editorial reins at *Rue Morgue*.

During the same FanTasia festival, artist **Gary Pullin** stopped by the same table after a screening of Lucio Fulci's 1981 classic *The Beyond*. "I gave him a crappy business card that I made in college and said I do graphic design, and I'd love to get involved with your magazine," Pullin says. Earlier, his roommate had shown him a copy of issue 3 with its Tom Savini cover story. "It blew my mind that there was a horror magazine from Toronto." Soon, Pullin developed the Gothic nameplate that graces *Rue Morgue*'s covers to this day. By 2001, he would be its art director.

BUILDING THE MONSTER

In a sound bite, media-obsessed world, Rodrigo Gudiño is an unlikely person to be fronting an artistic movement. While always ready to engage in a passionate discussion about filmmaking and the horror genre with friends, he's not the instant-on self-promoter that the film industry, or even the music industry, is used to. He would be the first to tell you that he has learned from both how *not* to do things.

Born in San Diego, Gudiño spent his first nine years in the Tijuana suburb of Playas before moving to Toronto. By 14 he was back in Mexico City, and a few years later, Toronto again. It was while he was working toward his BA in literary studies and philosophy at the University of Toronto that he racked up skills in writing, editing and page layout working on the student newspaper.

Inspired by magazines like *Weird Tales* and *Rod Serling's The Twilight Zone Magazine*, he was writing short stories during his last year at university, but realized he needed more writing experience overall if he was ever going to get anywhere with it. He applied to every magazine in Toronto, he remembers. "I got accepted by two: one was *RPM*, the other was *The Catholic New Times*."

RPM Weekly was a Canadian music magazine that started in 1964. To someone like Gudiño who was 26 and really into music, it

Gary Pullin
Before creating the look of *Rue Morgue* as art director of the magazine, Pullin designed the packaging for a number of products including Kayo, a chocolate drink similar to Yoo-hoo sold in the Chicago area. Throughout his career, he's designed everything from T-shirts and CD covers to jewelry and Web sites.

Culture of Horror
In its 12 year history, *Rue Morgue* has covered many different aspects of horror culture beyond the ghoulish films that are its stock-in-trade. Here are just a few:

* Horror themed breakfast cereals
* Vintage horror board games
* Classic Aurora monster models (above)
* Horror video games
* The dark paintings of assisted-suicide proponent Dr Jack Kevorkian
* Horror movie poster art
* Hieronymus Bosch figurines (below)
* Murder ballads
* Gruesome skateboard art
* Death photography
* Horror sculpture, photography and art
* Horror-themed music

seemed a dream job. Once there, he learned to write everything from spot news to reviews and opinion pieces. "But also I learned a lot of tricks from the music industry itself, which is always trying to break new bands or make something out of nothing," he says.

It was around this time that he began to notice something happening in his local Toronto video store: Suspect Video. The horror section had blossomed with offerings from all over the world. And it wasn't just videos anymore. Trading cards, music, games, books and clothing—the darker side of entertainment had become a large part of the popular culture.

This new renaissance, combined with his own literary leanings, led Gudiño to fire off an excited e-mail to an editor at *Fangoria*. "I pitched him the entire *Rue Morgue* idea," he says. "I essentially said, 'Have you thought of older films from the '50s or even before, or expressionist horror films? There's all these toys and fashion, everything—the **culture of horror**.' I think I gave a breakdown of all the different things I could cover for *Fangoria*. And my last question was, 'Are you interested in any of these?' The e-mail I got back from him was just the word 'no.' I don't even think the 'N' was capitalized."

Staring at the computer screen, it suddenly hit him. "Why don't I just do it myself?"

Meanwhile, the *RPM* dream job was turning into something else. The whole reason he wanted to write was that he had things to communicate to others. "In the music business, I learned how to write in a way you say nothing," he says. "A lot of journalists do that. It's a skill. You're able to write 200 words reviewing a CD which says absolutely nothing about whether you liked it or not."

While on his lunch break, he happened to duck into a gift shop where his attention was again drawn to all the Halloween-themed items on offer. "It dawned on me that perhaps the popular culture's fascination with horror was somehow reflective of the 20th century's interest in existentialism, alienation and anxiety," Gudiño later wrote in issue 72, the magazine's 10th anniversary issue. "The possibility of exploring, however superficially, this wider context excited me beyond the possibilities of a mere horror magazine."

Paying homage to literary idol Edgar Allan Poe, he christened his venture *Rue Morgue*, a French-English pairing that seemed distinctly Canadian.

For six months, he spent every spare moment outside of his full-time *RPM* gig designing the magazine and writing articles. Much-needed editing and proofing help came from Mary-Beth Hollyer, a friend from his student newspaper days who would help keep the magazine afloat as associate editor during its formative years. Finally, he laid the entire issue out—a process made all the more painstaking by the use of a pokey 386 computer.

"I wasn't very well off at the time," he says. "I needed a Pentium; I needed lots of stuff." There were also the student loans he was still paying off. All told, the first issue would cost him $1,000 Canadian. "In a way, it was counterintuitive to spend all this money on what, in effect, was a pipe dream."

Once the first issue was ready in October 1997, he hit the streets of Toronto, giving it away to any store that would stock it, and sending the rest off to every horror-related company he could find. In less than two years, it would gain distribution in the key US market. The only thing that was going to prevent *Rue Morgue* from remaining a pipe dream was getting it in front of fans and companies that would recognize it for what it was—the opening salvo in the New Horror movement.

GIVING IT LIFE

Verging on financial embarrassment, Gudiño hired the magazine's first employee, Jody Infurnari, on a strictly commission basis. A fellow *RPM* staffer, Infurnari's devotion to PR and marketing made him an ideal pick.

SPEND $ TO MAKE $

"In a way, it was counterintuitive to spend all this money on what, in effect, was a pipe dream," says Rodrigo Gudiño about his launch of *Rue Morgue* during some pretty lean years.

Early on, Gudiño read a study of magazine practices that suggested most titles that failed spent less than 5 cents an issue on promotion. He decided to spend the equivalent of $1 an issue.

Rue Morgue received a much-needed influx of capital when Marco Pecota came on board, lending Gudiño office space in exchange for a piece of the action. The two met when Gudiño reviewed (not quite glowingly) a board game based on *Dante's Inferno* that Pecota had created.

Back to that 1998 FanTasia festival. *Rue Morgue* had been around for about three issues, and artist Gary Pullin liked what he saw—potential. It might've had a fanzine-like patina, but Gudiño was clearly on to something.

Pullin, on the other hand, had been cooling his heels at the design firm Dollery Rudman Freibauer for about a year since moving from his native London, Ont., designing product packaging. Soon after he met Gudiño, he was freelancing for *Rue Morgue*, starting with a complete redesign of its logo.

"I didn't want to go too **Famous Monsters** with it and I didn't want to go Gothy because we're not a Goth magazine," he says. "The idea [for the lettering] was to come up with an emblem that you may see on old castle doors, or something that may be chiseled into a tombstone. When I added the crescent moon between the words, it just really stood out to me because it's a classic icon of any horror story or film."

Unable to afford his own computer, the artist used those at the packaging company at the end of the workday after the bosses had gone home. Though Gudiño wanted to hire him full time, the money wasn't there yet. Not wanting to lose Pullin's talent, he put him on a monthly stipend of $300 Canadian to handle much of each issue's graphic design jobs, including covers. "He said, 'If you can hold off and just stick it out for another year at the packaging firm, I want to hire you as our art director,'" Pullin remembers. "I did that and I'm glad I did."

The truth was, ghoulish and ghastly was grist for Pullin's creative mill and had been since childhood. "In the '80s, I was really into the gore/splatter stuff and I was drawing Jason, Freddy and all kinds of atrocities," he says. Back at Conestoga College, he was always the one people turned to when they were looking for a good horror flick to screen in a classroom late at night.

Toward the end of 2001, Pullin was hired as the full-time art director and started redesigning *Rue Morgue* with issue 24.

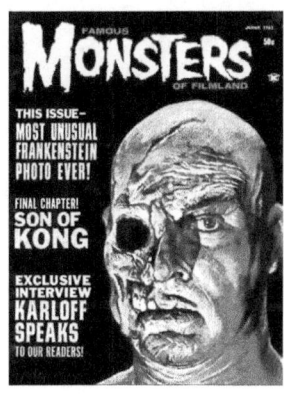

Famous Monsters of Filmland
Launched by publisher Jim Warren (the man who would unleash *Creepy, Eerie, Vampirella* and other black and white horror comic magazines years later) in 1958, *Famous Monsters* was perhaps the most successful fanzine in history. Under the loving hand of the late Forrest J Ackerman (he died Dec. 4, 2008 at 92), *FM* brought readers—mostly young children and teens—pun-filled articles and black and white pics from the classic monster movies that had recently fallen into American TV syndication. Everything from the Universal monsters (Dracula, Frankenstein, etc.) to Vincent Price's Poe films were grist for *FM*'s mill before it ran out of steam in 1983. Ten years later, Ray Ferry revived the *Famous Monsters* name with a new magazine that gradually imploded under the weight of lawsuits and a disastrous relationship with Ackerman. Those interested in an extremely one-sided-yet-oddly-gripping account of these events are referred to Ferry's book *Life Is But A Scream! The True Story of the Rebirth of Famous Monsters of Filmland*.

WHAT'S IN A NAME?

Even big names in the genre have contributed pieces including Bill Moseley (*The Devil's Rejects, Repo! The Genetic Opera*), Rob Bottin (makeup effects wizard best known for Carpenter's *The Thing*) and Kiss' Gene Simmons.

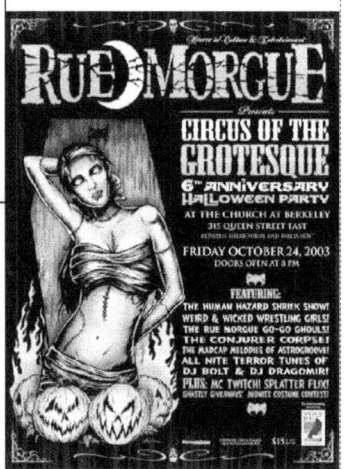

THE NEXT GENERATION

By 2002, the magazine was gathering momentum. Now that he was in a position to hire people to write for *Rue Morgue*, Gudiño was getting editorial submissions from all over, including from several big name genre journalists. It was time to step back and establish what the magazine's guidelines would be going forward.

"I turned everybody down," he remembers. "And the reason was I felt that having journalistic experience wasn't a good thing, at least not for this kind of magazine. I didn't want people who were jaded, but people who were very raw and more inexperienced, who would be starving to express their opinions and maybe sometimes say irresponsible things, but they would come from a very heartfelt place." In other words, no *RPM*-style fluff. If something was crap, *Rue Morgue*'s duty was to call it crap.

In the meantime, Gudiño and company had been busy growing the *Rue Morgue* brand beyond the magazine. In October 2001, they started programming a monthly movie night—dubbed CineMacabre—at The Vatikan Bar in Toronto.

Local writer and performance artist Monica S Kuebler started attending those screenings in 2002. The previous summer, she'd been laid off from her audio engineering gig at Magnetic North, a film and TV post-production company in Toronto, thanks to a ripple effect from the Hollywood strikes, and now was stuck in an office management position she quickly nicknamed "hell job." For a modest cover charge, she found a brief escape at CineMacabre.

At one show, she found a flyer promoting another *Rue Morgue* event: its annual Halloween party. The organizers were looking for go-go dancers. What did she have to lose?

After shaking her groove thang and meeting Gudiño at the party, she wound up doing some freelance work for the magazine before being hired as *Rue Morgue*'s assistant editor and first "Webmistress." In March 2007 she became associate editor.

It didn't take a lot of pushing to get Kuebler to call things the way she saw them in the very first pieces she submitted. "I wrote a column called 'Beneath the Cauldron of the Flesh' or something like that, essentially reviewing those softcore porno/horror films," she says. "Needless to say, it's easy to be very cutting about those movies because very few of them are any good whatsoever. For every one of those that's half-decent, you get seven that are just unwatchable."

Before long, she developed the magazine's horror literature beat, a natural extension of her own literary interests and experience.

At that time, *Rue Morgue* was tucked away in a 1920s-era movie theater that had been converted into office space at 700 Queen Street East. "Rod had an office with a door on it; Jovanka was in this weird old fireplace-looking room that didn't have a door on it. There were these insanely high movie theater ceilings, and then a loft area where the kitchen was. And in the back there was a little movie screening area. The rest was all open concept. So Gary and I sat in this little office space in the middle of this giant room. There were movie posters and props and toys all over it, but there was no place to grow in."

Monica S Kuebler, associate editor of *Rue Morgue*. The font Koobler (below) from Zang-O-Fonts is named after her.

AaBbCcDdEe

THE VUCKOVIC COMETH

Once *Rue Morgue* had passed its third year, Gudiño felt a little better about its future. He'd read that most new magazines go belly up in three years or less; by Year Three it was making enough to pay a few salaries, he says. "But in terms of the big picture, it wasn't making money until Year Seven."

However, there was a new wrinkle emerging.

For a while now, Gudiño had been thinking less about steering the magazine's editorial content and reviewing the hundreds of DVDs it accrued each year, and more about picking up a camera and making his own films.

That drive was there "even before I started the magazine," he

> "I can't think of anything better to do with my life than be able to read horror novels and write about them. That's pretty damn amazing as far as jobs go."
> —MONICA S KUEBLER

Jovanka Vuckovic succeeded Gudiño as editor in chief in 2006, bringing a new vibrancy to the tone of the magazine and its events.

admits. "The magazine is almost like a tool to make it easier for me to be a director." While he never developed a hard-and-fast plan for his moviemaking career, "I thought I can pursue a directing vision, and investors and studios won't care as much because they're not looking at me as a director, they're looking at me as a marketing entity."

In 2002, Jen Vuckovic, the woman who had won a subscription to *Rue Morgue* at FanTasia 1998, began helping Gudiño and company at horror conventions and other events. Since reading the magazine, she'd been impressed by the scope of its coverage, with pieces on everything from HP Lovecraft's nonfiction classic *Supernatural Horror in Literature* to the philosopher Søren Kierkegaard. "This was a thinking-person's genre magazine," she says. "We're all horror fans, we've all grown up. But magazines really haven't grown up with us."

If *Rue Morgue* was the odd magazine out on the newsstand, Vuckovic herself felt like its human equivalent—she was still trying to find her place in the world.

Born in Toronto in 1975 to Serbian parents, she quickly found her tastes did not run to the mainstream. As she wrote in a Dec. 5, 2006 entry on the magazine's blog, The Abattoir, "Though I've always been a writer and an artist, I've also been equally connected with the scientific side of my brain—and morbidity preoccupied both. I find science fascinating, along with death and dying."

During high school, she'd participated in a cooperative education program that placed her behind-the-scenes with the Ontario Provincial police. Later, at McMaster University in Hamilton, Ont., she studied forensic anthropology, but ultimately left it behind when she found herself unable to switch off her empathy for the dead people that came across the dissection table. "People told me tricks for getting past it, but they didn't work," she says.

Discouraged, she decided to engage the artistic side of her brain by trying her hand at creating visual effects for film. "Like all of the jobs I've gotten, I kind of dive into them headfirst without knowing what I'm doing."

Lying her ass off, she told her employers that she had experience, had lost her demo reel (damn!) and, most importantly, would work for nothing to prove herself.

"I'd go in late at night and I'd stay there all night until I figured out how to make the shot work," she says. "I'd be going through the tutorial guides and everything. By the time they came in the next morning, the shot would be finished but they didn't know I was there all night working on it. I totally faked it. But as I was faking it, I learned how to do it."

She worked on it all: sci-fi, a lot of made-for-TV flicks; she adopted pseudonyms such as Jen Tripp when she handled projects for the Canadian Broadcasting Corp. "I tried very hard to keep that part of my life not public," she says.

Then she went and let the cat out of the bag by winning a Gemini award for a 1999 CBC movie called *Must Be Santa*. "Much like *A Christmas Story* is now aired every year around Christmas time, because it was funded by the CBC, they will continue to air this film until the day I die," she says. "So I have [a **Gemini award**] in my living room at the bottom of a bookshelf somewhere, and sometimes people come over and say, 'Is that a fucking Gemini? Where'd you get that?' Then I've got to explain about this whole former life. Then they go, 'Whoah, what did you do before that?' Then their jaws drop when I tell them about the physical anthropology stuff. It's been an interesting ride so far."

Despite being constantly under-the-gun deadlinewise with her effects job, Vuckovic was also spending more time with Gudiño

DIDN'T JOVANKA VUCKOVIC HAVE ANOTHER NAME?

"When I first started at *Rue Morgue*, because my name is kind of complicated, I had said I have this nickname ["Jen"] that people sometimes call me, although I don't answer to it. Maybe I should just use it to make it easier on the readers. And Rod completely disagreed with me and told me I'd regret it.

"I used it for a year and I switched back because I think it was just too difficult. I never got used to that nickname. Besides, *Rue Morgue* was something that I was very proud of, unlike the visual effects stuff, and I wanted to put my name on this."

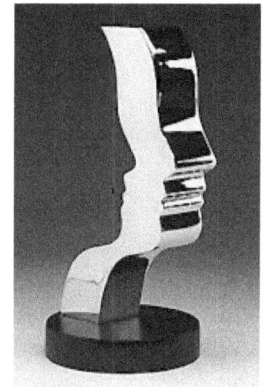

Gemini Award
The Canadian equivalent of the Emmys, the Gemini Awards are bestowed on what are considered the best television productions of a given year by the Academy of Canadian Cinema and Television.

> "I get up,
> I go to work,
> I make a
> magazine,
> I do it all for
> Satan."
>
> —— **JOVANKA VUCKOVIC**
> *quote from her MySpace page*

and the gang. Finally, confronting him with the dearth of women's bylines in the magazine, she offered to write something for him. A few months later, things got really weird.

"He sat me down at lunch and said, 'I want *you* to take over *Rue Morgue*,'" she remembers. "After I picked myself up off the floor, I was like, 'Why me? I don't know anything about magazine publishing!' He said, 'Yeah, but I'd rather hire somebody who's going to maintain the vision and the integrity of the magazine rather than an accomplished editor who's going to make decisions that are going to compromise the magazine.'"

Hands down that conversation was one of the hardest Gudiño's ever had at *Rue Morgue*, he says. "But the transitional process was a two-year process, and that made things easier for me and for her because, by the time the two years were up, I was definitely ready to get out." He was already planning his first short film: *The Eyes of Edward James*.

Vuckovic took over the reins with the January 2006 issue.

Since then, the magazine has gained an even more distinctive personality, thanks in large part to the way its stable of writers regularly savage the worst that cinema has to offer. Stuart F Andrews' issue 78 summation of indie film *Pop Skull* as being "a challenge to sit through...without hate-fucking the fast-forward button" remains a shining example of film criticism that *New Yorker* film critic Pauline Kael would've envied, however quietly.

The publication also has become even more eclectic, not only in the subject matter it covers—"monster cereals," horror hip hop, etc.—but also in the way it relates horror to the mainstream world. For example, where Gudiño used the editorial page "Note from Underground" to explore some of the more philosophical aspects of horror, Vuckovic often takes it as an opportunity to get at the darker elements of life itself.

Take issue 74, which featured a cover story on the 2007 adaptation of Jack Ketchum's *The Girl Next Door*. Coping with a personal

Rue Morgue founder Rodrigo Gudiño (left) directing a scene for his first short film, *The Eyes of Edward James*.

loss, she used that issue's "Note" to explore how watching *Girl*, easily one of the most punishing films of the last 20 years, resonated with the grief she was already feeling, and actually helped her to find some solace. Meditations followed on how growing up in the Serbian Orthodox tradition led her to adopt the watching of the slasher classic *Black Christmas* as an annual Yuletide tradition; the psychology behind her tattoos; and even the little-known arm-twisting that studio marketing departments engage in to try to get their latest projects on magazine covers.

Perhaps the most profound "Note" came in issue 69 which, oddly enough, sported an innocuous *Monster Squad* cover. In it she responded to a rape victim's letter asking why she (the letter writer) enjoys films that depict rape. Where most journalists would have conveniently left the letter at the bottom of the stack, Vuckovic tackled it head on. After addressing why many find rape in exploitation

> "I find it interesting that among some of the cruelest movies I've seen, like the *August Underground* films, the men behind the camera are some of the sweetest guys. [*August Underground* director, actor, writer] **Fred Vogel** is a big giant Teddy bear, yet he makes these horrible, punishing films."
>
> — VUCKOVIC

Fred Vogel
The driving force behind Pittsburgh's low-budget Toetag Pictures, Vogel first made waves directing and starring in the serial killer flick *August Underground* in 2001. Best described as Douglas Buck without the social commentary *(see sidebar, p. 167)*, Vogel has come by his splatter street cred honestly. In 2005, he was arrested in Canada on his way to *Rue Morgue*'s Festival of Fear convention for ferrying "obscene" materials into Canada, including *August Underground*. Charges were later dropped.

flicks so offensive, she concluded, "If you're slowly chipping away at the pain by allowing yourself to be with it (an actual technique used in cognitive therapy for post-traumatic stress disorder), you're loosening it, little by little, which isn't a bad thing."

Horror luminaries such as Steve Niles *(see p. 64)* bristle at the suggestion that dark works of the imagination are sometimes inspired by tortured childhoods or traumatic lives—a valid response to mainstream journalists' insistence on trying to oversimplify the complexities of life. But if we're completely honest with ourselves, a significant number of people who embrace dark films and culture are no strangers to tragedy themselves. The benefits of catharsis that can be derived from horror should not be so cavalierly dismissed.

In hindsight, Gudiño's replacement not only brought new life and purpose to the editorial page, the outgoing Vuckovic also brought to the table an engaging, extroverted personality that continues to charm directors, artists, readers and convention goers. She became the face of *Rue Morgue*.

NEW DIGS, NEW BLOOD

Change was clearly in the air in 2004. Gudiño was spending more time working on his film, Vuckovic had ditched her longtime nickname Jen for her given "Jovanka" (pronounced *Yo-VAHN-Ka*), and the CineMacabre movie night had moved to the Bloor Cinema to handle its swelling crowds.

Before the year was up, the magazine would host its first horror convention—the Festival of Fear—thanks to a savvy alliance with Hobbystar Marketing's FanExpo Canada.

In November, it also found itself a more permanent home in an enormous $800,000 Canadian, 8,000-square-foot vacant funeral home on Toronto's West side. "It can't be torn down because it's a historic building," Vuckovic wrote in an Abattoir entry. "Nor did the owners want to sell it as another funeral home because they own two others in the area and didn't want competition."

Quickly dubbed the *Rue Morgue* House of Horror, the former WM Speers Funeral Home—built in 1898—was retrofitted to house the growing arms of the *Rue Morgue* brand. While retaining its rows of pews, the chapel was converted into a screening room, the viewing room became office space for the magazine's editorial staff, etc. It has been the site of film viewings, a wedding and other unnatural rites.

The magazine was growing in other ways, too. Advertisers such as Columbia TriStar and Anchor Bay had been showing their support by taking out a healthy amount of advertising; a number of

The *Rue Morgue* House of Horror, formerly the WM Speers Funeral Home, was retrofitted to house the growing *Rue Morgue* brand in 2004.

high-profile film directors were anxious to talk to anyone who said they were calling from *Rue Morgue*; and the Rue Crew was gearing up to make the jump from bimonthly to 11-times-a-year come January 2005. Since Vuckovic would be moving up to the editor-in-chief position in about a year, it was vital that they find themselves a managing editor.

Gudiño and Vuckovic both had their eye on an Alberta freelancer who had been writing for the magazine for some time, but Dave Alexander really didn't want to make the 2,000-plus mile move.

"Mostly it was just being scared to change," Alexander says now. He turned the magazine's employment offer down twice. Yet when he found himself in Toronto to interview director Kevin Smith for *Spin* magazine about the episodes of *Degrassi High* he was shooting, he decided he had to meet the folks at *Rue Morgue* in person.

After spending three days with Gudiño, Kuebler, Vuckovic and Pullin, "I realized this would be a huge mistake if I didn't come out here. It was the family that I didn't know I had."

Dave Alexander getting to grips with genre-legend Robert Englund (or vice versa).

WITH FRIENDS LIKE THESE

From his experience covering Canada's music scene, Gudiño knew firsthand how difficult it can be covering a sector of the entertainment industry without "going native." He'd certainly seen it happen with the horror press.

Once he was on a horror movie set talking to a writer for another magazine. "He asked me if I'd seen this movie or that movie," Gudiño remembers. "I said, 'Well, did you like *this* horror movie?' And he said, 'Of course I liked it. It was a horror movie.'"

He laughs. "I thought to myself, Well, wow, there you go. That's it in a nutshell."

This attitude has a negative impact on the films that are actually made, he says. "One of the limitations of Hollywood, and one of the reasons I would never, ever run *Rue Morgue* out of Hollywood, is because you're friends with everybody. They're working in the business and 90 percent of them are making things that aren't very good. And if you're there with them, it's really going to compromise your integrity."

That's one of the reasons Gudiño rarely writes reviews anymore, Alexander says. "When you go away to conventions or film festivals and a lot of artists like the magazine and we're in contact with them, you end up building friendships in the industry, and you have to be careful to make sure you're still being fair and balanced. Ultimately you're accountable to the reader."

FROM MAGAZINE TO ARTIST COLLECTIVE

Though it's difficult to say when the transition took place, it was around this time that it became apparent that *Rue Morgue* was evolving from a magazine into something else.

Traditionally, an artist collective consists of people who work, and often exhibit, in a shared space. The resulting artworks usually benefit from the cross-pollination that occurs when creative people

> "There's a million bad horror movies that get made. We get to see a lot of what not to do and a lot of bad clichés and what to avoid and what's cheesy. On the flipside, we get to see some fantastic stuff that people outside of the horror genre have no idea exists because it's not opening at the local multiplex."
> —DAVE ALEXANDER

Burning Effigy Press
Rue Morgue associate editor Monica Kuebler co-founded Burning Effigy Press, which has published works of fiction by several writers including *Rue Morgue*'s Dave Alexander and Liisa Ladouceur.

work closely together, sharing ideas in the process.

With this iteration of the Rue Crew, each member was heavily involved in the pursuit of one art form or another in the handful of hours they didn't spend toiling away at the magazine.

A seasoned poet herself, Kuebler co-founded **Burning Effigy Press** in 1999 to produce chapbooks and anthologies of fringe poetry and prose. In January 2007, the press was relaunched to include a new focus on dark fiction, and scored its first coup a year later when Nicholas Kaufmann's chapbook, *General Slocum's Gold*, made it onto the final ballot for the Horror Writers Association's Bram Stoker Awards.

"I was like how can the very first horror thing I touch do that," Kuebler says, still amazed. "In a way it's kind of daunting. Now where do I go? Are any of the others ever going to live up to how well that book's done? I hope so."

Alexander and *Rue Morgue* copy editor Liisa Ladouceur have, respectively, a short-story chapbook and a collection of dark poetry slated to be published by Kuebler's press.

Former office manager Audra Jacombs and her husband are filmmakers. She also pitched in as production coordinator on Gudiño's second short, 2007's *The Demonology of Desire*.

Pullin continues to lend his trademark "ghoulish" style to everything from magazine covers and band posters to his own art prints and T-shirts. In 2008, he also delved into designing nightmares for the screen, beginning with a short film, *Fallow*, co-directed by Alberta-transplants Colin Landry and…Dave Alexander.

"We try to help each other achieve these artistic goals," Alexander says, "which is a good counterbalance for the amount of time and effort and energy that we pour into *Rue Morgue*. We talk all the time and we work on each other's stuff." In the case of *Fallow*, that extended to the magazine's graphic designer, Justin Erickson, working on the film's poster, and Kuebler's filmmaker husband, Brenton Bentz, producing.

Meanwhile, Vuckovic is writing a feature film screenplay for "a genre legend" who not only wants to produce it, but also wants her to direct it, she says. "It's my next career goal."

On the music scene, *Rue Morgue* started its own Internet radio station, *Rue Morgue* Radio, in 2005, hosted by the magazine's music critic, Tom "Tomb" Dragomir.

On and on it goes. Yet does all of this add up to a full-fledged artist collective?

"I think it might be developing more in that way as we've gelled as a team and gotten more efficient, so that we actually have time to do stuff outside of work time," Alexander says "We work crazy long hours, but everyone's got something on the go outside."

> "I don't need to watch someone being very graphically, very realistically dismembered. Maybe because I've had a lot of tragedy in my life and witnessed a lot of people near me suffering through near tragedy, maybe that's what has changed my ability to swallow that extremely realistic style."
>
> —KUEBLER

COVERING THE NEW HORROR

Since the emergence of region-free DVD players and the Internet, the number of horror films available to today's English-language audiences has grown considerably.

Though not adverse to running cover stories about big studio releases such as *Grindhouse* and Rob Zombie's *Halloween*, *Rue Morgue* has devoted a considerable number of covers and ink to fare rarely found at the local multiplex.

Take Spanish director **Nacho Cerdà**. If North American horror fans knew his name at all prior to the 2006 release of the English-language feature *The Abandoned*, chances are it was because of *Rue Morgue*. His films *Genesis* and *Aftermath*, part of a loose trilogy of shorts exploring death and mourning, were each given prime cover placement. Ditto a cover story package dedicated

Nacho Cerdà
The director's most intriguing film may be ahead of him. For such a sinister genre, horror films have relatively few conspiracies to call their own. Yet Cerdà's forthcoming documentary, *Coffin of Light*, looks at the 1970s Spanish cinematographer-turned-director Sergio del Monte, who was murdered just three days into the filming of his first feature.

to the short stop-motion works of Robert Morgan (*The Cat With Hands*), the Quay Brothers (*Street of Crocodiles*) and Jan Svankmajer (*Little Otik*).

One of the most interesting cover story choices came with issue 74 in December 2007: the just-about-straight-to-DVD release of *The Girl Next Door*.

Directed by Gregory M Wilson, this adaptation of Jack Ketchum's fictional treatment of the 1965 murder of 16-year-old Sylvia Likens is easily one of the most disturbing pieces of cinema to emerge in the last 20 years. Although aesthetically adventurous in its reimagination of 1950s Americana, and not overly gory (what does that even mean these days?), its depiction of the abuse and murder of its title character will stick with you long after viewing it. Coming as it did shortly after that year's *Captivity*, *Girl* provided an intriguing coda to the short-lived torture porn trend *(see p. 34)* for any publication willing to look at it in truly critical terms.

Kuebler's seven-page cover story tackled this "difficult to categorize gray area between 'horror' and 'drama,'" bringing to it an insight partially built on past research into the film's literary source material for previous *Rue Morgue* pieces.

The cover image Pullin and the editors chose was a sepia-

> "A lot of times... the studios don't give us too much to work with. Some of the images that we get are of people looking into the sky with their eyes wide open."
>
> —GARY PULLIN

toned close-up of the title character, eyes closed, with thin streaks of blood on her face. If nothing else, it is a near-perfect embodiment of the "beautiful bruise" New Horror aesthetic, where disturbing imagery is rendered in stark, beautiful colors, daring you to look away and to take it all in at once.

"It's a challenging cover for a lot of *Rue Morgue* readers," Pullin admits, and one that drew an unusually large number of complaints.

"They look at the image and it offends them, but they're buying a horror magazine."

Has *Rue Morgue* ever encountered content too extreme to publish?

"There was one movie called *Slaughtered Vomit Dolls*..." Pullin says. "They took out an ad but we had to censor it. We don't like censoring—what offends one person might not offend another. But when you've got a bloody vagina, that's probably not going to make it onto the cover of our magazine." [NHH]

PART THREE

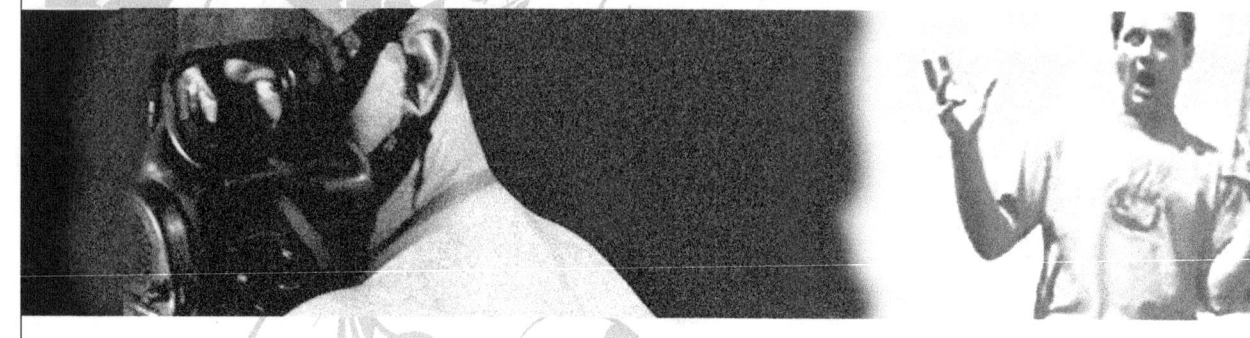

TOMORROW'S TERRORS

What keeps the New Horror "new" is the continuous influx of talent behind the camera, specifically those individuals who have grown up (or are even in the middle of growing up) on the classics of the genre.

One of the most inspiring examples of this is Austin filmmaker **Emily Hagins** (p. 190) who wrote, directed and distributed her first feature—a zombie flick called *Pathogen*—kicking the whole thing off at the age of 12. Fortunately for posterity, that entire filmmaking process was captured in a frank-but-funny documentary called *Zombie Girl: The Movie*.

In California, adventure-starved horror fan **Sean Clark** (p. 212) chucked a career in the mortgage industry (before the worldwide housing implosion) to pursue his hobby full time. With **Horror's Hallowed Grounds**, Clark tracked down the locations where several classic horror films were shot, often outwitting those who were less than sympathetic to what the *Phantasm* funeral home and the *Session 9* insane asylum mean to horror fans worldwide. Ultimately, he wrote and became the associate producer for 2008's **The Black Waters of Echo's Pond**.

Miami horror comic writer **Joe Monks** (p. 220) made the jump to directing horror flicks with **The Bunker**—a few years after he lost his eyesight to diabetes.

TERROR AT TWELVE

EMILY HAGINS

PART OF THE APPEAL OF HORROR FILMS LIES IN THE FEELING YOU GET THAT SOMEONE, SOMEWHERE WOULD BE UTTERLY MORTIFIED THAT YOU'RE WATCHING THESE SCENES OF IMAGINARY DEPRAVITY. AND IF THEY KNEW THAT CHILDREN WERE WATCHING IT? EVEN BETTER...

In 2003, 11-year-old Emily M Hagins and her mom parked themselves in the Alamo Drafthouse Cinema's downtown location for that year's Butt-Numb-A-Thon. The 24-hour film festival that Harry Knowles, founder of the Ain't It Cool News Web site, holds to celebrate his birthday each year is known for its eclectic mix of films, as well as for the extreme nature of some of those offerings.

But if Emily was the least bit rattled by the likes of Chan-wook Park's ultraviolent revenge thriller *Oldboy* or Alexandre Aja's splat-terific *Haute Tension*—just two of the gems screened that year—these weren't what she took away from the experience. No, it was *Undead*, that year's zombie comedy from Australia's Spierig brothers, that resonated with her days after the event.

"It was just a lot of fun," she says. The more she thought about it, the more the budding filmmaker realized that a zombie flick could make an impressive first feature.

Equal parts cinematic inspiration, video camera availability and unflagging family support spurred Emily to spend the next two years working on her own vision of a zombie apocalypse: *Pathogen*. During that time she would write, shoot, edit and distribute the film, all while going to school and learning the craft from the ground up. And in a thoroughly postmodern twist, she did all of this while an adult film crew covered her every move for a documentary project of their own.

Taken together, both *Pathogen* and the resulting documentary, *Zombie Girl: The Movie*, don't simply entertain, but offer a rare glimpse of the creative process unencumbered by the jaded industry posturing that rules the day.

'I HAD A 10-YEAR-OLD MAKING VATS OF FAKE BLOOD'

If Emily Hagins was destined to become a filmmaker, she couldn't have picked a better place to live than Austin, Texas.

> "When I was in junior high school, I went to class and played some sports but I wasn't very good, and I didn't really have any hobbies. I have no frame of reference for [Emily's movie making] other than doing homework and watching a lot of television."
>
> — JERRY HAGINS,
> *Emily's dad*

A comfortable distance from the rat race of Hollywood, the city has become something of a mecca for independent filmmakers. Those who don't come to study the craft at the University of Texas' Department of Radio-Television-Film or avail themselves of the studio space at **Austin Studios**, come to check out the South by Southwest (SXSW) film, music and interactive media festival held there each year.

Of course Austin is more famous for its vibrant music scene, which was one of the aspects that attracted Megan and Jerry Hagins to the area when they moved there in 1993 from Philadelphia shortly after Emily was born. Megan, now a graphic designer for the City of Austin, played guitar. Her husband, a spokesman for the Texas Department of Insurance, has been a student of traditional folk music —the banjo specifically—since his college days.

Emily was born on Oct. 27, 1992, an event preceded by a miscarriage and a scare that this pregnancy, too, would end in misfortune. The subsequent bond that formed between mother and daughter was a close one, and early on found its expression in a shared love of film. When she was in third grade, the pair started to go to the Alamo Drafthouse two or three times each week. By then, Emily had been dubbed "the Movie Girl" in school.

However, it wasn't until a year later that Emily picked up a movie camera for the first time. Hoping to cheer his daughter up when she was home sick from school one day, Jerry showed her how to make short films with the camera he'd just received from Megan that Christmas. Intrigued, she quickly adopted the equipment. "It's now referenced as my camera," Emily admits. "I feel bad about that."

Meanwhile, influences were everywhere; none more so than Peter Jackson's *Lord of the Rings* trilogy. Emily and Megan both fell in love with the films, haunting the Drafthouse to see them again and again. Mesmerized by Jackson's cinematic vision, the 10-year-old wrote the New Zealand director a letter. He replied soon after,

Austin Studios
In 2000, the Austin Film Society (of which Emily is a member), in cooperation with the City of Austin, converted airplane hangars on the grounds of the former Robert Mueller Municipal Airport into five production stages, now called Austin Studios. *The Texas Chainsaw Massacre* remake and *Grindhouse* are just two of the films shot there.

Emily Hagins sets up a shot for *Pathogen*.

thanking her for her kind words and telling her how nice it was to hear from someone in Austin where his American friend, Harry Knowles, lived. Soon, Emily and Knowles were in touch.

By this time, Emily had already made a handful of short films, most starring the family dog. Recognizing in Emily a kindred spirit, Knowles suggested she attend one of several camps that sought to introduce young people to filmmaking. Unfortunately at 10, Emily was still too young to qualify for any of them. Well connected with the area's film community, Knowles quickly got in touch with a friend and occasional contributor to Ain't It Cool News, filmmaker Rebecca Elliott.

"Harry was like, 'Hey, you've gotta check out this little girl's work,'" recalls Elliott, an Oklahoma native lured to Austin by its thriving film community.

Elliott and longtime filmmaking partner Jed Strahm were preparing to hold auditions for *Organic*, a movie about a "college grade-changing caper gone bad," Elliott says. She told Knowles that if Emily came by, she'd put her to work.

"She was very quiet and shy," recalls Elliott, who was in her mid-20s at the time. "But when people would come up to audition, Emily would hand them their scripts to read. And they're like, 'Who is this little child telling us what to do?'"

When it came time to start shooting, Elliott and Strahm invited her to the set. "I knew that she was a smart kid and was there to learn. There were jobs to be done, quite frankly," Elliott says, laughing. "I was like, 'Oh cool, free child labor—excellent!'"

Though they'd briefed **Emily's parents** about the script, *Organic* was still intended to be shot as an R-rated film, which made it difficult to have her on set for every scene. They opted instead to have her shoot some behind-the-scenes footage, which Emily later edited into a standalone DVD.

However, another job quickly emerged for Emily—mixing up three different varieties of fake blood for the shoot. "Sometimes you don't think about it when you're in the midst of this ridiculous project that's taking over your life," Elliott says. "Later, when you sit down and think about little things like that, you're like, 'I had a 10-year-old making vats of fake blood!'"

"Rebecca really treated Emily almost like a peer," Jerry Hagins recalls.

"It was a very good learning experience for me," Emily says, and one that would later influence how she ran her own movie set. While these experiences started her on the path to filmmaking, it would take Butt-Numb-A-Thon to light the match.

THE PATH TO *PATHOGEN*

Hoping to really give Emily and her mom a thrill, Knowles invited them to his annual all-day cinematic celebration in 2003. Crammed in amongst screenings of *Gingers Snaps: Unleashed* (see p. 116) and other flicks was a showing of the third *Lord of the Rings* film, *The Return of the King*, complete with a Q+A featuring Peter Jackson

Emily's parents
Jerry Hagins (above, with Emily) is still amazed at all that his daughter has accomplished so far. Though he admires her tenacity, he still wonders what made her think that it would all work out. "I guess no one told her it was impossible," he says. "I did have a theory about that, though this is probably kind of wacky. If you've ever watched kids television, a lot of it has kids in situations where it looks like things are impossible and they're told, 'Just don't give up, keep trying.' So they keep trying and, of course, they succeed because it's kids TV and it has happy endings. I think it suggests to kids that they really shouldn't give up." Below, Emily with her biggest fan, Megan.

and writers Frances Walsh and Philippa Boyens.

"That's why he let me go—I was such a *Lord of the Rings* dork," Emily says. But Jackson's tight schedule, a mob of *Rings* fans and Emily's own shyness prevented her from talking to Jackson that day.

That year's festival wasn't all hobbits and wizards.

"Regularly at Butt-Numb-A-Thon, we show really offensive stuff," admits Alamo founder Tim League. "I remember Harry and I actually saying, 'Oh shit, Emily's here.' We were like, 'Well, her mom knows what this [festival] is, so she's just gonna have to have a little desensitization today.' And that she did."

One of the treasures dug up for that year's festival was 1967's exploitation tale about a 15-year-old girl who sleeps around called ***Teenage Mother*** (with the tagline, "Means 9 months of trouble"). While it's pretty tame fare for the most part, it does end with a video of a real childbirth, complete with episiotomy, and the audience has the front-row seat.

Elliott was at the festival and remembers, "That was the one that I literally looked back—I just had to see Emily's expression. She's just wide-eyed, and her mom's sound asleep beside her."

Yet the 11-year-old's real education came courtesy of Butt-Numb-A-Thon's showing of *Undead*. "I was terrified of all horror movies and anything scary" up to that point, Emily says. *Undead* changed all that.

As every beginning filmmaker does, Emily quickly took stock of her assets. "We're not rich, that's the first thing I should point out," Emily says. But the Hagins family had acquired a second video camera by this point, a Hi8, and she had a few friends. Instant cast, she thought. Quickly she learned that friends and work rarely mix.

This is confirmed to a certain extent in a scene from *Zombie Girl: The Movie* in which Emily sums up her own philosophy about tackling *Pathogen* with Yoda's piece of wisdom from *The*

Teenage Mother
Though *Undead* was the movie at Butt-Numb-A-Thon 5 that most affected Emily Hagins, there was no shortage of impressive content at that screening. One that stands out for filmmaker Rebecca Elliott was the 1967 exploitation flick *Teenage Mother*, which features a real-life episiotomy scene. "That was the one that I literally looked back," Elliott says. "I just had to see Emily's expression."

Butt-Numb-A-Thon 5 (2003) lineup also included:
* *Haunted Gold*
* *The Lord of the Rings: The Return of the King*
* *The General*
* *Oldboy*
* *Ginger Snaps: Unleashed*
* *Haute Tension*
* *The Rotten Fruit*
* *The Passion of the Christ*

The 2003 Australian film *Undead*, written and directed by Michael and Peter Spierig, not only gave Emily an appreciation for horror movies, but inspired her to make her own.

Empire Strikes Back: "Try not. Do or do not. There is no try."

"It just doesn't work," she admits. With the exception of Alec Herskowitz who plays Sam, her friends proved extremely difficult to direct. One person in particular, the last to be jettisoned from the production, proved particularly tricky. "We had to keep reshooting because she'd change her hair," Emily says. "She had really long hair and then she cut it really short. Then she dyed it black. We just had to keep starting over. Finally, I had to say we couldn't keep doing that, and I had to tell her that we were going to have to hold auditions. We weren't friends anymore. Our friendship was kind of not so good by then anyway." It didn't help matters that the girl's house was being used for some of the scenes.

Frustrated, Emily placed an open audition call on AustinActors.net for a new crop of actors.

"That's when I realized *[Pathogen]* was going to move forward and move forward really quickly," Megan says. "From that point on, I think it was carved in stone."

> "I really don't want to do chick flicks. I guess I want to make movies that have good stories above all else, and I've never really seen a chick flick with a phenomenal story."
> ——EMILY

POSTMORTEM

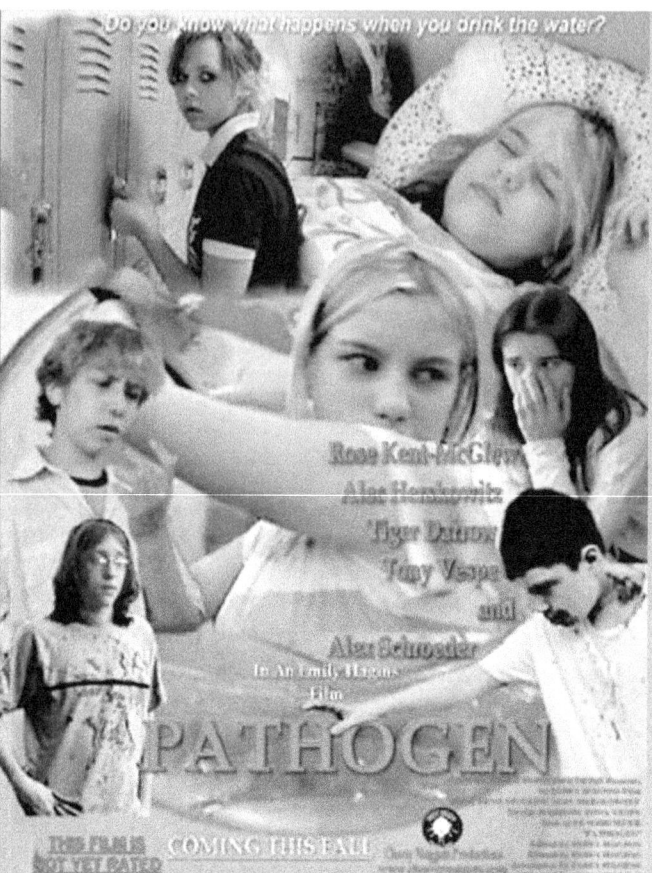

PATHOGEN

However interesting you find the origins of *Pathogen*, there comes a time when you have to get past all that, sit back and watch the thing. And that's where the problems begin.

That's because whatever you take away from this tale of an experimental cancer cure that seemingly touches off an epidemic of worldwide zombifications is entirely dependent on the frame of mind you bring to it. This is not a skilled-but-somber meditation on the follies of human existence, but a first time feature directed on a shoestring by a 12-year-old. If you haven't come looking for a lighthearted good time, you're watching the wrong movie. As director Emily Hagins told the crowd at *Pathogen*'s premiere in 2006, "If you seriously think something is funny...feel free to laugh because it's *funny*."

And there *are* funny moments. Occasionally these are down to times when the script's action runs headlong into its $7,000 budget: a nanotechnology research lab bearing a laser printed paper sign that reads "Nanotech Lab," for example.

The acting, too, is remarkably all over the place, though first-timers Tony Vespe as smart ass slacker Cameron and Alex Schroeder as the doomed Stacy turn in notable performances considering their lack of experience. It's at this point you have to remind yourself the average age of the actors in this movie is about 13.

This all leaves professional actress Tiger Darrow in the unusually awkward position of sticking out like a sore thumb precisely because of her acting expertise. Oddly, by the halfway point, this actually begins to work in *Pathogen's* favor as the whole movie takes on the feel of a *Simpsons* Treehouse of Horror episode.

As Austin film critic (and *Pathogen's* on-screen janitor) Christopher Cargill observed in the documentary *Zombie Girl: The Movie*, perhaps the most interesting part of this whole film is that "Here's zombie movies through the eyes of a 12-year-old girl."

(L to r): Aaron Marshall, Erik Mauck and Justin Johnson recorded the making of Emily's movie *Pathogen*, paring down about 147 hours of video into the documentary *Zombie Girl: The Movie*. Says Marshall, "When on set, I would usually hang back, suggesting shots or interviewing Emily while Justin and Erik shot the interview. Unless it was a day where we wanted to shoot with three cameras, like the *Pathogen* premiere. There I chose to take the camera that stayed on Emily the whole day—she's hard to keep up with!"

DUELING CAMERAS

Filmmakers Erik Mauck and Justin Johnson were working across town at Austin's cable access channel—the former in its equipment room, the latter teaching camera classes—when they first saw Emily's AustinActors.net posting.

At the time, they also hosted the channel's show *Between the Scenes*, which covered the making of local indie films. It didn't take them long to see the potential for a feature-length documentary about a 12-year-old girl directing her own movie.

The pair met Emily and her parents in March 2005, Johnson says. The next month, they shot their first interviews with the family on a couple of Sony DSR-PD170 MiniDVs, and set out on a nearly four-year odyssey that would try the patience and stamina of everyone involved.

In the summer of 2005, the pair was introduced to film editor Aaron Marshall by a mutual friend. Together as codirectors, all three set out to capture every phase of Emily's venture.

For the next year and a half, that's just what they did, Johnson says. "And I would say about three months into shooting, we knew

Emily was 12
In August 2005, Emily became the youngest recipient of a $1,000 Texas Filmmakers Production Fund grant.

Tiger Darrow
The actress also helped Emily design a couple of posters for *Pathogen (see p. 198)*. "I have one of the misprints where at the top it says, 'Do you know *know* what happens when you drink the water,'" Emily says. "It always makes me laugh."

Record sound
After reading about *Pathogen* on the Ain't It Cool News Web site, professional sound editor Tim Rakoczy (who handled sound for the *Planet Terror* portion of *Grindhouse* as well as *Sin City*) volunteered to help with the film's sound. "We looked him up and we're like, 'Oh wow, awesome!'" Emily says. "He did a really great job."

this was going to be a story about Emily and her mom."

In particular, they picked up on the tremendous amount of support that Megan provided for the production.

"Since **Emily was 12** at the time, her mom had to take on an enormous responsibility in terms of putting everything together because Emily was a kid, so she didn't really have any organizing skills," Johnson says. "Sometimes when we're just organizing short films even now after doing this stuff for eight or 10 years, I still miss stuff and screw up a schedule. She's 12 and having 15 people show up on a certain day. Just that alone, I think, would be hard to do at that age."

Emily is all too aware of her limitations in this department, she says. "I was trying to balance all of these things and I would forget things. I really needed somebody to contact actors and crew and let them know what changes there were because that was always the last thing on my mind. I'd call people the night before and be like, 'Hey, can you come tomorrow,' and it sounds so bad and it's so unprofessional. Especially when people are working for free, that just makes them not want to do it. I would think about props and location and script and all that stuff, and make sure everything else was ready, and then I'm like, 'Oh wait, I need actors!'"

Emily also was teaching herself the filmmaking craft as she went. She'd replaced most of her friends with a handpicked cast, including local professional actress **Tiger Darrow**, Emily's father Jerry as a bureaucrat, and one-time mentor Rebecca Elliott as scientific researcher Sue.

Figuring out how to **record sound**—already one of the greatest challenges that filmmakers face—became a great deal harder as the shoot went on. She planned to record sound separately via a makeshift boom mic—a shotgun mic taped to a long paint roller—but hit a snag when the camera they were using for sound was stolen during a home burglary. "Luckily, our house is pretty cluttered so they didn't steal our main camera," Emily says. "It was hidden under a bunch of papers and stuff on the table."

TENACITY

After about six months, the tensions already inherent in film production were multiplied on both sides. Emily and her parents were stretched thin by the day-to-day challenges of meeting a rigorous shooting schedule around work and school hours. Mauck and Johnson were walking the documentarian's tightrope between honoring their subjects' wishes and remaining close enough to get those perfect shots, even if it meant intruding on the Hagins' lives a bit more than they had anticipated.

"It was a little intimidating because their cameras were so much bigger than mine," Emily says. "And it was a little frustrating sometimes because I'd be having trouble putting the tripod together or something like that, and they'd be standing 4 inches from my face with the camera. I was like, 'Ah, just help me!'"

Says Mauck, "It's been my experience in making documentaries that no matter how much you try to prepare people for how intense it's going to be, it's not until you actually get in there and start being there for every moment of their lives that things start happening. It's never what they think it's going to be."

A type of cat-and-mouse game emerged in which the subjects of the documentary would try to stay a step or two ahead of the documentary makers. "I think there were times where they were like, 'If we don't want them to film, we just better not say anything about it,'" Johnson says.

Normally accommodating, Emily and Megan had their own hands full trying to get all the footage they needed in the small amount of time Megan could take off work. Where first-time feature makers such

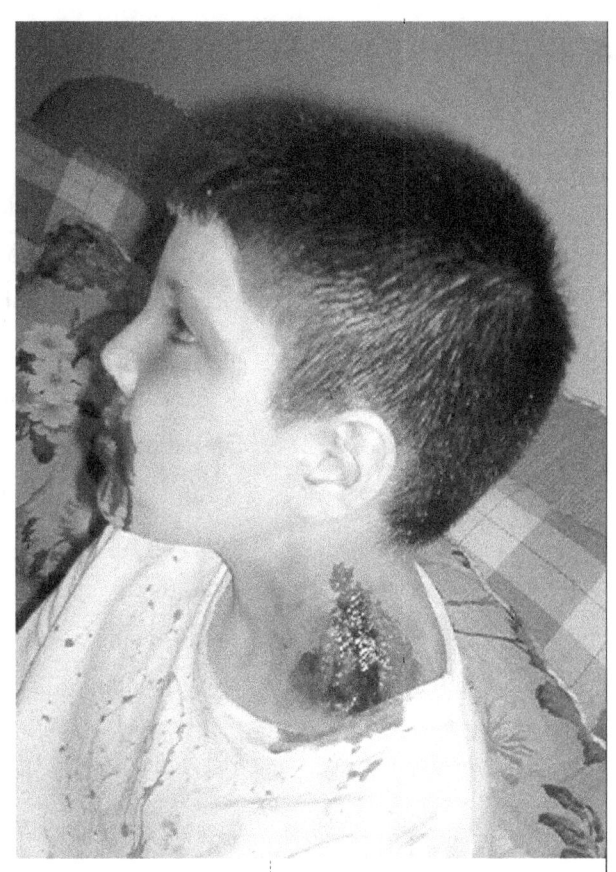

Emily put a lot of what she learned mixing blood on the set of Rebecca Elliott's movie *Organic* to good use for her own *Pathogen*.

The original downtown location of the Alamo Drafthouse closed in June 2007 after its 10 year lease ended and the rent for the next 10 years was raised significantly, founder Tim League says.

as Vincenzo Natali *(see p. 78)* struggle to keep their debut projects in a single, controllable location, Emily was determined to broaden the scope of *Pathogen* to include many locations—a doctor's office, a hospital, her own school, the local IGA grocery store—to give it the feel of an entire city, and possibly the world, facing annihilation by the zombie plague. Naturally, this required many locations, which multiplied the work necessary to keep it all straight.

By June 2005, nearly all principal photography had been completed on *Pathogen*. From Day One, the filmmaker had envisioned a climactic battle between her hero, Dannie (Rose Kent-McGlew) and a horde of flesh-eating zombies. Now she and Megan had managed to talk a local grocery store into letting them shoot the confrontation inside its doors, with the final showdown right outside. There was just one more thing she needed.

"She was pretty adamant about having a crane shot," Elliott recalls. It so happened that one of Elliott's filmmaking partners, Neil Reece, had fabricated a camera crane. "Once Emily found out she had access to something that could launch a camera 20 feet in the air, she was on board."

The taping of this climactic scene, complete with crane shot, saw Emily and her mostly-zombified cast shooting well into the night, with groups of increasingly sleep-deprived parents hanging out in the parking lot, waiting to whisk the actors home the moment the director shouted "cut." But the next day she made a discovery that pretty much yanked the rug out from under her.

"We were about to have this big wrap party and my mom asked me to check the tape," Emily remembers. "I'd left the tape in from the night before. That was that big day of filming at the grocery store and I hadn't locked the tape—we had recorded over about 15 minutes of footage. So at the big wrap party I had to tell them that we had to go back and reshoot. It was kind of like, 'I've just got to get through this, we're so close to finishing.' It was such a big shoot."

Unfortunately, one of the extras she had recruited for the previous night's scene had left quite a bit of fake blood in the store's bathroom, freaking out the management who thought someone had truly hurt themselves. After much apologizing, the group was allowed to reshoot the scene there.

"Over that year and a half she never gave up," Megan says. "She sat down and cut the whole movie together in one week, while I was at work during the summer."

On March 25, 2006, *Pathogen* premiered at the Alamo Drafthouse, less than three years after—and at the same venue—that Emily had seen *Undead*.

On its last night, "They showed the movie *Earthquake* and they rigged the theater so whenever there's an earthquake in the movie, the theater would shake and things were falling off the tables and ceiling tiles were falling," Emily recalls. "They literally tore it apart on closing night. We took our seats from the theater and threw them in our backyard." The Alamo reopened at its new location in November that same year.

Along with Emily's family and the rest of the cast, Rebecca Elliott, aka *Pathogen*'s Researcher Sue, also was there to see just »206

> "She did not rule with an iron fist. She's very effective. She doesn't get too excited. She's always had that quality about her, which is a really good quality to have in those high stress situations, especially dealing with your parents. Can you imagine making a film and then having to deal with your parents the whole time?"
>
> —— REBECCA ELLIOTT, *filmmaker, about Emily's directorial style on* Pathogen

POSTMORTEM

There are many reasons people settle down with a horror-themed film; life affirmation usually isn't one of them. But *Zombie Girl: The Movie* isn't like other documentaries.

In this day of DVD featurettes, "making of" documentaries are nothing new. But interviews and footage of the director on set usually amount to little more than slick PR pieces for the films they're packaged with. If the creative process is anywhere to be seen, it's dwarfed by the director's own oft-repeated shaggy dog stories and a budget that could pay for *Pathogen* five times over.

If *Zombie Girl* succeeds, it does so for two reasons. First, its structure follows that of the classic hero's journey popularized in the 1980s by mythology scholar Joseph Campbell. The movie opens on a shot of a wide-eyed but nervous Emily Hagins naively outlining her plans for *Pathogen*, and ends with her post-*Pathogen* victory. During the 80-plus minutes in between, we see her tackle challenge after challenge, from drumming up extras for the film's climax to trying to convince her father that she has to film in the street because zombies always walk in the street.

Secondly, it is nearly impossible not to root for the young director. Perhaps there is a scene of Emily angry, spiteful, petulant or rude in the 140-plus hours of *Zombie Girl* footage that was left on the cutting room floor, but we never glimpse those here. During the tensest moments of what was a nearly two-year ordeal, we see a young girl thoroughly in

> "There was a movie that Emily saw, I don't remember what it was...but I remember her talking about how they just want to show these girls screaming and all this stuff. And I was like, 'You *did* miss out on the whole slasher thing. You were 2.'"
>
> — **JUSTIN JOHNSON,** *co-director,*
> Zombie Girl: The Movie

control of herself and capable of defusing difficult situations rationally, with overworked parents on one side, and an overworked group of hyper under-15s on the other.

There are many approaches that filmmakers Justin Johnson, Erik Mauck and Aaron Marshall could've taken. What they ended up with is a piece that's often light-hearted yet never disrespectful of what Emily and her crew are trying to pull off. The two film crews' journey is a joint one, something all involved seem to quietly acknowledge.

Emily's mother Megan frequently is singled out for praise for the amount of time and energy she expended helping her daughter with *Pathogen*, and her efforts are on great display here. Special effects artist, props procurer, boom mic operator, craft services provider, not to mention fellow movie enthusiast, all while holding down a full-time job. Not as often recognized is her father, Jerry. If Emily inherited her love of film and her artistic streak from her mother, it becomes clear in *Zombie Girl* that she gained her concentration and unflappability from her father.

If you harbor the slightest interest in making movies, you may just find yourself digging out the old video camera after watching *Zombie Girl*.

And if Emily looks familiar, chances are good that you probably saw someone remarkably similar in childhood mirrors back when the word "no" was still a challenge rather than a life sentence.

«203 how far the little girl who had once mixed her stage blood had come.

"I made a deal a long time ago with all of my collaborators that I would never appear on camera ever again," Elliott says. "For Emily? I'm like, 'Oh sure, it's for Emily. She's 12. No one's ever going to see this.' Flash forward a year later and I'm staring at myself on the big screen at the Alamo Drafthouse, just kind of shaking my head. Good idea, Rebecca. Researcher Suuuue."

ZOMBIE GIRL

Despite *Pathogen's* full-circle premiere at the Alamo Drafthouse, and even the sale of more than 500 copies of the *Pathogen* DVD, everyone involved with the production knew that the journey wasn't yet complete.

For a year and a half, Mauck, Johnson and Marshall had orbited Emily and the production continuously, yet *Zombie Girl* would not be completed until August 2008.

"The edit itself took about two years," says Marshall, who cut down about 147 hours of footage into a slim 91-minute feature. "The story itself was fairly obvious. It was a matter of finding ways of pulling the story out of what we had to work with."

During that time, the movie editor, now in LA, also helped run commercial auditions and tackled other editing jobs, including the assembly edit for Mitchell Lichtenstein's 2007 horror comedy, *Teeth*.

Meanwhile, Johnson had moved to St. Louis in November 2006, which left Mauck alone in Austin, where he still occasionally bumped into Emily at Drafthouse shows, and even saw her at South by Southwest in 2008.

Finally, on Sunday, Sept. 21, 2008, *Zombie Girl* had its world premiere at Fantastic Fest at the Alamo Drafthouse's new location.

Johnson, Mauck and Marshall spent hours hanging up posters and chatting to potential moviegoers that weekend to ensure a decent size crowd for their 4:30 PM premiere. Whatever they did, it

SOUTH BY SOUTHWEST

Ever on the lookout to see new movies and get up close to filmmakers, Emily volunteered at 2008's South by Southwest, and ended up taking care of some of the festival's film panels. Part of that involved telling panelists when they were nearing the end of their speaking time. "Harry [Knowles] was on a panel with Harlan Ellison," Emily says. "Because I know Harry, I went up there and said, 'I'll give you a five minute signal for when you're getting close to the end of the panel.' He said, 'Yeah, I'm not going to listen to you.' And the panel ran two hours over. It was a long day."

Zombie Girl: The Movie, the documentary about Emily's moviemaking efforts, premiered at Fantastic Fest 2008 at the Alamo Drafthouse, the very same place that Emily was first inspired to embark on her moviemaking career.

worked: About 150 of the theater's 185 seats were filled. The second screening pulled 55. "It doesn't sound like a lot, but most of the films that had a lot of people were the ones where there was some sort of buzz going," Johnson says. "Ours I don't think too many people had heard of." To put it in perspective, this was the same 2008 festival that saw the US premieres of Darren Lynn Bousman's *Repo! The Genetic Opera* and Pascal Laugier's *Martyrs*.

A film festival frequently belongs to the directors of narrative film, more so genre festivals such as Fantastic Fest. Yet there were a few moments during the two showings of *Zombie Girl* that really impressed Johnson and company.

Probably the biggest audience reaction *Zombie Girl* received came during a moment when Emily, on her way to *Pathogen*'s premiere, says she would never release her films over and over again like George Lucas does. "The entire theater burst out into this huge applause," Johnson says. "I'd shown the film to many people before and that was never really a moment where I'd ever gotten any reaction from anybody. But it was a genre fest and all of these people had probably bought the *Star Wars* series hundreds of times. You

'THE ELIJAH WOOD STORY'

This is probably the weirdest thing that happened to us. The whole time we were shooting Emily and Megan, they always talked about how they loved *Lord of the Rings* and that's what got Emily started in making movies. She loved Elijah Wood. Right around the time of Emily's 13th birthday, we'd pretty much been shooting for about seven months.

It was going to be her birthday party and we decided to go and not bring cameras, but bring a present and come as friends, which ended up being one of the biggest mistakes we made as filmmakers.

She had her birthday party at this Pedazo Chunk Video Store. Harry Knowles was there. (It's his sister's store.) And I guess Elijah Wood [was in] Austin and knew the girl who owned the video store, and was just going to come by to see if she wanted to get dinner later.

Wood walks in on Emily's birthday party and all these kids start freaking out. The whole time I'm thinking, "Of course this would be the one time we don't bring a camera." I just had to walk outside because everything else that happened from then on was just footage that I was seeing that we weren't getting.

We hadn't really talked to Emily's dad that much, and he came outside and was like, "Well, now you've got a story to tell."

—JOHNSON

couldn't even hear what she said afterwards because people were clapping for 20 seconds. Me and Erik kind of looked at each other and were like, 'This is really wild.'"

However, there was another scene that really seemed to move members of the audience. Emily is standing at the front of the old Alamo Drafthouse introducing *Pathogen* before its premiere and the camera cuts to Megan, beaming with pride. "Later on, I had heard a lot of people were crying during that portion of the film," Johnson says. "I went back up to that theater later that night and one guy said it was the only film at Fantastic Fest that ever made him cry."

The Hagins family was pretty impressed with *Zombie Girl* for the most part. All three of them had actually seen the documentary prior to its premiere, but seeing it in a theater full of people on the big screen was its own odd experience.

"I look at it in different ways," Emily says. "From a totally me perspective it's like, 'Wow, I said that? That was really dumb. I totally take that back.' That's every couple of minutes, just totally embarrassed. I think nobody's really gonna remember that in the long run. But now all those really dumb things that I said when I was 12 and 13, they're on film forever.

"From the perspective of pretending it's not me, I see there are some things I did wrong on *Pathogen* that I did wrong on *The Retelling* [her next feature], too, so I'm trying to figure out ways that those things don't go wrong again."

For Megan's part, there's at least one tense scene between Megan and Emily captured in *Zombie Girl* that cracks her up. "I don't think I came across as very nice," she laughs. "But I don't think they focused on the things I was reacting to. There was some goofing off on the parts of the kids. It was also a little difficult because I was taking time off from work or had to get up early and work in the morning, and it was hard to have any time wasted because of that. But I enjoyed the movie. I thought it was very entertaining."

Right after that scene, *Pathogen* lead Rose Kent-McGlew

"It was kind of surreal to see the events unfold once again three years later," says Researcher Sue herself, Rebecca Elliott (above), about the *Zombie Girl* premiere. "I was again reminded just how long the entire process actually was from that first meeting I had with Em' all the way to the premiere at the Alamo, and now this latest premiere rounding out the saga. It also made me thankful again for being a part of such a unique experience."

Pathogen star Rose Kent-McGlew nearly steals the show in the behind-the-scenes documentary *Zombie Girl: The Movie*.

describes the tension of that moment between mother and daughter being thick enough to cut with a knife.

"Megan did tell me that she went up to Rose after the movie and told her, 'I hope you don't think I was mad about what you said,'" Johnson says.

Meanwhile, Jerry found the film to be a very inspiring piece of work. "Of course it's a little sobering to see your own life and family and household in a film, with the dog barking and a messy living room and stuff like that. But looking past that, it would be a documentary that I would want to see if I didn't know any of the people involved."

As the *Handbook* was going to press, Emily was hard at work finishing up post-production on her second feature. *The Retelling* is based loosely on the Japanese folktale of **Hoichi the Earless**, perhaps best known for its inclusion in the 1964 classic *Kwaidan*.

Having learned her lesson with the paint-roller boom mic, Emily rented professional sound equipment and had a dedicated sound person this time around: fellow sophomore Leo Schuster. "He read five different sound books and really worked his butt off to know the equipment before we filmed," she says. "It sounds great."

Hoichi the Earless
Megan lived in Japan for a couple of years before she and Jerry were married. When Emily was trying to come up with a story for her next film project, Megan lent her a book of Japanese folktales, which included the story of *Hoichi the Earless*. In that tale, priests try to protect a blind minstrel, Hoichi, from the attentions of some music loving ghosts by covering him from head to toe with Japanese writing, rendering him magically invisible. However, a ghost glimpses Hoichi's ears, the only body parts not covered by the writing, and rips them off.

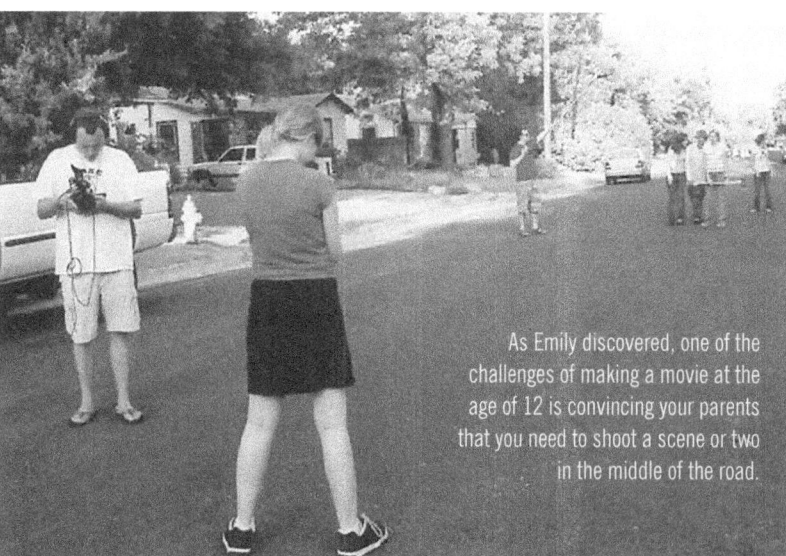

As Emily discovered, one of the challenges of making a movie at the age of 12 is convincing your parents that you need to shoot a scene or two in the middle of the road.

Like her first film, this one came in at around $7,000, with a massive garage sale pulling in about $750 alone, and a $10-per-ticket fund-raiser at the Alamo Drafthouse's South Lamar location bringing in another $800. Thus is the life of the low-budget filmmaker.

"I'm just trying to get as much done as I can" before school starts, the filmmaker says, one eye firmly on her first festival submission deadline. "Both my editors are home schooled, so that's good."

For nearly four years now, Emily Hagins has been the poster child for the plucky, resourceful independent filmmaker. She's also read quite a few newspaper, magazine—and now book chapter—leads that play her age above her accomplishments.

"I'm OK with that now because it's helping me reflect on the experience," she says. "But I hope with the next couple of movies I make, it will be more about the movie instead of my age." [NHH]

> "I don't want to do horror movies forever. My new one, I kept telling people, 'It will *not* be a horror movie, I'll do something different.' And then with *The Retelling*, I liked the story so much, it kind of is a horror movie."
>
> — EMILY

FROM FANDOM TO FILMDOM

SEAN CLARK

IN 2005, SOME THREE YEARS BEFORE THE CREDIT CRUNCH AND MORTGAGE MELTDOWN TAG-TEAMED THE WORLD ECONOMY INTO SUBMISSION, AN LA-AREA LOAN OFFICER DITCHED HIS DAY JOB TO INDULGE HIS LIFETIME PASSION FOR HORROR...

State Lunatic Hospital
Says Clark of his Danvers asylum visit, "It was pitch black in there; all the windows were boarded up. If you shut your flashlight off, you couldn't see your hand an inch from your face. The scariest part is you could be walking on the 6th floor down a hallway and look into a room that's collapsed six stories down, and you're looking all the way down to the bottom."

Though Sean Clark recently broke into the film world by rewriting much of the script and shooting second-unit for a horror feature called *The Black Waters of Echo's Pond,* it is as a guide to scare cinema's greatest locations that he first caught fans' attentions. From the real-life settings for the eerie waterfront of *The Fog's* Antonio Bay to *Halloween's* fictional Haddonfield, Ill., Clark has explored, written about and photographed them all, whisking hundreds of horror fans along for the ride.

HALLOWED BE THY NAME

It was dark that night, and cold. The 24-hour security truck had passed on down the service road in front of the abandoned **State Lunatic Hospital** in Danvers, Mass. Sean Clark and his friends watched it slip into the darkness from their hiding places behind the bushes, before hitting the ground running for the first wall that stood between them and the eerie institution that had been the setting for the 2001 classic *Session 9*.

"Every step you take out there, you step on a leaf and it's like *crunch*," he remembers to this day. "Everything seems so exaggeratedly loud."

Knowing the local sheriff's office is less than a mile away didn't help matters. Still, he knew they were all in good company. *Session 9* writer/director Brad Anderson *(Transsiberian, The Machinist)* had allegedly slipped into the legendary 313,00-square-foot structure urban-explorer style to see it all for himself prior to making his movie.

Clark's nighttime raid on Danvers was a far cry from the paper pushing he'd done for some 15 years in the mortgage business prior to hanging up his calculator permanently at 35. Though he already had three small, horror-film-related businesses going on the side at that time, what he'd really been hankering to do was to break into horror films.

Growing Up with Horror

Sean Clark's mother and father were pretty young when they had him—17 and 18, respectively—he points out, and pretty heavy into horror films themselves. As a result, some of his earliest memories revolve around seeing *The Texas Chainsaw Massacre* and *The Exorcist* in theaters when he was 4 or 5. "We were living in a friggin' trailer park in Anchorage, Alaska," he says. "They couldn't afford babysitters, so they took me."

Even as his parents outgrew the genre and the family moved to California when Clark was 6, his mother still took him and his friends to any flick they wanted to see, often against the ticket sellers' advice. Once his mother was running late, so her son and his friends tried to buy tickets to *Friday the 13th Part IV* at the local mall, only to get booted into a showing of *Romancing the Stone* instead. "I was like, 'We've seen every one of these damn movies, give us a break,'" Clark recalls. "Of course we ended up going to see it later, but I remember having to sit through *Romancing the Stone* pissed off."

Horror's Hallowed Grounds
Clark spun his love of horror films and filming locations into *Horror's Hallowed Grounds*, an online feature that takes readers to some of the most familiar landmarks in American horror movie history.

Moustapha Akkad
Syrian-born Moustapha Akkad, who executive produced every *Halloween* film from the original to 2002's *Halloween: Resurrection*, was killed in November 2005 as the result of injuries he sustained when a suicide bomber blew himself up at the Grand Hyatt in Amman, Jordan.

"I finally decided that if I'm seriously going to pursue filmmaking, I've got to dedicate my life to it," he says. "I've already got my hand in so many cookie jars, I can't have a 9-to-5 job on top of everything else."

There was no question that living in Los Angeles improved his chances of getting behind the camera, but that first great door-opening deal had so far eluded him. It would be one thing if he'd simply never managed to get his foot in the door, he says, but "I could sit here and tell you story after story of people who have looked me in the eye and said, 'This is a done deal,' and then it just falls apart."

He first hit upon the idea of visiting the real-life settings of great horror films back in the mid-1990s when he made *Halloween the Retrospective*. He went out, shot contemporary footage of the first film's locations, and edited in some clips from the movie for reference.

"It's funny how that video made the rounds," he says. "People were getting 10th generation copies. I actually got a guy who contacted me [in 2004]—he tracked me down. He's like, 'I want to interview you on my college radio show about this film you did.' And I'm like, 'You have no idea what has happened since then.'"

What had happened was that Clark had developed his film-location obsession into a television/blog concept called *Horror's Hallowed Grounds*. At the time he was trying to develop it as a TV series for The Horror Channel, an on-again/off-again American cable channel. "I don't want to say it was a waste of my time because it motivated me," he says.

FERTILE *GROUNDS*

Clark had done some work on the official documentary *Halloween: 25 Years of Terror*, when he had the opportunity to pitch the idea of a slicker version of his *Retrospective* to Malek Akkad, son of the late *Halloween* executive producer **Moustapha Akkad**.

Akkad loved the idea and gave him three weeks to make it happen. The resulting 24-minute short was edited down to a slick 17 minutes and included on the DVD.

In the meantime, things were getting sticky with The Horror Channel, whose representatives were starting to suggest they owned part of the *Horror's Hallowed Grounds* idea. Over the next several months, Clark bounced around from horror Web site to horror Web site until he landed at BloodyDisgusting.com.

Throughout all of this upheaval, he had been traveling to horror film locations around the country, posting contemporary photos of the sites alongside stills from the corresponding movies on which-

Here are just *some* of the film locations that Clark has visited over the years:
The Fog
The Texas Chainsaw Massacre
Friday the 13th
Poltergeist
The Amityville Horror
The Lost Boys
Dawn of the Dead

During his *Horror's Hallowed Grounds* career, Clark infiltrated the *Phantasm* cemetery (above) and the *Nightmare on Elm Street* house (below). He also shot a 17-minute short for *Halloween: 25 Years of Terror*, including an interview with PJ Soles (right) on the streets of the fictional "Haddonfield."

TO A "TEE"

Clark's projects include Horrorshirts.com, which offers a large selection of one-of-a-kind tees riffing on everything from Stephen King's *It* to cult cinema fave Tom Atkins. He's also part owner of Convention All Stars (conventionallstars.com), which represents a wide variety of horror films stars on the convention circuit. Finally, Silver Shampain Novelties (silvershampainnovelties.com) sells several horror-related masks and props.

ever Web site he happened to be contributing to at the time.

Today, links to most of these can be found on his MySpace page: horrorshallowedgrounds.com.

"I've always been a location nerd," Clark says, though he didn't really get into visiting horror film locations until he met *Phantasm* star Reggie Bannister. "I started grilling him for *Phantasm* locations and he was like, 'You know, man, that was right by my house.' He was telling me how he used to work at the actual cemetery where they shot *Phantasm*." The two have been close friends ever since.

If you check out his *Horror's Hallowed Grounds* article about *Phantasm*, Clark hints at having taken some extreme measures to actually get into the Forest Lawn casket room.

"I had to completely lie my ass off," he admits. He told the funeral home that his dying grandmother sent him there to personally take pictures of the coffins they had so she could choose one for herself. "The guy told me it's against the law; I don't know if that's true. But I had to actually sit down with the guy and fill out paperwork on my fake grandmother. I'm sitting there going, 'Man, this is a new low.' And then the worst part is I walk in there and they've completely remodeled the room—it's nothing like it was in the movie, except for the doorway. I remember saying, 'Wow, this looks really new—did you guys remodel this recently?' 'Oh, about two years ago.' Great."

FROM FAN TO FILM WRITER

With the exception of the *Halloween* footage, the only *Horror's Hallowed Grounds* project to actually be shot was a segment about *The Texas Chainsaw Massacre*.

During the first two months of 2007, Clark was in negotiations with Fearnet to develop the show for that horror cable channel, he says. "Then they came back and said that it wasn't in their budget for the year, which seems silly to me because it's got to be the cheapest show ever made."

However, no sooner did that project fall through than Clark's friend Mike Shahoud gave him a script to look over for a film he was associate producing. "I thought it was pretty cool and fairly unique," Clark recalls, "except it looked like the evil version of *Jumanji*."

The script—about a game that brings out the worst in its players—was written by the film's director, Gabriel Bologna, son of actors Joseph Bologna (*Transylvania 6-5000, Alligator II: The Mutation*) and Renée Taylor (*Alfie, The Producers*). Shahoud suggested that Clark meet with the director and explain how he would make the movie better.

"I'm thinking this guy's probably not gonna listen to some dumb horror kid," Clark says. Yet Bologna not only listened to him, he asked the "horror kid" to rewrite it. The result is the forthcoming flick **The Black Waters of Echo's Pond** starring Danielle Harris (Rob Zombie's *Halloween, Urban Legend*), Robert Patrick (*Terminator 2: Judgment Day*) and Electra and Elise Avellan—best known as the Venezuelan twins from the *Planet Terror* segment of *Grindhouse*.

"The thing about Gabe is he's not a horror fan at all, he'll admit that," Clark explains. "He said, 'I want you sitting next to me every day when I'm directing because I want to know if I'm doing something wrong as far as horror is concerned.' You just don't get that freedom as a writer. Usually in Hollywood you're banned from the set."

With his foot finally on the filmmaking ladder, Clark is anxious to get his own feature film ideas into production. If and when that happens will, of course, depend on how *Echo's Pond* is received. For the moment, this horror fan is simply enjoying the process, even if he has one eye permanently peeled, waiting for the other shoe to drop.

"So many times have opportunities presented themselves that ended up not happening that I wasn't counting on the movie at all," he says. "It wasn't until I was sitting on set and we were filming the first scene that it hit me: This is really happening!" [NHH]

The Black Waters of Echo's Pond
At press time, Clark was finishing up writing and production work on *The Black Waters of Echo's Pond*, a horror flick directed by Gabriel Bologna.

VISION-IMPAIRED VISIONARY

JOE MONKS

YOU CAN'T HELP BUT THINK THAT IF JOE MONKS' FIRST FEATURE HAD BEEN A THROWBACK TO THE '80S-ERA FEEL GOOD FLICKS LIKE *STAND AND DELIVER* OR A GENTLE ROMANTIC COMEDY ABOUT TWO ODDBALLS WHO FIND LOVE ON FACEBOOK, YOU'D KNOW HIS NAME BY NOW...

That's because the Queens-born Miami director is blind, a situation seemingly tailor-made for a dozen fawning newspaper profiles, if not Oprah's kingmaking seal of approval.

Nothing doing though because Monks' first feature film, *The Bunker*, is a gritty, at-times ugly little riff on the torture porn trend. Young Julia (Saskia Gonzalez), daughter of a New York congressman, is kidnapped and held captive by a brutal thug (Terry M West) who has a talent for torture and degradation. Think *All the President's Men* if Woodward and Bernstein had actually managed to turn up blood on Nixon's hands and you're not far off the mark.

"You either get it or you don't," Monks says of visceral horror. "You can take anybody to see a stupid comedy, they'll laugh. Good comedy is good comedy. It's tougher if horror's your genre. You're not going to take somebody who's just come from seeing *The Horse Whisperer* to *The Texas Chainsaw Massacre* and get a concession out of them if it's not their thing."

'THAT'S ALL SHE WROTE'

Joe Monks doesn't spend a lot of time discussing his blindness, but realizes that every struggling filmmaker needs an angle. To the best of his knowledge, he is the only blind director working in film today, and even dubbed his production company Sight Unseen Pictures to emphasize the point. He wasn't always blind; that would come later. But his love of horror was there from the very beginning.

Born Feb. 21, 1968, he grew up on a steady diet of horror comics ranging from **DC's** *Ghosts* to Warren's *Creepy* and *Eerie* black and white comic magazines. When he was at the Bronx's Fordham University in the late '80s, he had the opportunity to meet up with faculty member Rev. William O'Malley who played Father Joe Dyer, the priest who gives Father Damien Karras Last Rites in *The Exorcist*.

"He was joking around about careers and how you never expect things will turn out the way they do," and spent some time explain-

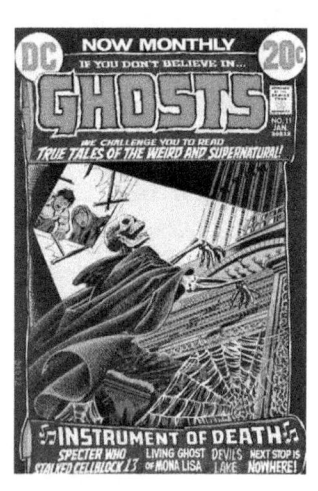

DC's *Ghosts*
While much has been written about the horror comics of EC (*Tales from the Crypt, The Vault of Horror,* etc.) and Warren's black and white horror mags (*Creepy, Vampirella,* etc.), the slightly less gruesome titles published in the 1970s and 1980s by DC Comics had their own hand in shaping some of the younger horror talents of our day. While the most popular title of that time was easily *The House of Mystery*, DC also unleashed other anemic scare rags including *House of Secrets, Weird War Tales* and *Ghosts*.

ing what it was like working with *Exorcist* director William Friedkin, Monks recalls. At one point, Friedkin asked the clergyman if he trusted him. "And Friedkin just slapped him in the face, hard. Just coldcocks the guy—whack! And he says, 'OK, now go and do this.' He's relating this story about how his hands are really shaking and he's really quivering on set. He says, 'A man just slapped me in the face and told me to go do my job!'"

Soon after graduating from Fordham, Monks began writing and publishing his own horror comics with titles like *Cry for Dawn* and *The Night Terrors*, and hit the road much of the year to flog them at conventions. At the same time, he was editing men's magazines for the publisher of *Cherry* and *High Society* to make ends meet.

For much of his life, Monks had battled diabetes. In 2001, while he was balancing his day job and his burgeoning comics business, the disease began to whittle away at his eyesight. Over the next 18 months, he endured several surgeries as he lost and regained some sight in each eye.

"After the seventh or eighth month, it was pretty much negligible vision," he says. "After the final surgery, it was like that's it, that's all she wrote. You can only edit men's magazines so long without having any eyesight."

For six months, he stayed at his editing job. "They were kind of hoping I'd gain back something," he says. "But eventually when I left that job, I had to go back to the comics full time because I really had no idea what I'd do otherwise. I really wasn't about to learn how to punch keys at the local courthouse coffee shop."

BUILDING *THE BUNKER*

In 2003, shortly after "the lights went out," Monks learned that one of his horror comic stories, "Chance Meeting," had been optioned for production on Japanese television.

He wrote the script and took a small part in what became the 30-

> "I know there's a place for *Child's Play* + *Leprechaun* and all that stuff, but I've gotta say those kind of movies, they're just not for me. If somebody's going to take me in there and say listen, give me your 8 or 9 bucks for a movie ticket, I want them to take their best shot. And I don't think most of those films are their best shot."
>
> — JOE MONKS

Hart D Fisher

Hart D Fisher has been at once praised by the underground horror community and condemned by the mainstream for his comic book publications, most notably books that feature the gruesome eccentricities of real-life serial killers. "We're really doing the same kind of thing, just doing it in two different ways," Monks says. "Hart embraces the outlaw, bad boy, boogeyman image. He definitely enjoys taking the pointy stick and poking people in the eye with it at times."

minute, direct-to-DVD video *Flowers on the Razorwire* directed by **Hart D Fisher**. Borrowing the title and framing device—a bloodthirsty dominatrix who extracts chilling stories from her victims— from a comic series written by Fisher, Monks quickly realized that films were what he really wanted to create for a living.

Monks next wrote *The Bunker,* a creepy tale about a sadistic thug who imprisons the daughter of a prominent politician in his chamber of horrors. He intended it to be the second direct-to-DVD installment of *Flowers on the Razorwire*, and naturally expected Fisher to direct it. When Fisher found himself tied up with prior music video directing commitments, Monks decided to direct it himself. "We were so far into it already," he says, "I just figured I know this material as well as anybody."

He went out and bought a Panasonic DVX-100A camera, recruited fringe horror star/writer Terry M West as his villain, and proceeded to transform his Miami living room into the titular bunker.

Building a set with walls that folded in and out like the flaps on a barn-door camera light, he and wife Pam managed to limit the 12-by-14-foot "bunker" to a portion of their L-shaped home.

"When it was supposed to be there for a month, it was no big deal," he says. "We'd gone down the budget and I'd looked at renting everything from a soundstage to just a commercial warehouse in Miami, so we'd have total control over the set," he says. However, it ended up sitting in Monks' home for a good year.

Still, "I knew that if we didn't get something and we had to go back and shoot scenes later, there'd be almost no way to do it. So it was like, 'Well, we could just build it here.'"

Though clearly a low-budget flick, *The Bunker* is a tale more smartly told than many of its competitors, and far less punishing than most of the fare that gets tipped into the torture porn bin today. The character Julia is subjected to a number of physical and psychological punishments, but nothing terribly over the top by 21st century horror standards.

"We could've beaten this girl and bruised her and bloodied her up over and over again," Monks says, "but I think that loses its impact pretty quickly."

DIRECTING AROUND THE BLIND SPOT

As entertaining as it is to discuss the nuances of horror cinema with Monks, sooner or later one has to ask the obvious question: Just how the hell do you direct a movie if you can't see what the camera does?

Fortunately for Monks, he'd known and talked film with *Bunker* villain West for more than 15 years. When it came time to block out and frame sequences in the movie, "I gave him my cinematic references," Monks explains. "I'd say I want this to be a three-shot, kind of like the scene in *Jaws* where they're swapping the tattoo stories, and this scope of field, so he was right on top of it with me."

Monks also kept in close contact with director of photography Salvador Lleo de la Fe, and ended up sketching simple storyboards on a memo pad to get across the details. "It was you here, you here, you here, these are the expressions I want, and this is the emotion I want to get across," Monks says. "I'd give them my references and then we'd do a couple of takes and I'd listen. Then I'd confer with the people who I trusted most around me at the time."

While *The Bunker* is probably not going to be the goriest film you see—distribution is still being worked out for the DVD—its language may raise the occasional eyebrow. Monks purposefully put several choice expletives in the mouth of his imperiled protagonist, in part as a reaction to the relatively PG-rated whinings that erupt from many horror film characters today.

"It seems like their dialogue has been pre-cut for television broadcast or cable access in a hotel room somewhere," Monks says." No, these

> "The people who were there from the beginning, everybody who came along was willing to do crazy things: to take a needle, to lay in an alley when it's 35 degrees, pretty much in nothing but bra, panties, high heels and a piece of plastic laying over them, covered in stage blood that was quickly turning to jelly because of the weather."
> — MONKS

people are going to be screaming and cussing like drunken sailors! I've heard that a number of people who've reviewed [The Bunker] are like, 'Wow, these people are really flipping out. The profanity's amazing!'"

IN *THE BUNKER*, DOWN AND DIRTY

Shot on the streets of New York City, Long Island, Los Angeles and Fort Myers, Fla., for around $80,000, *The Bunker* wrung the most out of the resources it had to work with, especially its cast and crew. Among other things, leading lady Saskia Gonzalez took a needle in the arm on camera.

"The original idea was that I was supposed to shave my arm and take that needle," Monks says. "She said, 'No, my friend's a phlebotomist, we practice on each other because she's an EMT. We'll bring her on set and she'll work the actual needle in a close-up, and you'd just better get it in one take.'" They did.

Even Monks got in front of the camera for a scene, standing in for West. "I had to shave my head," he recalls. "I don't have the greatest of bald heads. But I was willing to be bald for two weeks because we needed a shot that looked exactly like Terry, where you saw him pushing a body out the door.

"It's what you do if you want to make your film come out. And Saskia not washing her hair for a week—tell a woman 'don't wash your hair for a week,' you're asking for a lot."

While there is an obvious pride in Monks' voice when he talks about the obstacles he's overcome to get *The Bunker* made, it's clear that he knows his blindness is something that's bound to make Hollywood's gatekeepers nervous.

"I only had one shot to make this first movie," he says. "I'm only going to get one chance to impress somebody, get a job, get a script picked up because really, let's be honest. I don't know how enlightened the world is, but it's not like there are a lot of blind people out there directing films. As far as I know, I'm still the first." [NHH]

> "It's like when people peel back an onion. Inside is the wetter, messier, gooier part of the onion that's going to make your eyes water even more. There's a place for that, and I think that's what a lot of those films that people have labeled 'torture porn' decided to do. I think that feeds the adrenaline rush."
> — MONKS

CREDITS

Our tremendous thanks go to all who opened their photographic archives to the *Handbook*. Every effort has been made to give credit to the copyright holders in this volume. Please address any corrections to asberman813@gmail.com so that we may assign credit to the proper copyright holders in future editions of this book.

FRONT COVER *Wolf Creek*
BACK COVER *Inside, Saw II, Splice*

P. 10
Courtesy PMK/HBH

PP. 15, 18, 20-23, 25, 27, 28, 32, 38, 41, 42 Courtesy of Eli Roth

PP. 34-36, 96, 101, 105, 111-113, 115, 116, 121, 125, 134, 142, 145, 147, 149-151, 153, 155, 158-160, 162, 197, back cover (*Saw II*) Copyright Lionsgate

P. 44, 48, 54, 57, 60, 63, Cover Courtesy of Greg McLean

P. 65
Photo by Tim Bradstreet

P. 68
Photo by Alyson Hurt

P. 70
Illustration by Ben Templesmith

P. 74
Copyright Columbia Pictures

P. 83, 88
Courtesy Vincenzo Natali

P. 78, 92, 93, back cover (*Splice*) Photo by Steve Wilkie, Copyright *Splice* (Copperheart) Productions Inc.

P. 99
Courtesy Karen Walton/Photo by Sébastien Raymond

P. 100
Courtesy Karen Walton

P. 109
Courtesy Emily Perkins

P. 115
Copyright Cindy Sherman

PP. 128, 132 (*Paradis*), 133, 136, 137, 139-141, back cover (*Inside*) Courtesy Julien Maury + Alexandre Bustillo

P. 132
Copyright Dark Sky Films (*Ils*)

P. 132
Copyright Dimension Extreme (*Dalle*)

P. 135
Photo by Alain Bachellier/Creative Commons

P. 161
Copyright The Weinstein Co.

PP. 164-165
Courtesy Kristie Macor/ The Hogtown Project, www.hogtownproject.com

P. 167
Copyright Douglas Buck

PP. 168, 186, 187
Courtesy *Rue Morgue*

PP. 169, 174
Courtesy Gary Pullin

PP. 172, 179, 181
Courtesy Rodrigo Gudiño

P. 175, 184
Courtesy Monica S Kuebler

P. 176
Courtesy Jovanka Vuckovic

P. 182
Courtesy Dave Alexander

PP. 190, 194, 195
Courtesy the Hagins family

P. 198
Courtesy Cheesy Nuggets Productions

PP. 199-201, 203-205, 207, 209 (Rose Kent-McGlew), 210, 211 Courtesy of *Zombie Girl: The Movie* LLC

P. 202
Courtesy Alamo Draft House

P. 209
Courtesy Rebecca Elliott

PP. 212, 216, 217
Courtesy Sean Clark

PP. 220, 224, 226
Courtesy Joe Monks

ACKNOWLEDGEMENTS

You don't write a history of an artistic movement, however brief, without relying on the kindness of strangers. Thanks first must go to interviewees who often overrode the protestations of their publicists ("but how does talking to *him* get your movie on magazine covers" next week?) and found an hour or two in their busy schedules to reminisce with someone who, however keen, knows next to nothing about the Hollywood system, nor how the industry outside the US works. Darren Lynn Bousman, John Fawcett, Katie Isabelle, Greg McLean, Vincenzo Natali, Steve Niles, Emily Perkins, Todd Cherniawsky—generous people all.

Thanks must also go to Eli Roth for the generosity he showed in digging up pictures. The man e-mailed me a good 20 images soon after I asked for one or two, and did so one image at a time. He was equally generous with his time, both in speaking with me directly and sending me detailed e-mails about different aspects of his career, until we were both certain the chapter you find herein is as accurate an account of his life and work as possible.

Inside writer/director team Alexandre Bustillo and Julien Maury met me more than halfway across the French-English language divide. Between them they communicated some extremely complex ideas about their work to me in my native English, when the best my high school French could manage was to ask them how they were. I also have them to thank for the bounty of behind-the-scenes *Inside* photos within these pages. Merci beaucoup, messieurs.

Ginger Snaps writer Karen Walton gets *The New Horror Handbook* "Above-and-Beyond" Award for all of her help reconstructing the birth of that coming-of-age classic. Despite heavy deadlines of her own, she always found time to answer my questions with infectious enthusiasm and in great detail, no matter how personal they might get. For this book she even scared up a photo of her childhood home, the place that inspired her lifelong suspicion of suburbia, and which ultimately led to *Ginger Snaps*. You rock, Waltz.

To filmmaker Emily Hagins and her family, Rebecca Elliott, and Zombie Girl documentary makers Aaron Marshall, Justin Johnson and Erik Mauck, my sincere thanks for helping me better understand a director in the making.

Finally, this book probably wouldn't have happened at all—well, it wouldn't have been written by me, anyway—without the guys and gals who keep *Rue Morgue* magazine alive and kicking. While I've always gravitated to horror films, it wasn't until I picked up my first issue of *Rue Morgue* in 2003 that I really caught the fever. Its intelligent feature stories and snarky reviews made me appreciate the medium, and introduced me to films and directors that now mean a great deal to me today. When it came to writing the *Rue Morgue* chapter, everyone there gave generously of their time, bared their souls, and in one case helped me get past a particularly stubborn publicity firm to communicate with a director one-on-one. Thanks to Jovanka, Dave, Monica, Gary, and of course founder Rodrigo. All hail the Rue Crew. —**A.S. BERMAN**

Index

8 Films to Die For 134
24 34
30 Days of Night 7, 9, 66, 70-74

A

Abandoned, The 185
Academy of Canadian Cinema and Television 177
Ackerman, Forrest J 173
After Dark Films 134
Aftermath 14, 185
Ain't It Cool News 28, 192, 194, 200
Aja, Alexandre 131, 154, 192
Akkad, Malek 216
Akkad, Moustapha 216
À l'intérieur (See *Inside*)
Alamo Drafthouse Cinema 192, 193, 196, 202, 203, 206-209, 211
Aleister Arcane 66
Alexander, Dave 61, 164, 182-185
Algonquin Round Table 166
Alien 63, 80, 91
Alone in the Dark 46, 131
Amant, Lionel 139

American Film Institute 20
Amityville Horror, The 217
Amityville Horror, The (remake) 46, 131
An American Crime 130
Anchor Bay 181
Anderson, Brad 215
Anderson, Paul Thomas 154
Andrews, Stuart F 178
Arcane Comix 69
Argento, Dario 55, 138
Atkins, Tom 218
At the Movies 39, 74
Audition 28, 29, 53, 133
August Underground 180
Austin Film Society 193
Austin Studios 193
Avellan, Electra and Elise 219

B

Backpacker murderer 52
Bad Taste 47
Ballard, JG 94
Balun, Chas 69
Banff Television Festival 101

Bannister, Reggie 218
Barbarash, Ernie 84
Barès, Laurent 134
Barker, Clive 69, 94, 144
Bart, Roger 38
Basket Case 17
Báthory, Elizabeth 37
Bava, Mario 55
Bell, Tobin 149, 150, 153
Bent, Lyriq 153, 155
Bentz, Brenton 184
Best, Thom 113
Betsworth, Gary 167
Between the Scenes 199
Beyond (production co.) 49, 58
Beyond, The 169
Bigfoot (comic) 71
Bijelic, André 82, 85, 86, 90, 91
Birds, The 29, 136
Black and White 17
Black Christmas 179
Black Christmas (remake) 92
Black Waters of Echo's Pond, The 189, 214, 219

Blanks, Jamie 47
Blood & Donuts 92, 106
BloodyDisgusting.com 217
Bloor Cinema 167, 180
Boll, Uwe 46, 131
Bologna, Gabriel 219
Bologna, Joseph 219
Boogeyman 46, 131
Bosch, Hieronymus 14, 134, 170
Bottin, Rob 174
Bousman, Darren Lynn 77, 142-163, 207
Boyens, Philippa 196
Boys Club, The 101, 113
Bram Stoker Awards 184
Briggs, Chris 28
Brightman, Sarah 159, 160
British Board of Film Classification 36
Brody, Adrien 92
Brownsville 13
Bruce, Lenny 12
Buck, Douglas 167, 180
Buffy the Vampire Slayer 73, 98, 109, 159

Bunker, The 189, 222, 224-227
Buñuel, Luis 75
Burg, Mark 148
Burning Effigy Press 184
Bush, George W. 13
Bustillo, Alexandre 77, 128-141
Butt-Numb-A-Thon 192, 195, 196

C

Cabin Fever 12, 18-29, 38, 40, 42, 46, 144
Cameron, James 81
Campbell, Joseph 204
Campbell, Nicholas 111
Canadian Broadcasting Corp. 177
Canadian Film Centre 82, 86, 88, 101, 102, 106
Canadian Film Development Corp. 108
Canal+ 139
Cannes International Film Festival 119, 130
Cannibal Holocaust 33
Captivity 35, 186
Cargill, Christopher 198
Carpenter, John 6, 20, 80, 174
Cars That Ate Paris, The 47
Catholic New Times, The 169
Cavuto, Neil 13
Cerdà, Nacho 14, 185
Cherniawsky, Todd 110, 111, 114, 120-121
Chubb, Ken 107
CineMacabre 174, 180
Cinemagic 67
Cinémathèque Française 41
Clarke, Melinda 107
Clover, Carol 56
Coffin of Light 185
Columbia Pictures 66
Columbia TriStar 181
Columbine 108, 109
Convention All Stars 218

Cook, Robin 110
Count Gore de Vol 66
Craig, Johnny 69
Crash 94
Craven, Wes 80
Creepy 66, 67, 173, 222
Cronenberg, David 80, 81, 92, 94, 103, 106, 108, 111
Cry for Dawn 223
Cube 77, 80-95, 101, 148
Cube2: Hypercube 86, 88
Cube Zero 84, 86, 88
Cuthbert, Elisha 35
Cutting Moments 167
Cypher 90

D

Dale, Holly 106
Dalí, Salvador 75
Dalle, Béatrice 132-134, 136, 138
Danvers State Lunatic Hospital 214, 215
Dark, The 127
Dark Forces: Secret Battles of WWII 63
Darrow, Tiger 198, 200
Davis, Jack 69
Dawn of the Dead 217
DC Comics 222
Dead Alive 47
Dead Ringers 103
DeBello, James 25
de Boer, Nicole 87
Deep Red magazine 69
Degrassi High 182
del Toro, Guillermo 92
Demonology of Desire, The 184
Descent, The 74, 131
Desperate, The 146, 147, 148, 153
Devil's Rejects, The 46, 131
DeWilde, Philip 111
de la Fe, Salvador Lleo 226

de la Iglesia, Álex 139
de La Tour, Georges 134
De Palma, Brian 167
Diary of the Dead 116
Dimension Films 58, 61
Disaster Movie 161
Dollery Rudman Freibauer 173
Dracula (novel) 72
Dragomir, Tom "Tomb" 164, 185
Dunstan, Marcus 153, 156
Dyszel, Dick 66

E

Earth: Final Conflict 90
Earthquake 203
Ebert, Roger 39
EC Comics 37, 69, 222
Eclipse Comics 69
Edelstein, David 34
Eerie 66, 67, 173, 222
Elevated 101
Elliott, Rebecca 194-196, 200-203, 206, 209
Ellison, Harlan 206
Empire Strikes Back, The 197
Englund, Robert 182
Erickson, Justin 165, 184
Escape From Alcatraz 91
Escher, MC 83
Eugenides, Jeffrey 114
Every Other Day is Halloween 66
Evil Dead, The 14, 20, 25, 33
Exorcist, The 56, 63, 67, 68, 80, 136, 215, 222, 223
Exorcist stairs 67, 68
Eyes of Edward James, The 178, 179

F

Falconio, Peter 52
Fallow 184
Famous Monsters of Filmland 67, 173

FanExpo Canada 180
Fangoria 67, 136, 166, 167, 170
FantaCo Enterprises 69
FanTasia Film Festival 163, 167, 169, 172, 176
Fantastic Fest 163, 206, 207, 208
Fawcett, John 82, 96-127
Fearnet 218
Feast 153, 156
Ferry, Ray 173
Festival of Fear 180
Fig Newton 13
Film Finance Corp. 51
Filmoption International 111
Final Girl 56, 122
Fisher, Hart D 224, 225
Fleiss, Mike 28
Fletcher, Brendan 111, 117
Flowers on the Razorwire 224, 225
Followes, Michael 114
Folsey Jr., George 20
Folsey, Ryan 20
Forman, Milos 17
Fox News 13
Frankenhooker 17
Freddy vs. Jason 117
Frédiani, Vérane 139
Friday the 13th Part IV 215
Friedkin, William 223
Frontière(s) 134, 161
Fulci, Lucio 136, 169
Fulford, Robert 108
Funny Games 29
Fydolla Ho 158

G

Gaines, William 37, 69
Gein, Ed 52
Gemini Award 177
General Slocum's Gold 184
Genesis 185

Gens, Xavier 132, 134
German, Lauren 31, 40
Ghosts (comic) 222
Gibson, Will 48, 53, 54, 60
Gilliam, Terry 94
Ginger Snaps 46, 47, 77, 92, 96-127
Ginger Snaps: Unleashed 116-117, 121, 126, 127, 195
Ginger Snaps Back: The Beginning 105, 121, 123, 124-25, 127
Girl Next Door, The 130, 178, 186
Gonzalez, Saskia 222, 227
Gorno 7
Goya, Francisco de 14
Gray Matters 67
Greutert, Kevin 152
Grindhouse (movie) 185, 193, 200, 219
Guadagni, Nicky 87
Guantanamo Bay 33, 34
Gudiño, Rodrigo 164-187
Gudjonsson, Eythor 30

H
Hackl, David 151
Hagins, Emily M 189-211
Hagins, Jerry 192, 193, 195, 200, 205, 210
Hagins, Megan 193, 195-197, 200-203, 205, 208-210
Hall, Karen Lee 108
Halloween 20, 56, 214, 216, 218
Halloween: 25 Years of Terror 216
Halloween the Retrospective 216
Hampton, Danielle 110
Haneke, Michael 29
Hard Candy 73, 117
Harris, Danielle 219
Harvey, Grant 127
Haute Tension (aka *High Tension*) 131, 132, 134, 154, 192, 196

Head, Anthony Stewart 157, 158, 159
Hellbound: Hellraiser II 118
Hellraiser 132
Hernandez, Jay 30
Herskowitz, Alec 197
Hewlett, David 87, 90
High Rise 94
High School for Performing Arts 13
Hilton, Paris 160
Hoban, Steve 92, 106, 107, 126, 127
Hoffman, Gregg 148
Hoichi the Earless 210
Hollyer, Mary-Beth 171
Horror's Hallowed Grounds 189, 216-218
Horror Channel, The 216, 217
Horrorshirts.com 218
Hostel 9, 12, 13, 20, 27-30, 33, 34, 35, 37, 38, 39, 41
Hostel Part II 14, 20, 27, 31, 33, 34, 35, 36, 38, 40, 42, 43, 130
House of 1,000 Corpses 46
Hurricane Katrina 13
Huston, Danny 73, 74

I
I Am Legend 67, 69, 75
IDW Publishing 70
I Know What You Did Last Summer 46, 80
Ils (aka *Them*) 132, 134, 139
IMAX Corp. 61, 106
Infurnari, Jody 171
Inside 7, 77, 84, 128-141
Iraq war 9, 12, 13, 33
Irons, Jeremy 85, 103
Isabelle, Katharine 98, 101, 104, 105, 110-112, 115, 116, 122-126

J
Jackson, Peter 19, 47, 193, 195, 196
Jacombs, Audra 164, 184
Jarratt, John 46, 50, 53, 59, 60
Jaws 60, 226
Jewison, Norman 82
Johnson, Eric 116
Johnson, Justin 199, 200, 201, 205-208, 210
Jones, Alan 154
Jones, Paul 118, 119
Jordanova, Vera 31
Juno 131

K
Kaderabkova, Jana 30
Kael, Pauline 178
Kafka, Franz 85
Kaufmann, Nicholas 184
Kehr, Dave 131
Kent-McGlew, Rose 202, 209-210
Kerekes, David 33
Kern, Joey 25
Ketchum, Jack 130, 178, 186
Kevan, Scott 19, 20, 23
Kevorkian, Jack 170
Kidder, Janet 116
Kill Bill 31
King, Stephen 24, 35, 80
King of the Dead 69
KNB EFX Group 29, 127
Knowles, Harry 28, 192, 194, 195, 206, 208
Koules, Oren 148
Kuebler, Monica S 164, 174, 175, 182, 184, 185, 186
Kwaidan 210

L
Ladd, Jordan 22-23, 25
Ladouceur, Liisa 184
La Fabrique de Films 139
Land of the Dead 101
Landry, Colin 184
LaRose, J. 154, 158, 162
Laugier, Pascal 207
League, Tim 196, 202
Lees, Joanne 52
Lemche, Kris 101, 105, 112
Let the Right One In 7
Lichtenstein, Mitchell 206
Lifeboat 91
Likens, Sylvia 130, 186
Lionsgate 26, 108, 112, 144, 147, 157, 161
Livid 133
Long Weekend 47
Lord of the Rings, The 19, 47, 193, 195, 196, 208
Lost Boys, The 217
Lucas, George 207
Lugosi, Bela 70, 73, 98
Luhrmann, Baz 49, 94
Lynch, David 40, 43, 139, 157

M
Macfadyen, Angus 152
Machinist, The 215
Mad Movies 132, 136
Magrath, Cassandra 46, 53
Malick, Terrence 47
Marshall, Aaron 199, 205, 206
Marshall, Neil 74, 131, 154
Martin, Bob 166
Martinelli, Gabriella 94
Martini, Megan 126
Martyrs 35, 161, 207
Maslany, Tatiana 116
Massicotte, Stephen 127

Matarazzo, Heather 27, 31, 36-37
Mauck, Erik 199, 201, 205, 206
Maury, François 136
Maury, Julien 128-141
McDonald, Bruce 106
McGee, Robert 110
McLean, Dwayne 101
McLean, Greg 4, 9, 14, 44-63, 134, 154
Melton, Patrick 153, 156
Men, Women and Chainsaws: Gender in the Modern Horror Film 56
Messengers, The 116
Meyer, Dina 153, 154
Midnight Meat Train, The 144, 161
Miike, Takashi 28, 29, 37, 53
Milat, Ivan 52
Miller, Andrew 87, 90
Mitchell, Elvis 41
Mitchell, Radha 59, 60
Monks, Joe 189, 220-227
Monster Squad, The 179
Morassi, Kestie 46, 53
Moreau, David 132
Morgan, Robert 186
Moseley, Bill 160, 174
Motion International 108
Mulholland Dr. 40, 139
Murdoch, Bradley 52
Must Be Santa 177
My Dinner with Andre 82
MySpace 39, 178, 218

N
Nail, The 71
Natali, Vincenzo 77, 78-95, 101, 120, 148, 202
Necromerchant's Debt, The 156
Nedeljáková, Barbara 30
Nelson, Brian 73

New Horror 4, 6, 7, 9, 14, 77, 167, 171, 185, 187, 189
New Yorker, The 166, 178
New York Times, The 131
Nightbreed 94
Night of the Living Dead 41, 66
Night Terrors, The 223
Niles, Steve 7, 9, 64-75, 180
Nothing 90
Now Magazine 89

O
O'Malley, William 222-223
Oldboy 24, 192, 196
Organic 194, 195, 201
Others, The 19

P
Page, Ellen 73, 117, 130, 131
Palud, Xavier 132
Pang Brothers 116
Papillon 91
Paradis, Alysson 132, 136, 137
Paranormal Activity 152
Passion of the Christ, The 34, 145, 157, 196
Pathogen 189, 192, 194, 196-210
Patrick, Robert 219
Patterson, Scott 153, 155
Pearlstein, Randy 18
Pecota, Marco 165, 172
Pedazo Chunk Video Store 208
Penn, Chris 101
Perkins, Emily 98, 101, 104, 105, 109, 111-118, 122, 124, 126
Phantasm 189, 217, 218
Phillips, Bijou 31
Phillips, Nathan 46, 53
Phillips, William 89
Picnic at Hanging Rock 47, 50
Pieces 17, 30
Pin… 90
Planet Terror 200, 219

Polley, Sarah 82, 92
Poltergeist 217
Pontypool 106
Pop Skull 178
Prom Night II 101
Psycho 51, 133
Puchon International Fantastic Film Festival 90
Pullin, Gary 165, 168, 169, 172, 173, 182, 184, 186, 187

Q
Quay Brothers 186

R
Raimi, Sam 25, 73
Rakoczy, Tim 200
Ray, Christina 127
Ray, Nica 167
Reece, Neil 202
Repo! The Genetic Opera 144, 146, 153, 156-163, 207
Retelling, The 209, 210, 211
Return of the Living Dead 3 107
Ribière, Franck 139
Richardson, Derek 30
Ring, The 19, 24
Rocky Horror Picture Show, The 144, 156, 157
Rod Serling's The Twilight Zone Magazine 169
Rogers, Mimi 105, 112
Rogue 9, 50, 52, 54, 55, 58, 59, 60, 61, 62, 63
Romancing the Stone 215
Romeo + Juliet 49, 94
Romero, George 6, 41, 48, 66, 116
Roth, Eli 9, 10-43, 52, 130, 144, 154
RPM Weekly 169, 170, 171
Rue Morgue 61, 77, 164-187
RZA, The 13

S
Sarkozy, Nicolas 135
Saturday Night magazine 108
Savini, Tom 166, 169
Saw 7, 29, 34, 46, 144, 145, 147, 148, 150, 152, 153, 154, 156, 158, 161
Saw II 46, 145, 146, 148, 149, 152
Saw III 150, 151, 152, 153, 155, 158
Saw IV 117, 130, 153, 155, 156
Saw V 151, 152
Saw VI 152
Scary Movie 61, 161
Schroeder, Alex 198
Schuster, Leo 210
Scream 24, 80
Screen Australia 51
See No Evil 33
Sept. 11th 6, 9
Sergio del Monte 185
Session 9 189, 215
Shahoud, Mike 219
Sherman, Cindy 115
Shivers 108, 111
Sight Unseen Pictures 222
Silent Hill 59, 101, 118
Silver Shampain Novelties 218
Sin City 200
Sirius Satellite Radio 166
Sisters 167
Sitges International Festival of Fantastic and Horror Cinema 54, 163
Sixth Sense, The 19
Slade, David 7, 33, 72, 73
Slaughtered Vomit Dolls 187
Smith, Darren 156
Smith, Kevin 182
Smith, Shawnee 145, 150, 153, 158
Soderbergh, Steven 85

Soles, PJ 217
Soomekh, Bahar 149
South by Southwest 132, 193, 206
Spierig, Michael and Peter 192, 197
Spin 182
Splat pack 154
Splice 81, 92, 94, 120
Stalker 91
Stargate Atlantis 90
Starlog 67
Star Wars 208
Strahm, Jed 194, 195
Strong, Rider 20, 25
Sullivan, Brett 117, 127
Sundance Film Festival 56
Suspect Video 167, 170
Suspiria 55, 138
Svankmajer, Jan 185
Switchblade Romance (See *Haute Tension*)

T

Tales from the Crypt 69, 222
Tarantino, Quentin 29, 31, 39
Taylor, Renée 219
Teenage Mother 196
Teeth 206
Telefilm Canada 107, 108
Templesmith, Ben 9, 70, 72, 90
Tenebre 138
Texas Chainsaw Massacre, The 20, 28, 52, 193, 215, 217, 218, 222
Texas Chainsaw Massacre 2 160
Texas Filmmakers Production Fund 200
Them (See *Ils*)
Thomas, Jeremy 94
Timpone, Tony 166
Titanic 81
Toetag Pictures 180
Toronto After Dark 163
Toronto International Film Festival 11, 26, 89, 126
Toronto Star 111
Torture porn 7, 12, 34-35, 75, 130, 144, 186, 222, 225
Total Film magazine 154
Trimark 108
Tripp, Jen (See Vuckovic, Jovanka)
Turning Paige 111
Twisted Pictures 147, 148
Twitter 70, 90
Tyson, Mike 13

U

Unapix 108
Un chien andalou 75
Undead 47, 192, 196, 197, 203

V

Van Wilder 146
Vartan, Michael 60
Vault of Horror, The 69, 222
Vega, Alexa 157, 160
Vespe, Tony 198
Vincent, Cerina 19, 21, 22, 25
Virgin Suicides, The 114
Vogel, Fred 180
Vuckovic, Jovanka 164, 167, 175-180, 182, 185

W

Wahlberg, Donnie 152, 153
Walker, Charles 36
Wallace Avenue Studios 81
Walsh, Frances 19, 196
Walton, Karen 82, 98-102, 105, 106, 108, 109, 113, 114, 118-120, 127
Wan, James 147, 148, 153, 154
Warren, Jim 67, 173, 222
Waters, John 157
Weekend of Horrors 166
Weir, Peter 47, 50
Weird Tales 169
Weird War Tales 222
West, Terry M 222, 225-227
Whannell, Leigh 147, 149, 153, 154
White Noise 46
Wilson, Gregory M 186
Wilson, Patrick 73
Wint, Maurice 87
Wolf Creek 4, 9, 14, 34, 46, 47, 50, 52-62
Wolfe Creek Crater National Park 52, 53, 54
Wood, Elijah 208
Wrong Turn 118

X

X-Files, The 146

Z

Zang-O-Fonts 175
Zdunich, Terrance 156, 157
Zollo, Fred 40
Zombi 2 136
Zombie 136
Zombie, Rob 46, 71, 106, 131, 154, 185
Zombie Girl: The Movie 162, 189, 192, 196, 198, 199, 204-209

Also by A.S. Berman

Meet the people behind your favorite British TV characters!

Whether you're one of those people who hunkers down in front of the TV every weekend to get your fix of Britcoms courtesy of your local PBS station, or you're working your way through classic British shows one DVD at a time, you're probably a fan of British television's golden age. Between 1970 and 2000, PBS and cable television brought some of the finest British programs ever made to our shores, and with them, introduced us to actors, writers and producers who have gone on to become legends, even in homes thousands of miles from their own.

30 Years of British Television brings you interviews with 14 of those legends. Their memories, their words.

BearManor Media
bearmanormedia.com

Retail book orders over $99 always receive FREE US SHIPPING!

www.ingramcontent.com/pod-product-compliance
Lightning Source LLC
Chambersburg PA
CBHW081147230426

43664CB00018B/2829